D1040263

ERIC CANTONA

ERIC CANTONA

FourFourTwo | *great footballers*

Rob Wightman

Published in Great Britain in 2002 by
Virgin Books Ltd
Thames Wharf Studios
Rainville Road
London W6 9HA

Copyright © Rob Wightman 2002

The right of Rob Wightman to be identified as
the author of this work has been asserted by
him in accordance with the Copyright, Designs
and Patents Act 1988.

This book is sold subject to the condition that it
shall not, by way of trade or otherwise, be lent,
resold, hired out or otherwise circulated
without the publisher's prior written consent in
any form of binding or cover other than that in
which it is published and without a similar
condition including this condition being
imposed upon the subsequent purchaser.

A catalogue record for the book is available
from the British Library.

ISBN 0 7535 0662 9

Typeset by TW Typesetting, Plymouth, Devon

Printed and bound in Great Britain by
Mackays of Chatham PLC

Contents

Acknowledgements

Naturally, I have quite a number of people to thank for the help, contributions and advice that have enabled me to research and write this book.

On the publishing side, I should acknowledge the efforts of Cormac Bourne and Jonathan Taylor. I'm also grateful to Matt Allen, Dave Anderson, Joe Bernstein, Rick Broadbent and Ian Ridley for sparing the time to help with contacts and to offer advice.

The combined wisdom of Erik Bielderman, Paul Davies, David Meek, Andy Mitten and Martin Tyler has also been essential, and I thank them all for their time and efforts. Moreover, I would like to acknowledge the contributions of Franck Sauzée, Lee Sharpe, Richard Shaw, Gary Speed and Howard Wilkinson, all of whom helped me build up, I hope, a more accurate and colourful picture of Eric Cantona.

Sadly, there were a number of players and managers who did not wish to be interviewed, which is a shame. I record the fact, if not their names, merely to express my disappointment that the book was not able to benefit from the invaluable first-hand contributions I believe they would have been able to provide.

However, some football clubs and associations were both kind and efficient in the assistance they provided, and I would like to thank the following: Olympique Nîmes for background material; the Football Association, the Newcastle United press office, Hibernian FC, Bradford City and the Coventry City press office for help with setting up interviews; and the UEFA press office for the information they provided.

I must also say a huge thank you to Sam Pilger, whose chat and advice were a genuine help. And I acknowledge my enormous gratitude to Justyn Barnes for all his encouragement, enthusiasm and counsel – it must be my shout with the beers!

As ever, I'm grateful to a number of old friends for their help and kindness: Vicky and Adam for their hospitality at Rockingham Palace on my visits to Manchester; Sid for lending me the *Ooh Aah Cantona* video; everyone at my local hostelry for providing a congenial atmosphere in which to relax of an evening; and all the usual suspects, including Ben, Charlie and JP for our various chats during the book-writing process.

Without the backing I have received from my parents, writing this book would have been a far harder task. I'm particularly grateful to my mother for the proofreading and my father for firing my enthusiasm for the French language, my knowledge of which was extremely valuable for research purposes. I would also like to thank Jim for all his encouragement and understanding, and for being as enthusiastic about Barcelona–Real Madrid as I was. Special gratitude is also due to Tamsin for her total support and consistent ability to make the light at the end of the tunnel shine more brightly.

Finally, I'm grateful to Eric Cantona himself for being the most fascinating subject about which to write, and for being the ultimate hero in a four-and-a-half-year epic that transformed the way I view Manchester United and football.

Rob Wightman
December 2001

Introduction

There can be few greater accolades for a player and the way in which he approaches his career than when one of the most successful club managers in football history describes him as the best prepared he has ever dealt with. Sir Alex Ferguson viewed Eric Cantona, arguably his greatest ever signing, as a model professional whose conscientious attitude towards training made him a role model for the young players coming through Manchester United's much-vaunted youth system.

From the moment the Frenchman strutted into Old Trafford a love affair began that was clearly meant to be. There has always been a massive burden of expectation placed upon the shoulders of any major new signing at United. But if you are a striker, the level of that expectation can be simply unbearable since you are following in the footsteps of genuine legends like Denis Law and George Best. Just ask Alan Brazil, Peter Davenport or Garry Birtles, good players all of them, how it felt to not quite make the grade at the Theatre of Dreams. With Eric Cantona, it was different. Everything was different.

As 1992 drew to a close, the Frenchman was a lost soul. His troubled career had seen him play for six clubs in as many years. He had yet to find the consistent adoration that would inspire him or the freedom that would allow his myriad talents to flourish. On 27 November 1992, all that changed. The expectations at Manchester United intimidate weak players, the ones who will never be great, yet, in equal measure, they inspire the strong, the players for whom Old Trafford glory is their destiny. Certainly, Eric Cantona fell into the latter category.

Lee Sharpe, a man who received ample adulation from the Old Trafford faithful during his time at the club, summed up the principal dynamic of the Cantona–United relationship. 'I think fans at Old Trafford like players who are hard-working, attack-minded, and who support the club while they play there, who become Man United supporters. He came to United and spent years there and they idolised him, he idolised them. It was a good match.'

This biography is very definitely independent in nature, and I hope that by speaking to people from different sections of the game – players, coaches, journalists and fans – I have provided a variety of different perspectives that will offer a broad-based view of Eric Cantona's career, both in England and in France. I have steered away from the temptation to try to analyse Eric's personality too deeply. This is, after all, primarily a biography of a footballer and an attempt to assess and analyse his ability, as well as to decide where he belongs in football's unofficial hall of fame. How, for instance, does he rank alongside such legendary figures as Sir Bobby Charlton and George Best in terms of his impact at Old Trafford? Did he achieve – let's rephrase that: could he have achieved the same level of success with France and won an eternal place in the hearts of followers of Les Bleus as Michel Platini and, more recently, Zinedine Zidane have done?

People have tried to analyse Cantona's mind, to determine what makes him tick and why he is prone to outbursts of violent rage, but that is not the principal task with which I believe I am charged. It seems impossible to make a concrete and balanced judgement of someone who was so utterly adored or totally loathed by the football establishments, fans, players and referees of France and England alike. For every supporter of Cantona there is a detractor because, quite simply, for each of Eric's great triumphs and good qualities there is also an item in a catalogue of flashpoints and sheer bloody-mindedness. No, to try to actually judge someone as a person, to write in such a way as to try to influence or even dictate what others think of Monsieur Cantona, would be wrong. I shall instead, as Eric perhaps should have done once or twice himself, adhere to an old adage and let the football do the talking.

Martin Tyler, the Sky television commentator, suggested when I was researching this book and reviewing the
events of 1996 that I must find it hard to believe what
happened after Cantona's comeback from suspension. He
was right. As I watched (several times!) the video of that
period, the magnitude of Cantona's extraordinary contribution to Manchester United's success that season struck
me afresh. Some observers claim that Eric's lack of a
European Cup winner's medal indicates that he did not
have great ability at the very highest level of the game. I
would wholeheartedly dispute that thesis. In many ways,
the achievements of the 1995/96 season rank alongside
the wonderful Treble of 1998/99 because, as Alan Hansen
will not care to remember, United genuinely won things
with kids. And the man who was instrumental in the
whole affair, whose goals, assists, even goal-line clearan-
ces contributed so much to that Double success, was Eric
Cantona.

Lee Sharpe, a member of that 1996 Double-winning
team who remembers the experience with great fondness,
told me of his abiding recollection of Eric's role in that
campaign. 'My lasting memory: just to be able to construct
something special when we most needed it and least
expected it. That was a big lift. When teams used to come
to Old Trafford and defend and we were pushing for the
League, to have someone in the team who could go and
win you the game at any second carries you through and
keeps you pushing for ninety minutes.'

When Franck Sauzée, Cantona's team-mate at Olympique Marseille and in the French national squad, first
went to play in Scotland, he was delighted to learn at first
hand just how deep an impact his former colleague had
made throughout the British Isles. 'In France, everybody
knows him. [As far as great players go] you have Michel
Platini, of course, Zinedine Zidane, of course, and after
that you have Cantona, of course. When I was in France
I knew that Eric was a fantastic player in England. He was
the king at Manchester United. But now, in Scotland, I can
talk about him and Man United and people are very happy
and enjoy talking about him and what he did at that club.

It was fantastic. French people love him now. When he was in France it was maybe a little bit difficult sometimes.'

It is the story of how Eric Cantona transformed himself from a figure of derision to many in his homeland into a man who captured the hearts of the manager, players, staff and fans at one of the world's biggest clubs that remains so fascinating. Had you told a fifteen-year-old apprentice at the French club Auxerre that he would find his spiritual home in the north-west of England, he would have been unlikely to believe you. But then everything about Eric Cantona leaves one with a lingering sense of incredulity.

1 Southern Accents and Northern Soul

There is nothing more stupid than a footballer who pretends to be more indispensable to the game than the ball.

ALBERT CANTONA

It is little wonder that the man voted the greatest player in Manchester United's history by readers of the club's official magazine should have found his spiritual home in English football. After all, Eric Daniel Pierre Cantona was born on 24 May 1966, two months before England lifted the World Cup after defeating West Germany 4–2 at Wembley.

This coincidence, the birth of one of the greatest footballers ever to play in England and the national team's finest triumph, was to spark the imagination of the marketing men at sportswear manufacturing giants Nike three decades later. '1966 was a good year for English football – Eric was born,' quipped the firm's billboards, the words placed alongside a head-and-shoulders shot of Cantona in typical pose: hair slightly ruffled, face unshaven, eyebrows meeting in the middle above a nose that was surely designed for sniffing wines of fine vintage, collar upturned (of course), and that look in his eyes that says, 'I am master of all I survey.' At the time, as the pivotal member of a Manchester United team that had emerged from 26 years of frustration to dominate English football, he was. And he knew it.

The place of his birth was Caillols, a rundown suburb bordering the 11th and 12th *arrondissements* of Marseille, its identity split between the cosmopolitan mêlée of France's second city and the idyllic setting of the

Provence countryside. As Cantona grew up it was a dichotomy that would fit perfectly with his favourite pursuits: the rural backdrop to his upbringing provided the larks, woodcocks and thrushes he, his father and his brothers were so fond of hunting while their neighbours remained in their slumber; the countryside also provided the colours and inspiration for his painting, another passion inherited from his father; and, of course, the city boasted the Stade Vélodrome, home to Olympique Marseille, one of the aristocrats of French football.

Cantona refers to great wealth in his background, not because his family was rolling in cash but because he and his brothers were well cushioned by the security and warmth large Mediterranean families provide. He was the middle son of three. His elder brother by three years was Jean-Marie, while Joël, who was also to play professional football in England with Stockport County, was a year and a half his junior. Material wealth was not seen as a necessity during his childhood. After all, he was later to write, he had the 'sunshine, the hills and the sea to enjoy'. 'I am a son of rich people,' he declared. 'But with us, riches have never been money or luxury or even expenditure. Frankly, I wish that all those children who ask for my autograph were able to have the same values which were transmitted to me by my family in the hills of Marseille. That would be a great start in life.'

The family home was a converted cave. Joseph, Eric's grandfather, was a mason by trade and had brought his wife Lucienne and son Albert to live in the cave in the summer of 1955. It covered an area of just nine square metres. By the time Eric was born, the cave was just one room in a house the family had built on top of it. The scenery around Caillols was picturesque. Families from the city centre would come out to the area and picnic on the hill where the Cantonas lived. However, the natural beauty and tranquillity of the surrounding area hardly made for a cosseted lifestyle. Eric's grandparents' first winter was the harshest since records began, and only a curtain separated the room from the freezing temperatures outside. One day during that cold period Joseph,

Lucienne and Albert were snowed in and it took them a whole day to dig their way out.

Like so many people in Marseille, Cantona's paternal grandparents were of immigrant stock. The family hailed from Sardinia, and Eric's father was brought up to speak the local language of the island at home with his parents. He was also taught to appreciate his natural environment and developed a love of hunting and walking his dogs – passions that were also handed down to Eric. Family activities were important to the Cantonas. They always ate together, and Eric and his brothers learnt to hunt with the male elders of the family.

Although the Cantona boys were brought up to understand and love what their surroundings could provide by way of entertainment, it wasn't long before they fell in love with the activity that entranced almost all boys of their age throughout the city of Marseille. They discovered football. The three brothers formed an effective trio, firstly at the infant school in Caillols, and later at the Grande Bastide secondary school. Eric also played at the local Caillols club, a well-known junior team which had previously boasted Jean Tigana as one of its star performers. Cantona believes, though, that he gained invaluable experience by learning to play the beautiful game with his peers in the streets and fields around his home. 'I must admit that football in the streets gave us a great sense of freedom and liberty. There's nothing surprising in the fact that our heroes learnt football in the open fields and on the streets. Look at Skoblar and Salif Keita and, later, the little boy with golden feet, Maradona, or even Platini. All of them have dribbled tin cans and aimed them at imaginary goals before they had the opportunity to make the stadiums of the entire world explode with happiness.'

In common with other youngsters (the name Alan Shearer leaps to mind) who have gone on to become great strikers, Eric started out as a goalkeeper, like his father. However, it wasn't long before his desire to be more involved in the game saw him move to an outfield position. A childhood incident had a profound influence on his approach to playing football. For his father, Albert, football ranked alongside hunting and painting, his other favourite pastimes, and he took a keen interest in how his sons were progressing at the sport. One day, after the Caillols team had suffered a defeat, Albert was critical of Eric's performance. However, unlike the father who rants and raves on the sidelines, bullying his son into making up for his own failings as a footballer, Albert's criticism was both wise and constructive. He clearly believed his son had been too intent on holding on to the ball in an attempt to outshine everyone else on the pitch, especially his brothers and an Algerian team-mate who was blessed with great skill and dribbling ability. Eric's father told him: 'There is nothing more stupid than a footballer who pretends to be more indispensable to the game than the ball. Rather than run with the ball, make the ball do the work, give it and look quickly. Look around quickly and you will be the best. Look before you receive the ball and then give it, and always remember that the ball goes quicker than you can carry it.' From that point on Eric developed an awareness of how and where other players were moving and adhered to the simple adage behind his father's words: let the ball do the work.

Cantona remembers another incident from his formative years that he describes as the time he 'learnt about how much stupidity and injustice there was all around'. In the summer of 1978, he and his pals in the Caillols Colts were on the crest of a wave. The team had stormed to victory in the region's cup competition, the Provence Cup, beating a side called Vitrolles 3–0 in the final. Caillols then had only to draw their last league game, against Vivaux-Marronniers, to complete the Double. Sadly, however, it wasn't to be. Eric's team dominated the game but ended up on the wrong end of a 1–0 scoreline.

The game was not without the sort of incident in which, it seems, only Eric could be involved. As his grandmother Lucienne watched, as she always did, from the stands, Eric took it upon himself five minutes before the final whistle to launch a single-handed mission to rescue the all-important point from the jaws of defeat. Picking up the ball deep in his own half, he beat six or seven of the opposition and found himself bearing down on goal, about to score and clinch the Double for Caillols. But his hopes of glory vanished in an instant, as a footballer's so often do, with a blast from the referee's whistle. The official stopped Eric in his tracks because his bootlaces were undone. Eric wrote: 'The rule is a formality: a footballer must have his laces tied. The match was over and tears flowed in the dressing-room.'

It is typical of Cantona to recall such events, to recount them and place them alongside what are surely more significant incidents, including the many triumphs of his professional career. However, you can't help but sympathise with the schoolboy who was deprived of his moment of glory because of something so trivial. Nor was it the last time Eric would fall foul of a referee.

At the Caillols club, they knew early on that Eric Cantona was destined for greatness. Club president Yves Ciccullo told the writer Rick Broadbent that even at the age of six Cantona stood out from the crowd. 'He always knew he would be a big star. I knew he would be a great professional. Lots of other players from here have become professionals, players like Jean Tigana, but Eric has superseded them all.' Broadbent recounted how he showed the president a picture of Cantona taken during the player's professional career. 'He was the same when he was a six-year-old boy,' Ciccullo said. 'Always very proud. This look is not an image, this is real Cantona. He did the same look when he was a young boy.'

While Cantona certainly admired the local heroes of Olympique Marseille – among them Josip Skoblar, the Yugoslav striker who scored 100 goals in his first 100 matches at the club in the early 1970s, and Roger Magnusson, the Swedish playmaker of the same era – he admits that from the age of eleven onwards he idolised the Dutch national team. He would fantasise about leading such a side. Eric envisaged being Neeskens, Cruyff, Rep and Arie Haan all at once! So entranced was he by this wonderful orange machine driven by the incomparable and magnificent Johan Cruyff that he was distraught to see them lose consecutive World Cup finals. On both occasions they were overcome by the host nation: West Germany in 1974 and Argentina four years later. Eric viewed these defeats as a betrayal of 'the beautiful play of the Dutch'. (Are we to assume, therefore, that the blast of a referee's whistle preventing Eric from scoring in that Colts match was, in his eyes, a similar betrayal of beauty?) Eric even confessed that he was so enamoured of the Dutch that he almost wanted them to beat France at the Parc des Princes when the two sides met in 1982.

Two men played pivotal roles in his destiny. Firstly, Cantona inherited his love of football from his father. However, it was at the Grande Bastide secondary school that he met the man who was to act as his true football mentor. Célestin Oliver, a veteran of the France team that finished third in the 1958 World Cup in Sweden, was a teacher at the school and instilled in his young charge the belief and self-confidence he needed to carve out a career at the very highest level of the game. Eric soon developed a deep respect for Oliver, of whom he wrote in his autobiography: 'His power on the field of the stadium of Caillols had a kind of legitimacy acquired by heroes who return from wonderful battles. Without doubt it was he who discovered that I had a driving need for success. With all the means at his disposal at school, Célestin Oliver pushed me towards victory, without betraying the beautiful game.' Of course not. According to Oliver, Eric Cantona was, in academic terms at least, an average pupil, but he shone on the sports field, where he showed his true intelligence. 'With the ball at his feet, he took his time deciding on the best option. He dared to do things with the ball,' Oliver told *Le Sport* magazine.

Although he was proud of his Marseille roots and enjoyed the climate and ambience of his home area, its hills, the sea and the sun, Eric's nomadic spirit became apparent in his early teens. As a fourteen-year-old he made a brave, mature and far-sighted decision to leave home and go to a place where he could begin to strive in earnest towards a career in professional football. Few football clubs would have been able to entice a youngster so utterly devoted to his lifestyle, background and family. But Auxerre was not most football clubs.

A representative of the French Football Federation, Henri Emile, had spotted Cantona's talent while running the rule over players to be selected for the regional team. His original remit, as he told the author Ian Ridley, had been to watch a player whose name he has long since forgotten. 'My attention was immediately drawn to this boy called Cantona,' recalled Emile, who was later to become assistant to the French national coach Aimé Jacquet. 'He was different. He had more intelligence than the others, was a level above them. He had good technique, spirit and initiative. He knew when to hold the ball, when to pass it, knew how to use it to do positive things.' Emile had no hesitation in recommending Eric to Guy Roux, Auxerre's long-standing, inspirational manager, and Roux invited Cantona and his father to visit Auxerre to discuss the possibility of the club taking him on as an apprentice.

Eric believed his relatives would understand the instincts that decreed he should leave the hills of Provence in order to find success elsewhere. Neither set of grandparents was French by birth. While his paternal grandparents' decision to up sticks and leave their native Sardinia had an air of the romantic about it, his mother's father had had far more pressing reasons for moving away from his homeland. For him, it was quite possibly a matter of life and death.

Cantona's maternal grandfather, Pedro Raurich, was morally and physically committed to the Republican cause during the Spanish Civil War of 1936–39. After fighting the Falangists for two years on the arid plains of Catalonia, the thirty-year-old Pedro was seriously wounded and forced to go north, to France, to receive medical attention and to recuperate. And it was on that side of the Pyrenees that he stayed when the war ended a year later, enduring concentration camps and deportation when France was occupied by the Nazis in the early 1940s. Pedro did not return to the country of his birth during the forty years that it was under the dictatorial hand of the Falangist leader Francisco Franco. Like many Spaniards who lived in exile during that era, Cantona's grandfather was never to see his parents again. Instead, he set up home in Marseille.

Eric reasoned that compared with such a long and enforced period of exile, his short spell away from Marseille would be no great hardship. However, despite the logical, mature arguments he uses in his autobiography to explain why, in 1981, he left his family to join Auxerre as an apprentice, there seems to have been a simpler factor behind his attraction to the Burgundy club. Originally he had planned to move to Nice Football Club, fewer than seventy miles along the coast from his home town. Despite the advice of his mentor and teacher, Célestin Oliver, Cantona rejected the opportunity to learn his trade at the club of two of his idols, the French international Roger Jouve, another product of Caillols, and the Pole Ivan Katalinski.

The rationale behind that particular decision appears to have been less than mature. When he visited Nice, Eric was disappointed not to have been gifted so much as a club shirt. However, a few weeks later, he returned from Auxerre with a number of jerseys and other souvenirs. That was the real clincher. On the journey home from Auxerre, almost 400 miles from Marseille, Eric made his decision as he admired his new possessions. Auxerre was the club for him.

At first sight, this may all appear rather puerile. But, in fact, Eric was quite sage in his assessment of the situation. He reckoned that if he were to endure the wrench of leaving family and friends, he should go somewhere he would feel at home, to a club that made him feel welcome. The gift of one of the club's red striped shirts was the masterstroke of perhaps the shrewdest coach in French football history. In an instant, Guy Roux had convinced the teenager that he would be happy and would progress at Auxerre. A difficult decision had been made easy.

However, convincing the rest of the family that he was making the right move was not so straightforward. His father argued that Nice would be a better choice. Because of its proximity to Marseille, Eric's parents would be able to visit him every weekend. His elder brother, Jean-Marie, was also opposed to the move. Eric retorted that young players from the south coast needed to head north to further their football education. Perhaps a glorious return to play for Olympique Marseille would one day materialise. 'I was convinced that one day or another I would return and I would bring the crowd to their feet in the north and south stands of the Marseille stadium where I used to go as a little boy, sitting on the shoulders of my father,' Eric wrote. As fate would have it, he would come back to join the team he had supported as a boy, but his spells at the Stade Vélodrome were to be soured by controversy.

In spite of their reservations, the Cantonas did not stand in their son's way. Shortly after his fifteenth birthday, Eric travelled to Auxerre to lay the foundations for one of the most eye-catching, famous (sometimes infamous) and colourful careers in football history.

It was May 1981. That summer was to be a happy time for Eric. Although he missed going hunting with his father and swimming with his friends, he settled well into life at Auxerre. Later, he was to recall: 'That summer of 1981, the atmosphere in the dressing-rooms at the ground of the Abbé Deschamps and the warmth of the hostel where we stayed during the week gave me great happiness. I had the impression that this club was paying attention to me and looking after me.'

It was a fabulous time to join Auxerre. The club had just finished its first season in the top flight of Le Championnat, the French league, and there were excellent players such as the Polish striker Andrej Szarmach for Eric and his fellow trainees to admire and aspire to emulate. According to Cantona, the Pole had single-handedly kept the club in the top division that season. He was therefore a good role model for Eric, who himself was to prove a similar inspiration for at least one club later in his career. Then there was Guy Roux, a manager of the highest ability who during his two decades in charge had transformed Auxerre from a local league side to a First Division outfit.

In the process, Roux had developed a youth system that was the envy of many of the top clubs in Europe. (Incidentally, at the time of writing Roux is still the manager of Auxerre, forty years after his initial appointment.)

During those early days with Auxerre, Cantona came to appreciate Roux's commitment to youth development. A decade and a half later he was able to look back on that era with sincere gratitude. In the early 1980s, many French clubs had fallen into the trap of trying to buy instant success by wheeling out the cheque-book to recruit the best available players. This, however, was not the Auxerre way of doing things. The club took its youth programme extremely seriously and was delighted to see youngsters develop into first-team players. Youth is the cornerstone of Auxerre's football philosophy. The club's full name, the Association de la Jeunesse Auxerroise (usually abbreviated as AJA), translates as the Auxerre Youth Association. The nurturing of young talent is as essential a part of its make-up as the production of wine is to the surrounding Burgundy region. It can be no coincidence that the longest and most settled period of Eric's professional career was at the Manchester United of Alex Ferguson, a club and a manager with a similarly high regard for the merits of home-grown talent.

At the Abbé Deschamps, Eric soon stood out among his peers, many of whom, as is always the case with trainees, were never to fulfil their dream of playing professional football. It wasn't long before Guy Roux called Eric into a practice match with the first eleven. The manager liked to introduce a few youngsters to the first-team squad from time to time, partly to give them experience but also to keep the older players on their toes. Eric took part in one such game in the spring of 1982; a team of youth- and reserve-team players took on established stars such as Joel Bats, Szarmach and Garande. Cantona's performance that day meant, 'I began to exist in the eyes of Guy Roux.' After coming on as a second-half substitute, Eric gave Lucien Denis, fifteen years his senior, such a torrid time with his skill and pace that the defender attempted to foul him whenever he got near enough to make contact. Denis's treatment of the youngster was so harsh that his team-mates were forced to have words. 'You don't try to rough up somebody who's making his debut and is just trying to show his ability,' Eric wrote later in his career. Perhaps an incident of this type made him aware of the responsibility of senior players to help up-and-coming youngsters find their feet, not take them away. It was a role he was to play perfectly at Old Trafford.

Eric began to attract more and more attention within the club as he quickly graduated from fourth-team football into the third team. Most of his colleagues in that side were eighteen or nineteen and struggled to understand why a boy who hadn't quite reached sixteen yet had been promoted to that level, but that wasn't something Eric allowed to bother him. The coaches had faith in him; most importantly, he believed in himself. Cantona freely admits that Roux had a profound and extremely positive influence on him. He was also delighted that the manager seemed to find time for his youth players as well as putting the first team through its paces. In 1996, the year when Manchester United were supposed, in the words of BBC pundit Alan Hansen, to 'win nothing with kids', Eric stated: 'It's common in many clubs to find a heartless attitude towards young players; an attitude in which they are used and then unceremoniously cast aside. Roux was different. His philosophy was to look after the young players, and I think that essential in a football club.' Cantona could relate to Roux because they came from similar backgrounds. The Auxerre manager had also been brought up in the country and taught to appreciate the woods, fields and wildlife that surrounded his grand-father's smallholding.

Eric's progress was soon noted at national level, and in May 1982 he was called up to the French youth team. Cantona was thrilled at being selected, especially since the youngsters were billeted in the same Lyon hotel as the senior squad, who were in town to play a World Cup warm-up match against Bulgaria. The youth team took on their Swiss counterparts as a curtain-raiser for that game and claimed a 3–2 victory, Eric netting the third goal. Cantona realised that he had taken a step towards his dream of representing Les Bleus, as the French national team is known in France.

At that time the France team comprised players of legendary status, among them Michel Platini, Alain Giresse and Jean Tigana. Despite their wealth of talent, France got off to a poor start at Spain 82, losing 3–1 to a Bryan Robson-inspired England. However, Platini and co. improved as the tournament wore on and won through to the semi-finals, where they suffered a cruel, controversial defeat in Seville at the hands of West Germany. It was a game that certainly raised Eric's adolescent hackles. He abhorred the injustice of a match in which Harald Schumacher, the German goalkeeper, went unpunished for pole-axing Patrick Battiston, an act that saw the Frenchman stretchered from the field. Watching such a game merely fuelled Eric's desire to succeed at the very highest level.

2 The Sorcerer's Apprentice

Eric was a character, and when something went wrong he would sometimes overreact because he felt that he was defending the good against the bad.

ERIK BIELDERMAN

The autumn of 1983 produced two major landmarks for Eric Cantona, one in his playing career, the other in his personal life. Both were important developments as he moved towards his destiny on and off the field.

On 22 October, Guy Roux decided it was time to put Eric's emerging talents to the test and threw him into his debut First Division match. Roux had a couple of reasons for selecting him for the eighteenth league match of the season against Nancy. Obviously he wanted to blood the seventeen-year-old, to give him experience and measure his progress at the highest level possible domestically. He also wanted to shake up his regular first-choice strike partnership of Garande and Szarmach. Garande was going through one of those sticky patches that even the best strikers experience from time to time. He was struggling for goals, and Roux clearly hoped to provoke a positive response by leaving him on the bench in favour of a rookie.

Eric didn't know Andrej Szarmach well but found him an ideal strike partner. He was impressed not just by the senior striker's ability as a footballer but also by his generosity of spirit. 'His simplicity, gentility and humility reassured me,' Eric recalled. Auxerre stormed to a commanding 4–1 lead, and thereafter the Pole tried desperately to set Eric up for a dream debut goal. It wasn't to be, but the young Frenchman did display a touch of the fearless self-belief that was to be a feature of his game throughout his professional career. Towards the end of the game he received the ball in his own penalty area. Without even looking up, he nutmegged an attacker who tried to challenge him. He later claimed it was 'sheer insolence and instinct'. Those words could be used to characterise much of his life as a footballer.

Insolence and instinct also came to the fore that season after a particularly unfriendly reserve-team game. The story goes that Eric was confronted by seven angry opponents in the Auxerre car park afterwards. Erik Bielderman, a well-known football journalist with *L'Equipe* who has known the player for many years, insisted that it is fact, not an element of the Cantona legend, that four of them required hospital treatment as a result of the fracas. 'All the stories are true. They are not legends. They are part of the history of Eric. Eric was a character, and when something went wrong he would sometimes overreact because he felt that he was defending the good against the bad. So from his own point of view that isn't something he regrets doing, I'm sure.'

These flashpoints aside, the 1983/84 season was full of highs. In the game against Nancy, Cantona played along-side men he admired such as Szarmach, Bats and Cuperly, and later in the campaign he also appeared against Lens. Back in the reserve team things also progressed well. Auxerre were Third Division champions (the French Third Division comprises reserve teams from First Division clubs) and Eric was second highest goalscorer behind one Bernard 'Nino' Ferrer, who struck twenty times in total. Nino had come to Auxerre from Vichy in the autumn of 1983 and had since developed a rapport with Eric that would produce great playing form for both men, as well as an enduring friendship.

What's more, Nino had a sister. Isabelle Ferrer was a student at the University of Aix-en-Provence, but during her holidays she would come to the Chablis region to stay with her brother while revising for her exams. Three years Eric's senior, Isabelle fascinated him. He was in love. Happily, she fell for him too.

Despite the achievements of the 1983/84 campaign, Cantona was forced to tread water for a year. He had reached the age of eighteen, when French youngsters become eligible for a year's compulsory national military service. According to Eric, Guy Roux was no great fan of the military – probably because it meant he lost promising players for a year at a crucial stage in their development. The manager told his young charge that since his year with the army was to be a total waste of time, he might as well try to enjoy himself. This Eric achieved.

For Cantona and Nino, there was to be no constant square bashing, no night exercises in the depths of winter. They entered the Joinville battalion, one of several sports sections for young men doing their national service. Eric described their base at Fontainebleau, near Paris, as a 'formidable school of fun'. In short, the two friends spent a year partying at night and sleeping during the day. It was more reminiscent of a Club 18–30 holiday than a spell in the military. Even so, Cantona has always insisted that that period had a positive effect on his career. He, like his peers, was emerging from adolescence with plenty of emotional and rebellious energy to expend. In those twelve months they were able to get an awful lot out of their systems – doubtless in more ways than one. 'For the group that gathered in the battalion,' Cantona maintained, 'it was vital to let off steam then before renewing our acquaintance with a more sane and balanced existence.'

Despite living in what appears to have been a virtual holiday camp during the week, he and Nino still had to return to Burgundy at weekends to play for Auxerre. Any dip in form, commitment or effort would soon have been noted and commented upon by the ever-vigilant Guy Roux. So there was some sort of calming influence, enough of a structure for them not to forget the long struggle ahead towards success in the professional game. The Auxerre manager's insistence that his players do their national service as soon as possible was pretty smart. The body of an eighteen- or nineteen-year-old will recover more quickly from partying to excess than that of an older player. Cantona has openly acknowledged and showed his appreciation of the common sense behind Roux's policy.

During that period Eric also gained vital experience of playing abroad since he was regularly selected to play for the French army team. His most memorable trip was a visit to Africa, a week in Gabon. He loved it there. He was touched by the warm reception the team got from the locals and enjoyed being taken on river trips in boats that were little more than hollowed-out tree trunks. Inevitably, he and the rest of the lads sampled the local nightlife. Of course, this hardly constituted the ideal preparation for games in unfamiliar conditions against opposition who 'showed great skill with the ball and were only short of tactical awareness'. No matter, Eric appears to have gained much from the experience.

This trip to Africa offers an interesting glimpse of one of the best traits of Eric's personality. From his autobiography it is clear that he was quick to embrace a foreign culture radically different to the one he was used to back home. How many times can that be said of an eighteen- or nineteen-year-old footballer when travelling abroad?

By Eric's own admission, he and Nino continued to enjoy their long nights out even on their return to Auxerre towards the end of the 1984/85 campaign, and things continued to go pretty well on the field. On 14 May 1985, Auxerre entertained Rouen. In the 64th minute, Eric made a run that caught the Rouen rearguard square, reached the through-ball, 35 yards from goal, before the advancing goalkeeper and slotted home coolly across the rain-soaked, muddy pitch. It was his first goal in professional football.

A fortnight later, Auxerre travelled to Strasbourg knowing that a point would secure a place in the following season's UEFA Cup competition. On the eve of the match Cantona, now nineteen, and Nino took what the former later referred to as 'a nocturnal stroll in the streets of Strasbourg'. They didn't return to the team hotel until 4 a.m., hardly the perfect way to ensure they were in the right physical and mental shape for a crunch game. Doubtless Guy Roux would have had palpitations had he known.

Despite his antics, however, Cantona was to be the team's hero, bridging the gap – as was so often the case throughout his career, especially during the glory years at Old Trafford – between all and nothing, success and failure, ecstasy and misery. An hour into the match things were not going to plan for the visitors to the Meinau Stadium. A crowd of 25,000 spectators had watched Strasbourg take the lead, and the Auxerre bench was getting twitchy as their dreams of competing in Europe started to fade. Cue Cantona. Like the *deus ex machina* of a Greek tragedy, he put everything in its rightful place, reversing Auxerre's fortunes with a stunning solo goal. 'Some minutes before the end,' he recounted, 'I get the ball in my own penalty area. Great spaces seem to open up before me and there is very little pressure on me, so I attack. I am marching towards Europe; I'm sure of myself. The equaliser has not yet been scored, but I feel that something very important is going to happen. That explains our love for the game. From that moment everything changes in my life. From 25m I strike. The ball ends up in the top right corner of the Strasbourg goal and this goal will send Auxerre into Europe.'

Amid the celebrations that followed that match Eric and Nino took the decision to quit the endless partying and concentrate on their football and their home lives. It was time to grow up. They realised that the stresses and strains being placed on their bodies by their off-field activities were not conducive to a long, successful career in professional football. Besides, Nino was to marry that summer.

Eric, too, was to make significant strides towards domestic security. As a guest at his friend's wedding, he was reacquainted with the groom's sister Isabelle, the literature student from Aix-en-Provence. Several weeks later, Isabelle travelled up to Auxerre to spend a fortnight with Eric at his flat. 'I certainly have never forgotten the visit,' Eric wrote, 'nor the moment when she was about to go back to Marseille when she jumped from the train on to the platform as it began to pull away and stayed for another two days.'

Whenever a small club progresses into a major competition, the players, fans, coach and officials pray that a plum tie will be pulled out of the hat. So it was for Auxerre early in the 1985/86 season. The UEFA Cup, for which they had qualified so dramatically courtesy of Eric's goal at Strasbourg, gave the small but developing French team a real taste of the big time: they were drawn against one of the genuine superpowers, AC Milan. The Auxerre players now had the chance to test themselves against players such as Franco Baresi, the *rosso neri* sweeper, and England striker Mark Hateley. It was a dream come true.

For Cantona, sadly, there was to be no opportunity to line up against the footballing aristocrats of Milan. A few weeks into the season he had contracted a nasty bout of flu which kept him out of the team for a trip to Nice. Unfortunately for Eric, the man who took his place was not just keen to hold on to it, but capable as well. Roger Boli, brother of Basile, the famous French international defender, scored and the team won, so when Auxerre played host to the mighty AC Milan in early September, there seemed little point in changing a winning team to accommodate a teenager who had recently been ill. The frustrated Eric was forced to sit on the sidelines as his team-mates recorded a famous 3–1 victory at the Abbé Deschamps Stadium. What's more, by Cantona's own admission, Boli had again performed with great confidence and composure.

The return leg at the imposing San Siro – or the Giuseppe Meazza, to give the ground Milan share with city rivals Internazionale its full, proper name – was a different story. The Italians swept Auxerre aside, beating them 3–0 to take the first-round tie 4–3 on aggregate. Eric appeared as a second-half substitute but was unable to affect the result. Despite the disappointment of defeat, he and his team-mates remained philosophical, recognising that they were young and that there would be plenty more European adventures to look forward to.

About a fortnight after Auxerre's exit from the UEFA Cup, Eric loaded the contents of his flat into his Peugeot 104 and headed for Aix-en-Provence to be with Isabelle for several months. However, this was no sudden flight of fancy, no fit of pique at being left on the substitutes bench for recent games. The ever-canny Guy Roux had suggested that Eric, still only nineteen, spend the remainder of the season playing on loan at Second Division Martigues. At first, Cantona was reluctant to take what could have been viewed as a step backwards – after all, he had yet to sign a professional contract and the last thing he wanted was for others to progress while he festered in some backwater. But on reflection, he awoke to what Roux was doing.

Auxerre was a small town of just 50,000 inhabitants and the manager was therefore able to keep abreast of exactly what each of his players was up to, even if it meant getting on his moped and trawling around the nightclubs in the countryside. Roux was fully aware of the burgeon-ing relationship between Eric and Isabelle Ferrer. At one point he even telephoned her to enquire as to the strength of feeling she and his young striker had for each other. On hearing that things were serious, Roux decided the best thing would be to facilitate the development of their relationship. By hindering it, the manager realised, he risked distracting Eric from his football. Hence the deci-sion to loan him to Martigues, just a few miles from Isabelle in Aix-en-Provence. As Eric was to recognise, Guy Roux wanted him to 'live on love and fresh air for several months'. And Roux was no fool. He knew Eric would live not in Martigues but with Isabelle in her small studio apartment.

The young footballer embarked on the journey south with his belongings packed into the car around him, including a large black and white TV in the passenger seat. He had only passed his test six weeks before and was now going to drive more than 400 kilometres in a heavily laden car. He couldn't even see anything in the car's mirrors, but nothing was going to stop him reaching Isabelle as soon as possible. That's love for you.

Although Eric had not yet turned twenty and Isabelle had just finished her studies, they both knew that what they felt for each other was the real thing. They enjoyed an idyllic few months together, exchanging ideas and feelings, exploring the countryside of Provence and the Camargue, each getting to know the other far away from the sorts of pressures that would impinge on their life once Eric turned professional. They had little money of course, but that was not an issue. Eric's upbringing had been modest and he was therefore able to enjoy simple pleasures. Even football, his other great love, failed to arrest his attention as the relationship blossomed – so much so that his parents began to worry, especially as Eric had had little contact with Guy Roux since his arrival in the south. 'Football hadn't died in me, but it was drowsing dangerously,' Eric later revealed.

On the field, things started well. Martigues were bottom of their division when Eric scored on his debut against Montceau, an event which, according to the club's then vice-president Jean Patti, 'lifted the whole club'. The team were apparently satisfied with what he contributed in his following fifteen appearances, even though they yielded only three more goals and he twice received his marching orders. After the first of these red cards, at Grasse in December, Eric's brother Jean-Marie, who was watching from the stands, badly gashed his hand while hurdling a fence. It seems he was intent on taking to task another spectator who had directed insults at Eric. The younger Cantona was again sent off against Cannes, but nobody at Martigues appears to have shown too much concern. 'He was withdrawn, but I think he was happy here,' Patti later remarked.

His nine-month sojourn with Martigues ended abruptly. Guy Roux, concerned that his young apprentice's focus had shifted away from football, travelled to see Eric in person. One evening in June 1986, when Martigues were playing promotion hopefuls Lyon at their Gerland Stadium, the Auxerre manager appeared in the stands. After the final whistle he tracked down Eric's father in the bowels of the stadium and told him it was time for his son to return to Burgundy. The following season he would play for the Auxerre first team as a professional. Eric was delighted. Although he had loved his spell in the south, it was time to resume his career in earnest. 'It was a double challenge: first, it was an attempt to put the formidable years of Szarmach behind the club so we could move on, and second, it gave me the chance to play as quickly as possible after nine months relaxing in the Second Division. The stakes were high, but this time I wasn't alone, as Guy Roux well knew.'

The Martigues adventure had had the perfect impact on Eric's outlook on life and his footballing future. Just as Roux had hoped, he had become more settled as his romance with Isabelle flourished. Moreover, she had agreed to return with him to Auxerre. When, in later years, he had the opportunity to look back and reflect upon that period, he wrote: 'Sometimes your life can be changed within a few months. I left Auxerre not being able to know if I would ever come back to the Abbé Deschamps Stadium. But now that day had arrived at last. My time away from Auxerre had put my career back on course. A top-level sportsman needs to find his equilibrium outside the football ground or the running track or the jumping pits.'

True to form, when Eric and Isabelle married in the summer of 1986 they sent out notices of their nuptials only once the knot had already been officially tied. Eric was glad to return to Auxerre. The newly-weds set up home some twenty kilometres outside the town, near the woods of Poilly in the department of Yonne. There, after training, Eric could indulge his passion for hunting, wandering through the countryside with his shotgun searching out woodcock and pigeon, as he had done during his younger years in Caillols. It was perfect. 'I was free to paint and to live twenty kilometres from Auxerre with my Isabelle and my dogs,' he enthused. 'And it was in this period of time that I made the majority of friends that I have kept until this day.'

Eric has insisted throughout his playing career that he needed the quiet and calm of the countryside to strike a contrast with the excitement of a big match. Come the start of the 1986/87 season everything in his life seemed to have fallen nicely into place – he even started seeing a psychoanalyst, not because of fears about his state of mind but because of an interest in the subconscious – and now, back at Auxerre, it was time to kick-start his career.

Individuality and the right to express himself as an individual have always been key elements of the Cantona psyche. Two days before a league match against Brest early in the new campaign, Guy Roux took his squad to Roscoff to prepare. Among their party, somewhat bizarrely, was a hairdresser whom Eric employed to shave his head so that he could 'feel the fresh rain and the strength of the wind on my skull'. What seems more likely, however, is that this was part of Eric's concerted thrust to make a major impact on the field. In short, he was determined to get himself noticed.

Roux telephoned Isabelle at home, concerned that Eric's change of appearance might not meet with his wife's approval. 'Like an egg, Isabelle, like an egg. Just like an egg,' he exclaimed. Isabelle, for her part, assumed Roux was pulling her leg and refused to believe the story until her husband slid into bed next to her late that night. She had something of a shock when she placed a hand on his now bald pate. Eric's team-mates, Nino Ferrer and William Prunier (who was later to join him briefly at Old Trafford) among them, were, of course, unaffected by Eric's baldness. They simply continued to train hard, setting their sights on a season of achievement that would match their ambitions, although according to Cantona 'they also had a spark of impertinence and insolence in their eyes'. Two of Eric's favourite qualities again.

Such a bald statement attracted the wrong sort of interest from sections of the media who had already identified the Auxerre striker as a potential source of colourful stories and eye-catching photographs. But the attention Eric received from the press at this time had not yet reached the almost intolerable levels it did in later years. His form on the pitch in 1986/87 was also eye-catching, his end-of-season tally 13 goals in 36 league appearances.

During the following campaign, 1987/88, Cantona continued to add gloss to a reputation that had now spread throughout France. Although he racked up only a modest 8 goals in 32 games, he developed a habit of coming to the fore on the big occasion. Eric shone against the superstars of Bordeaux that season, scoring a headed goal on the run not dissimilar to the one he was to score against Blackburn at Old Trafford in January 1995, just days before the infamous Selhurst Park incident, and he starred as Auxerre enjoyed a prolonged UEFA Cup run before their eventual elimination at the hands of the Greek side Panathinaikos.

Moreover, he received international recognition. On 12 August 1987 Eric made his debut for the national team in a friendly against West Germany at the Olympic Stadium in Munich. As the teams filed out of the tunnel, Eric walked abreast of Lothar Matthaus. France lost 2–1, but Cantona got his name on the score sheet. He was also a key member of the exciting France Under-21 team that was earning plaudits from fans, pundits and football folk alike. Inspired by Cantona, they were soon to capture the imagination of France's entire football-watching fraternity.

As he was in the process of winning through to the Under-21 European Championship final with France, his fortunes at domestic level were poised to take a dramatic twist. In the aftermath of a French Cup quarter-final defeat on 23 April 1988 at the hands of Lille, he told Guy Roux that he wanted to leave the club that had nurtured him since the age of fifteen. Stung by the bitter disappointment of being unable to fulfil his dream of lifting the French Cup with Auxerre that season, he slapped in a transfer request. Eric was determined to move to a club whose thirst for glory could match his own.

Naturally, Roux tried to dissuade him. In the dressing-room after the cup exit, the manager had reminded his team that they were still young and reasoned that their errors had been born of a collective and individual lack of experience rather than shortfalls in technical ability and commitment. Eric, however, was not convinced. He was only just 22 but had played a good eighty games in the First Division. So, he argued, he already had ample experience. Perhaps Eric was right, maybe it was time for him to move on, but the path he was to take proved, with the benefit of much hindsight, to be the wrong one. Or at least the wrong one at that time.

Experienced or not, one thing was indisputable: Eric was naive. News of his decision to leave Auxerre spread throughout the country just two days before France's Under-21 European Championship semi-final second leg against England at Highbury. CANTONA ABOUT TO DEPART screamed one headline. He had inadvertently heaped huge expectations and pressure on himself ahead of a crunch game which millions of his fellow countrymen would be watching on television. As it was he played a blinder, scoring twice.

Although Guy Roux was naturally reluctant to allow Eric to leave the club that had picked him up as a teenager and given him first-class footballing tuition, he may also have been a little relieved at the young star's departure. Firstly, there was the money: Auxerre received a then French record £2.3 million for Cantona. Also, Roux was a realist and knew that in the long term Auxerre could not provide him with the standard and profile of football he desired. Such realism would also have led Roux to the conclusion that even his ability to control difficult players might be stretched to the limit by Cantona's volatility. Even so, Erik Bielderman is convinced that Roux would have had his regrets: 'I'm sure Guy Roux was disappointed not to have had a longer association [with Eric] as a player and to have seen how good Eric was going to be.'

It is important to emphasise the crucial role played by the Auxerre manager in Cantona's formative years. Not only did he ensure Eric received expert instruction at France's best football school, he also, as Bielderman noted, had the strength of personality to cope with the young player's restive nature: 'I'm sure that if he had been at a club with weaker staff he might not have kept on the road to a professional career. So I think Guy Roux was at the early stage as important as Alex Ferguson at the end. They are the two men to whom Eric must pay respect for ever.'

Moreover, managers of their stature clearly revelled in the sort of challenge Eric presented. On more than one occasion during his spell at Auxerre, Guy Roux was forced to deal with the violent side of Cantona's character. In one such incident he received a club fine for giving goalkeeper Bruno Martini a black eye following an altercation while they were clearing snow from the Auxerre pitch.

The plus side of all this was that Auxerre had developed a player of supreme talent with the commitment and desire to climb to the very top of his profession. 'I think he was as technically gifted as the new generation of young French talent that you can see now,' Bielderman observed.

3 Return to Yesterday

I was no longer thinking about money because I had become the proprietor of quite another fortune, and that was the possibility of wearing the white shirt of Olympique Marseille.

ERIC CANTONA

There is an adage in football that if you are good enough, you are old enough. The flaw in this theory, though, is that, apart from raw talent, success in the modern game has much to do with getting sound advice from a reliable mentor, choosing the optimum moment for each career move and being the beneficiary of the odd healthy portion of luck.

When Eric Cantona decided to quit Auxerre he had just turned 22, was a regular member of the French Under-21 side and had also made his debut for the full national team. Naturally, therefore, he had plenty of potential suitors lining up to prise him away from the Burgundy club in a mega-francs deal. On the advice of his friend and Auxerre team-mate Pascal Planques, Eric signed up with an agent for the first time early in the summer of 1988, enlisting the services of Alain Migliaccio – who also represented Planques – to help him sift through the myriad offers he was receiving. Eric clearly recognised the need to have on board someone who had experience of dealing with the 'labyrinth of financial negotiations' that are part and parcel of a big-money move.

It may have been essential to get the details of any transfer right, but Eric has always maintained that money has never been a determining factor in any of his moves. Later, he wrote: 'Stupid people are convinced that a footballer goes only where the money is. If they don't want to die as idiots they should know that there are other things which also form part of negotiations. That said, in a set-up which can generate huge sums it's reasonable that the principal actors of the show ask for their share.' Bearing in mind the frequency with which he was to change clubs during his career and the contractual complexities involved, Cantona often had cause to feel grateful to have hired someone with Migliaccio's nous and knowledge of the market. Although they were later to part company, Eric expressly acknowledges his gratitude to his agent in his 1993 autobiography.

Between them, from June 1988, during the transfer scramble that slots in between the end of one season and the start of the next, player and agent weighed up the merits of the various propositions on the table. Several clubs could be eliminated straight away because they did not represent a sufficient increase in standard and profile. Eric also dismissed the idea of going to Italy – there had been a murmur of interest coming from the direction of Milan – because he didn't feel he had yet developed sufficiently to tackle the tight man-marking employed throughout Italy's ultra-defensive Serie A.

They soon narrowed down the list to two clubs, both of whom were capable of matching Cantona's financial demands and sporting ambitions. They were Matra Racing of Paris and the team he had watched as a boy perched on his father's shoulders. Yes, Olympique Marseille were prepared to offer an emotional and extremely lucrative homecoming to the local boy who made good. On the face of things, it was a simple decision: he was being offered a vast sum of money to return to the place where he had family, old friends and happy memories. And OM, as they are known throughout France, could offer him the top-drawer, high-profile football he craved. Simple, then. Eric Cantona would sign for Marseille.

Not so. For a start, his psychoanalyst had advised him not to move to his hometown club. Their sessions together had apparently reached such an advanced stage that the analyst had started predicting his client's future. He recommended that Eric try his luck on the other side of the stretch of water the French call La Manche – he should go to England. Of course, that is where fate eventually led him, but for the time being he ignored his analyst's prescient advice.

The other complicating factor to cloud his decision was that the offer from Matra Racing appealed to the romantic side to his imagination. Above all, he had been mightily impressed by what the club's president, Jean-Luc Lagardère, had told him. Both clubs had got as far as drawing up contracts which were awaiting Eric's signature when, at the end of the three-week period Cantona was granted to deliberate his choice, Lagardère produced a potential masterstroke. He invited Eric to dinner at his home, which almost resulted in the player signing for Matra Racing.

Not only was Cantona wowed by the fact that Lagardère had an original by the celebrated Catalan painter Joan Miró hanging on his living-room wall – the president was clearly a man of 'taste and culture' – he was also highly impressed by his suitor's footballing knowledge. Not all chairmen and presidents have a convincing grasp of on-field matters. Lagardère clearly knew how and where Eric operated, and he was keen for him to line up alongside the Uruguayan Enzo Francescoli, a player whose abilities Eric had long held in great esteem, in the Matra Racing forward line.

Cunningly, Lagardère had arranged to dine with the player the night before he was due to announce his decision. As Eric travelled back to his hotel that night, his head was in a spin. 'My choice had to be made the following morning at 11.30 and I still didn't know which one to go for. I was torn between the call of my hometown and the mad desire to wager on the future success of Matra.' He found Alain Migliaccio in the hotel bar, and explained the conundrum. His agent's advice was simple: 'Go and sleep on it.'

The attraction of playing for Olympique Marseille was not based purely on the romance Eric associated with the team of Skoblar and Magnusson that he had watched as a child. True, he had particularly vivid memories of seeing his heroes take on the indomitable Ajax, then European champions, at the Stade Vélodrome in October 1971, but there were plenty of other factors that made a transfer to Marseille appealing.

In 1986, the club had been bought by Bernard Tapie, a successful businessman and politician driven by an intense desire to bring back the glory days. When he took over, Marseille had only just recovered their place in France's top flight after suffering four ignominious years in the Second Division. His designs for the club were grand and he wanted the best that money could buy. Michel Hidalgo, still fresh from leading France to victory in the 1984 European Championship, was installed as manager, with Gérard Banide as team coach. Their remit was to recruit the finest, most exciting players available. Cantona, with his burgeoning reputation as a creator and goalscorer for both Auxerre and the national Under-21 side, fell into this category, so Banide was despatched to Burgundy to sound out their target about the possibility of a move to Marseille. Hidalgo saw Cantona filling the role of playmaker in his team, a plan that certainly appealed to Eric. Moreover, he would earn about twenty times his existing salary.

So in spite of the overtures made by Matra Racing, Eric's heart and head told him the morning after his dinner with Jean-Luc Lagardère that the only course of action was to sign for Olympique Marseille. As soon as he had informed Migliaccio of his decision, the agent telephoned Jean-Pierre Bernès, OM's commercial manager who dealt with transfer negotiations, to tell him that Marseille had got their man. A meeting was rapidly arranged for later that morning in a hotel owned by Bernard Tapie.

However, there was to be one final twist before the deal was completed. As Eric sat, pen in hand, about to commit himself to Marseille, the telephone rang. It was for him. Migliaccio's secretary was on the line with an urgent message: AC Milan wanted to buy him. Silvio Berlusconi, the media magnate and Milan president, had sent word that he wished to meet with Eric to discuss the matter. Cantona vacillated. Serie A was still attractive, despite his earlier assertion that its negative approach would stifle his creative flair. For a moment he allowed himself to dream of taking the field at the San Siro clad in the famous red and black stripes of AC Milan.

Bernès interrupted his reverie. 'What are you going to do?' he asked.

Eric retorted, 'What am I going to do? I'm signing for Marseille, and that's that!'

The pull of his hometown club proved too great a temptation for Eric to resist. Later in his career he would look back at the summer of 1988 and reflect: 'I had come back to the club of my childhood. With such a contract I was also doing good business. But there was no danger of that going to my head. I had had the good fortune to meet a young lady whose interests were not obsessed by show and flash. Isabelle had always preferred books to sports cars. She wouldn't let me lose my values, and besides, I was no longer thinking about money because I had become the proprietor of quite another fortune, and that was the possibility of wearing the white shirt of Olympique Marseille. The Vélodrome was waiting for Cantona.'

The Vélodrome was indeed awaiting Eric's presence, with both excitement and expectation. The Marseille president, manager, squad and fans were excited at the prospect of glory delivered by the most entertaining and gifted young footballer of a generation. These emotions were fuelled by the huge transfer fee of £2.3 million. In England, by means of comparison, Tottenham Hotspur had just become the first British club to break the £2 million barrier by signing another young player blessed with outrageous skill and a personality to match, Paul Gascoigne. 'Everybody was very excited,' Erik Bielderman remembered, 'and thought it was a great transfer because at the time Marseille were a great team and Eric . . . he was going back to his roots. At that time, Eric was regarded as the star to be and a world-class player, so the only club that had the money to afford such a player and was able to convince him to play in France and not for a big team in Europe was Marseille. Everybody was excited, but everybody also knew that the relationship between

Tapie and Cantona could be explosive because they are two strong personalities – and that's exactly what happened.' Franck Sauzée, who played with Cantona at Marseille in the 1988/89 season and for the Under-21 and full national teams, also believed that the marriage between player and club would be a match made in heaven. 'It was a very good move for Marseille when Eric signed. He was a striker and he had done absolutely fantastically with the Under-21 national team. It was a time when Bernard Tapie was trying to build a fantastic club and a big team in Marseille, and it was a very good signing for Marseille.'

Sadly, it wasn't long before the dream move back to Marseille to play for the team he had supported as a boy turned sour. Eric made a stuttering, though not disastrous, start to the 1988/89 campaign, failing to score in his first five appearances. He did, however, show off his ability as a provider of goals, and there were signs that he would strike up an excellent understanding with Jean-Pierre Papin, the legendary Marseille striker whom he was also to play alongside at international level.

Eric broke his goal-scoring duck on 17 August against, ironically, Matra Racing, the team he had so nearly joined. But this was not enough to persuade Henri Michel, the manager of the French national team, that Eric was worth his place in a sixteen-man squad for a forthcoming match against Czechoslovakia at the Parc des Princes. That decision alone was to prove a watershed in Cantona's career. Not only did it frustrate the player, it was to prove the catalyst to a controversial outburst of the type that would dog the rest of his career in France. At first, Eric's response was positive: he created a goal and scored twice against Strasbourg in the league just two days after the squad had been announced. However, he had yet to fully settle at Marseille and the last thing he needed was to feel rejected by the national team. Temporarily blinded by the media spotlight now being trained upon him, Eric needed understanding and counsel, not rejection. After the Strasbourg match, he exploded.

Television has an increasingly important role to play in the careers of professional footballers, and it is a double-

edged sword, providing both the sort of publicity marketing men crave and the opportunity for mishap and
controversy that managers and players fear. Eric's decision to give a TV interview shortly after the final whistle
in Strasbourg was ill-advised in the extreme. His adrenalin
still flowing after a stunning performance, he let rip at the
national team coach. 'I hope that one day people realise
that Henri Michel is the most incompetent manager in
world football,' he fumed. Had he stopped at that point,
he might just have got away with a ticking-off from the
French Football Federation. He continued. 'I was reading
an article by Mickey Rourke, who is a guy I really like, and
he referred to the people who awarded the Oscars in
Hollywood as shit bags. Well, I think that Henri Michel is
not far from being included in that category.' Eric,
sporting a faded denim jacket, his tousled hair still wet
from the post-match shower, beads of sweat seeping from
his brow, spat the words out with real venom.

It wasn't long before he realised that his emotional
outburst was a great error. When, later, he saw himself on
television and in other sections of the media, he recognised the disservice he had done himself. He was, he
admitted, 'afraid'. Even so, his remorse was hardly without limits. Cantona made a public apology and attempted
to explain himself to Henri Michel, but it seems he didn't
exactly lie prostrate at the manager's feet and beg for
forgiveness. After all, he insisted, 'I hadn't told any lies
but I had been clumsy. I needed to learn the art of
communication.'

Those in the upper echelons of French football were not
impressed. On the evening of 9 September, the French
FA's response was both immediate and drastic: Cantona
was banned from all international matches until further
notice, and that included the second leg of the Under-21
European Championship final against Greece, a game the
French youngsters would have been unlikely to be playing
save for Eric's goals and creativity. He was to be an exile
in his own country, and he was only in his early twenties.

A recurring theme throughout Cantona's career in both
France and England is that he needed to be selected all

the time, that he reacted angrily to any suggestion he was being rejected by the team. Erik Bielderman believes that if Olympique Marseille had supported Cantona in the way Manchester United did in the wake of the Selhurst Park incident, his career in France might have been very different. 'Each time Eric felt rejected, by the coach, by his team-mates, by the media or by the club, you lost him. That's what happened. After that situation with the French national team, Marseille didn't back him – perhaps they didn't have the choice, maybe they were under pressure from the French Football Federation – and Eric felt betrayed by Marseille.'

But Eric's absence from the national set-up was to be far shorter than expected. Henri Michel was fired after the team's failure to win in Cyprus on 22 October; the 1–1 draw meant Les Bleus did not qualify for the 1990 World Cup in Italy. The French Federation turned to the legendary Michel Platini for inspiration, and one of his first acts as manager was to recall Cantona.

However, at club level things went from bad to worse. In January 1989, Eric played in a charity match against Torpedo Moscow at Sédan. Overreacting to jeers from the crowd, he refused to go quietly when substituted and threw his shirt in the direction of the referee as he left the field. Bielderman observed: 'This image was used on every single occasion that someone did a piece on Eric Cantona. This image was symbolic of the French period in the same way that the Selhurst Park image became symbolic of Eric's time in England.'

By throwing his club shirt on the ground, Eric antagonised people in every stratum of the French football fraternity. Fans all over the world set great store by the club shirt and badge, which is why many players make great shows of allegiance to the colours they wear, perhaps kissing the shirt or the badge after scoring a goal. By contrast, any show of disrespect is tantamount to sacrilege in the eyes of the supporters. Bielderman confirmed that this was certainly the case with followers of Olympique Marseille. 'To throw a shirt is like saying "shit" to the fans and the club. You can express in the dressing-room your bitterness, but you have to respect the jersey, you have to respect the colours, and Marseille is a club where the colours mean a lot, where the fans are completely devoted to their club. So to put the jersey in the mud was very provocative.'

However, there were still feelings of sympathy for Eric within the dressing-room. 'I played in that game,' Franck Sauzée recalled. 'I think he was very nervous – everybody was nervous. We were not very happy because although it was a friendly game, it was a difficult friendly game. On the pitch he wasn't very happy. The story became a very important one for the Marseille fans and for Bernard Tapie as well. For us, the players, it wasn't a problem. But Bernard Tapie declared in the papers that no Marseille player had ever done that and it was the beginning of the breakdown [in the relationship] between Eric and Tapie.'

Cantona's actions had indeed incensed Bernard Tapie, the Olympique Marseille president, whose own activities, it would later transpire, made Eric look positively saintly by comparison. Tapie banned Cantona from playing for Marseille indefinitely, proclaiming, 'A player who throws his shirt on the ground, even if he has scored three goals in the match, must be sanctioned because that's not what we expect from sport. This doesn't correspond to the idea which I have of football in general and of football at Olympique Marseille in particular.'

After the shirt-throwing incident, Eric didn't receive the sort of support from the hierarchy at Marseille he would later get from Alex Ferguson and the board of directors at Manchester United. 'The personal relationship [between Tapie and Cantona] was not good, and when something happens and you don't like a person, you don't back him up,' Bielderman said. 'Fergie backed him up because as a player, as a man, he liked him. But if Eric had been disrespectful to the club and useless on the pitch and had a row with the coach or the players, obviously the reaction would have been different. I think Tapie is a volatile person, a strange character. He didn't care too much about dropping Eric from the first team. It didn't matter too much to him because he knew that the following day he could have a Desailly, a Deschamps, so he could be French champion and European champion without Cantona.'

Meanwhile, the French media stoked the fire of controversy that was already burning ferociously by getting one of the country's foremost psychologists to analyse the mind of Cantona, a campaign which was later to have resonance in England when one tabloid newspaper labelled him 'Le Nutter' post-Selhurst Park. However, quotes from one interview that Eric gave at the time offer some insight into what was really going on in his mind. 'Today's image of football is of sweat and muscles strained through effort. I dream of lightness, harmony and pleasure. I'm looking for a symphony, but the music of football these days is nothing but heavy metal,' he mused.

Directly after the Sédan incident, Eric decided a change of air and scene would calm him down and help him come to terms with events at Marseille. So he decamped to Barcelona to stay with his friend Michel Pinéda, who was playing in the Spanish league at the time. Cantona was able to relax in the bohemian atmosphere of the Catalan capital where he enjoyed the company of Pedro, his grandfather, whose advice he listened to intently.

On Eric's return to France, however, the enraged Tapie packed him off on loan to Bordeaux for the rest of the season with the consent of Marseille boss Michel Hidalgo. At one point Tapie even said he would send Cantona to a clinic to get to the root of his problems. It proved an empty threat. Although those associated with Olympique Marseille have generally cast Cantona as the villain of the piece, Franck Sauzée insisted that his team-mates were sad to see him go. 'When he moved away [to Bordeaux] we were very disappointed because we lost a fantastic player and it was a shame really.' Sauzée also dismissed suggestions that Cantona had caused trouble for Hidalgo during his first spell at the club. 'It [the relationship between player and coach] was fantastic, no problem. I think it was Michel Hidalgo who wanted to pick him. There was no problem at all. With the players as well, Eric was fantastic, no problem. I knew him before he came to Marseille, from the French Under-21 team, and it was fantastic. After that we played together in Marseille, with the French national team, and all the time it was a pleasure to play with him, to have him there as a player and as a friend. I have very good memories of him, they were fantastic moments in my career.'

So there is a need to separate myth from reality here. Cantona's reputation as 'Le Brat', the bad boy of French football, was only fair up to a point. For those who liked him and got on well with him, of whom there were plenty, he was a man who commanded respect both on and off the field. That is certainly clear from Sauzée's declarations.

Although Cantona made a reasonable enough impression at Bordeaux, scoring six goals in eleven appearances, it wasn't a happy period in his career. The team was struggling in the league – hence their willingness to take a chance on Eric – and not even the grace and guile of the French international midfielder Jean Tigana, like Eric a product of the Caillols stable, could lift the team from the doldrums.

Thus the four-month loan spell with the Girondins was largely uneventful, except for one incident, the significance of which Eric was not to recognise until he joined Montpellier the following season. One morning, as he was leaving the house to go to training, Cantona, a devoted animal lover, saw one of his dogs lying flat out on the terrace. Its whimpering spoke of the fact that it was seriously ill – dying, in fact. Understandably he stayed with his treasured pet, trying to tend to its needs, until the animal died. He missed training and didn't go into the club until the afternoon.

A couple of years into his time in England, Eric reflected on what had gone wrong at Marseille for the video *Ooh Aah Cantona*. He admitted that he had signed for the club because he came from Marseille and had supported OM as a boy, that it was a retrograde step. 'I really wanted to experience what my idols had experienced. The first year didn't go very well. I was really overawed, it was really such a massive change, I couldn't understand exactly what was expected of me. And, on top of that, going back to Marseille, seeing all my relatives, all my friends, sort of put me back in the past. I slipped back ten years. I went back to my amateur days.'

4 A Sort of Homecoming

A prophet is not without honour, save in his own country, and in his own house.

MATTHEW 13:57

At the start of the 1989/90 campaign Marseille again loaned Cantona out, this time to Montpellier, around eighty miles along the coast to the west of his hometown. The club was then managed by Aimé Jacquet, the future national team coach who would later end Eric's international career before leading France to World Cup triumph in 1998.

Although playing for Montpellier entailed earning just half the salary he had at the Vélodrome, Cantona was pleased to be leaving Marseille and Bernard Tapie behind. That said, his spell at Montpellier got off to an inauspicious start. Within a few hours of putting pen to paper, Eric was being sat down by the club president, Louis Nicollin, and warned not to start skipping training sessions. Cantona assumed he was joking, and said as much. He was therefore surprised to hear that an official at Bordeaux had warned the Montpellier president about 'acts of truancy'. Eric immediately realised that the story of how he had missed just one training session to attend to his dying dog had lost nothing in the telling. He was furious that one club, as he saw it, had attempted to blacken his name with another, but he was powerless to do anything about it. Besides, he had no regrets about what he had done. 'He who has regrets cannot look at himself in the mirror.'

At his new club he teamed up once again with Stéphane Paille, his strike partner from the salad days of the French Under-21 European Championship-winning side. This was a prospect that excited Eric. The season prior to his arrival, Montpellier had finished in the top half of the division, which encouraged the club's fans, directors and sponsors to believe that a European place was within the team's grasp in 1989/90. Those hopes were naturally fuelled by the signing of Eric Cantona and Stéphane Paille.

But despite the presence of Cantona, Paille, the flamboyant Colombian Carlos Valderrama and the emerging Laurent Blanc at centre-half, Montpellier were hardly one of Le Championnat's superpowers. Just one month into the season it became apparent that the team was more likely to be battling to avoid relegation than pushing for a place in the UEFA Cup come the end of the campaign.

Eric noted feelings of deflation, disillusionment and resentment within the club and among its sponsors and supporters; even the mayor of the town let it be known that he was far from satisfied with the situation. Cantona believed the blame for the team's failings could be laid at the doors of president Nicollin and manager Jacquet. 'The management of Montpellier had worked without any safety net,' he later claimed. 'They had expected a balanced team to develop in the space of a few weeks between old and new players. Our mission was to interpret *The Magic Flute* every Saturday at the Mosson Stadium. Thrills and goals in perfect harmony.'

However, he was also aware that in the eyes of many he and Paille, the club's big signings, were culpable. He soon began to sense a whispering campaign about him and his strike partner, and after a dismal defeat at Lille on 27 September his suspicions were confirmed. As he and his team-mates trudged through a corridor on the way back to their dressing-room, Eric overheard one of their number, Jean-Claude Lemoult, suggest to another player that Cantona and Paille were Montpellier's weak link. He was livid, and responded by throwing his boots in Lemoult's face. A fight, albeit a brief one, ensued. 'Inside the dressing-room the fight passed off like lightning. The door opens, it's finished,' Eric recalled.

The damage, however, was done. Cantona had managed to become embroiled in controversy just at the

time when it would have been smart to keep his nose
clean. It soon emerged in the media that Eric had come
to blows with a team-mate following the game at Lille.
Cantona admitted to TV and newspaper reporters that
there had indeed been an incident, but he stressed that it
had been blown out of proportion. This, however, was not
a view shared by Louis Nicollin, who slapped a ban on
Cantona after six members of the Montpellier squad
signed a petition demanding Eric be sacked.

As ever, of course, people simply divided into two
camps: those who loved him and those who hated him;
those who wanted him back in the team and those who
wanted him banished from the club. On this occasion,
Eric's friends within the team – Laurent Blanc, Stéphane
Paille and Carlos Valderrama among them – rallied
around him and the issue was resolved with his reinstate-
ment in the side after an absence of just ten days. From
a footballing perspective, it was a good job: Eric inspired
Montpellier to march on in the French Cup. They made it
through to the last sixteen where they were led to victory
by a swashbuckling Cantona hat-trick comprising a right-
footed half volley, a looping header and a brilliant solo
goal of the sort his future team-mate Ryan Giggs would
produce so famously in an FA Cup semi-final replay at
Villa Park as Manchester United strode to Treble glory in
1999.

In the quarter-finals, Eric was again on fire and scored
two more goals. In fact, he would have recorded another
hat-trick had one not been harshly disallowed. That
victory set up a tough semi-final encounter with St
Etienne, but Eric was once again the differentiating factor.
His winning goal – a right-footed volley at the far post,
meeting a well-weighted cross from Kader Ferhaoui – was
one he was to emulate at St James's Park in 1996 as he
embarked upon another crusade, that time to deny
Newcastle the Premiership title and return it instead to
Old Trafford after its year-long sabbatical at Ewood Park.
There is nothing quite like a successful cup run to boost
team morale, and Eric was later to recall how he and
Jean-Claude Lemoult, the player with whom he had

fought earlier in the season, celebrated that semi-final victory together. 'Jean-Claude Lemoult and I hug each other and we will meet up again later that evening in the wine bars of Nîmes.'

Although he may not have realised it at the time, 8 June 1990 saw Eric's finest hour in French club football. A crowd of 45,000 spectators crammed into the Parc des Princes to see Montpellier take on Matra Racing in front of François Mitterrand, the then French President. Eric cut an inspirational figure throughout as Montpellier sealed a famous victory by two goals to one in a match that needed extra time before a winner emerged. 'It certainly wasn't the most beautiful of finals, but it was a match full of suspense. The drama makes you forget everything else.' That was Eric's lasting memory of the final. After a night out in the French capital to celebrate their success, the team returned in triumph to Montpellier, where the club's fans lined the streets to greet their returning conquering heroes.

Montpellier may have struggled in the league in 1989/90, but it was during his spell there that Eric was eventually able to recover his best form and win back his place in the national team. But he had got into trouble again and the clash with Lemoult would certainly count against him when disciplinary committees deliberated what action to take. Still, Cantona was once more the talk of French football, for positive reasons, and Bernard Tapie was forced, to a certain extent, to eat humble pie and bring him back to the Vélodrome. Even so, the player insisted he had no desire to rejoin his old club. 'I didn't want to go back there. But my contacts with other clubs couldn't lead to any new openings. I belonged to Marseille and they alone could decide my future. I had just had a very good season. Among my achievements were the French Cup, nine goals for the national team, including victories like the one against Germany at Montpellier in February 1990, and that annoyed everybody in Marseille. They wanted me back in their fold.'

Despite all Eric's reservations, the early signs were good. Just a few weeks into the 1990/91 season, Tapie brought in a new manager with whom Eric was to get on well. Franz Beckenbauer arrived in September, fresh from leading West Germany to World Cup glory in Italy, albeit after a dour final against Argentina characterised by negativity and sickening play-acting from both sides. The Marseille president was desperate to win the European Cup and therefore enlisted Beckenbauer's help as a replacement for the previous manager, Gérard Gili.

Cantona responded well to Beckenbauer and produced his best goalscoring form in a Marseille shirt: he was on target seven times in twelve matches, including a brace against Caen. And he was also playing well for France. It seemed for all the world as if the right circumstances were in place, that Cantona now found himself in the appropriate ambience to become the hero for his hometown club he had always wanted to be. Chris Waddle, who had also been making his mark at the Stade Vélodrome since his arrival the previous season, recalled: 'Eric's got good technical ability. He enjoyed the training, and Beckenbauer was a big fan of his. I thought Eric was good as well. We played him and Jean-Pierre Papin up front, with me behind them or on the right-hand side and someone on the left. Beckenbauer liked him to get in the box a lot. He used to let him just lay up and get in the box. Beckenbauer used him more as an English centre-forward, to get him to try and come in at the far post, to use his head and his height.'

But on 28 October, Canto, as he was known in France, sustained damage to his knee ligaments as a result of a challenge on the Brest player Racine Kane. The injury kept him sidelined for three months and effectively sounded the death knell for his career with Olympique Marseille. The team missed him at first and struggled to produce the results their voracious fans and president required. The ever-demanding Tapie was not satisfied, and over the Christmas period he orchestrated a sideways move within the club for Beckenbauer and drafted in a new manager, the Belgian Raymond Goethals.

During the remainder of Eric's absence, the influence of Goethals saw Marseille get into a groove of good form, with Waddle supplementing Papin and Abedi Pelé, Cantona's replacement, in attack. 'By the time Eric was fit, we were playing well,' Waddle said. 'Abedi Pelé was playing up front with Papin, with me just behind, and Eric couldn't get back in the side. That's the way the system had developed from the 4-4-2 we had been playing when Eric was up front. Eric did like to drop off, to pass it, but we had a lot who could do that: Pelé, myself. Whenever players aren't in the side, and think they should be, they get cheesed off and it's very hard to accept. I don't think Eric and Goethals got on that well because of that.'

Cantona and Goethals certainly did not see eye to eye. 'Instead of the class and confidence of Beckenbauer, we now have the very individualistic Belgian humour of Raymond Goethals,' Eric fumed in his autobiography. 'I am sorry, but the gulf between us was insurmountable. Whereas I had confidence in Beckenbauer as long as he was in the active role as manager, I was now in the era of his successor and it was clear to me that I was going to be given the push.' Despite Cantona's frustration at not being picked on a regular basis, it is difficult to argue with Goethals' selection policy since Marseille went on to win Le Championnat, with 22 victories in 38 games, as well as making the semi-finals of the European Cup. Eric did collect his first championship winner's medal at the end of the campaign, but he made just six more starts and scored one goal after returning from injury.

In the late spring of 1991, moreover, it had become clear to Eric that Marseille wished to sell him. For his part, the player could no longer bear to work for a coach who did not pick him and a president who expected his players to act like doormats for the shoes of his inflated ego. Eric was convinced that Tapie, with whom his relations had turned sour during his first spell at the club, wanted rid of him once again. This was certainly the case after he refused to speak out in defence of his president after Tapie had made some less than complimentary comments about the French Football Federation. The president had never supported Eric during his clashes with French football's governing body, so Eric felt Tapie was not deserving of his loyalty. Besides, Eric Cantona has never paid lip service to anybody.

In June 1991, shortly after Marseille celebrated their season of famous achievement, Eric Cantona left the Stade Vélodrome to sign for Olympique Nîmes in a deal which saw Marseille recoup only half the £2.3 million they had paid for him three years earlier. Since his childhood he had dreamt of writing his name large in Olympique Marseille folklore, but it was not in his hometown that he would become a footballing legend. Cantona is generally not considered one of the greats at Marseille. After all, he was banned from the national team just seven games into his first spell at the club, and six months later was prohibited from playing for Marseille after the infamous Sédan incident. Posted on the club's official website are long eulogies on the careers of Jean-Pierre Papin and Chris Waddle, among others, yet of Eric Cantona there is just a short piece of text which begins: 'No man is a prophet in his own country. Before being admired in England, the son of Caillols, bought for a pot of gold from Auxerre, experienced plenty of difficulties in Marseille. It is true that his performances on the pitch were nothing less than mediocre and that his difficult personality did nothing to sort things out either. From the jersey thrown on the ground at Sédan to his rows with Goethals and Hidalgo, including the virulent curse he directed at the national team manager Henri Michel . . .'

Another season, another team. Cantona's arrival at Nîmes was greeted with the usual euphoria by club directors and supporters alike. Eric was appointed captain of the side and once again the level of expectation heaped upon his shoulders was enormous, especially considering he was still only 25. But things went badly in the league for Nîmes that season. The simple truth is that they were not as good a side as Eric had hoped and perhaps dared to believe. Although he consistently tried his hardest, he could only muster two goals in eighteen appearances. His frustration began to reach boiling point. In later years, Cantona recalled: 'So I went to Nîmes, a club which was on the way up and we all wanted enough time to turn it into a great club. What I hadn't banked on is that I wouldn't be given enough time, so I didn't want to waste any more of my time.'

During a game at St Etienne on 7 December Eric finally snapped. He jumped for a cross with a defender on the edge of the opposition penalty area, taking the ball down beautifully on his chest in typically cool fashion. The referee blew and indicated, wrongly, that Cantona had thrust an elbow towards the defender. Eric's response was to pick up the ball and fling it at the official. It struck him on the back of the thigh.

The irony of the situation was that had Eric not been blessed with the skill and balance to control the ball so perfectly, it would never have bounced back off the turf within his reach to be easily caught and, yes, shamefully thrown at the referee. But then, if the referee was so convinced he had used an elbow, why did he not want to speak to him first, to at least give him a warning or to caution him? Eric didn't stick around to argue. He had his back turned and was walking towards the tunnel before the referee had even had time to reach into his top pocket and whip out the red card. The front page of *L'Equipe* declared CANTONA TURNS HIS BACK. The headline was emblazoned above a picture of Eric from behind in jeans, white T-shirt and waistcoat, walking, a dog either side of him, along a country track. IS IT THE FIRST DEATH OF CANTONA? asked another article's headline. They were both right: the end of his career in French club football was nigh.

As a result of the incident at St Etienne, Cantona was summoned to appear before the French Football Federation's disciplinary committee. Despite all the fuss surrounding his actions, they imposed a ban of just four matches, hardly a life sentence. However, it was not so much the suspension as the attitude and words of the committee that prompted Eric to walk out on French club football for good. At the hearing, it became clear, when members of the committee referred to the fact that they had received complaints about his behaviour from several clubs, that he was being judged not solely on this one incident; previous ills were being thrown in for good measure. He was incensed, and demanded to be treated like any other player in the French league. That brought the following response from panel chairman Jacques Riolaci: 'You can't be judged like any other player. Behind you there is a trail of the smell of sulphur. You can expect anything from an individualist like you.' In retaliation, Eric walked up to each member of the committee and uttered the word 'idiot' in his face. His suspension was immediately doubled to two months, but that was irrelevant. He had set light to the bridges Riolaci had virtually invited him to burn. His career in France was over.

On 12 December 1991, at the age of 25, Eric Cantona announced his decision to retire from football with immediate effect. However, informed observers of French football believed Eric would soon change his mind and return to the game, though not in France. They were right, and Cantona was soon to be reincarnated abroad. 'It was not possible for Eric to play for a French club any more because of the media, because of the fans, because of the coaches, because of everyone,' Erik Bielderman noted. But on the other side of the Channel glory was awaiting Eric. This time, amid a chorus of oohs and aahs, he would not fail, and he would become the darling of the followers of at least one English club.

As a footnote to this chapter, it is worth recalling Olympique Marseille's 1993 triumph in the European Cup, having beaten AC Milan 1–0 in the final. Bernard Tapie had finally reached the promised land he had sought for so long. However, it later transpired that he had indulged in all sorts of illegal and underhand tactics to improve Marseille's chances of winning the game. It emerged that the club had bribed players from Valenciennes to deliberately lose a league match in order that Marseille could secure the French title early, giving them more time to rest before the game against Milan. As a result, Marseille were stripped of their title and demoted to the French Second Division. Tapie was sentenced to eight months in prison for his role in the scandal after judges at his trial failed to believe his defence, which he summed up as follows: 'I may have lied, but I lied in good faith.'

5 English Rose

No matter where I roam I will come back to my
  English rose,
For no bums could ever tempt me from she.
                                'ENGLISH ROSE', PAUL WELLER

After announcing his (first) retirement from football, Eric
spent several weeks trying to relax at home. He walked
on the beach at Grau-du-Roi, painted, listened to music
and played with Raphael, his young son. He may have
enjoyed these various activities, but his life seemed
incomplete without football.

In the meantime, national team coach Michel Platini
was desperate not to lose one of his key players for good
just a few months before the European Championship in
Sweden. Gérard Houllier, his assistant, suggested a possible course of action: they might be able to persuade
Cantona to join a club abroad, where there would not be
the same public scrutiny of his every move and word.
Houllier knew England well. He had spent a period of
time teaching in Liverpool, spoke the language, understood the culture and, critically, had extensive contacts
within the English game. What's more, the English league
was the only major one in Europe whose transfer market
remained open at that time of year. As history would
prove, the plan was a masterstroke.

Platini visited Cantona in Nîmes to implore him to
come out of retirement. He received a warm welcome.
Cantona had always held Platini in high esteem as a coach
and as a person. Moreover, he was now determined to
start playing again, but away from the spotlight that had
blinded him in France. So Platini and Houllier, aided by
Eric's lawyer and agent Jean-Jacques Bertrand (who had

recently taken over from Alain Migliaccio) and Jean-Jacques Amorfini, vice-president of the French Players Union, set about the task of finding him a team in England's top division. Houllier enlisted the services of an English agent, Dennis Roach, to forge links with a suitable club. Roach had once represented Trevor Francis, who was at that time manager of Sheffield Wednesday, so he offered Cantona to him. Francis, an acquaintance of Platini, was interested. Wednesday despatched their club secretary, Graham Mackrell, to France forthwith to thrash out an agreement.

On 23 January 1992, Mackrell and Roach met with Cantona and Amorfini at the headquarters of the Cacharel fashion house in Paris. Also present was Jean Bousquet, the president of Olympique Nîmes. Eric had begun proceedings to buy out his contract from his former employers, but that process was not yet complete so Wednesday would have to pay around £1 million to take him to Hillsborough in a permanent deal. This was not a state of affairs the English club was prepared to entertain. Instead, they brokered a loan deal.

A few days later Cantona arrived in Sheffield. His stay was not to be a long one. He remained in the city for a week, during which time he passed a medical, trained and even played in an indoor friendly at the Sheffield Arena. But then he walked out. Wednesday were being cautious about taking him on without first having a chance to check out his credentials at first hand and gauge whether he was likely to settle in England. Their approach to the matter was, it must be said, understandable, given the player's chequered history. During that week, Trevor Francis informed Eric that he was still only at Hillsborough on a trial basis. Cantona took umbrage. After all, he was an established French international, he came recommended by Michel Platini and Gérard Houllier no less, and he claimed there had been no mention of a trial period when the deal was agreed in Paris. 'Even if they had proposed such a trial period, I would not have hesitated in telling them that I had not been on trial anywhere since the age of fourteen, just before I joined

Auxerre,' Eric complained. In France there was widespread surprise at Wednesday's stance. Erik Bielderman recalled: 'Everybody was shocked that Sheffield Wednesday wanted to have him on trial. They felt that he was such a well-known player that he should not be treated like an apprentice.'

Just when it appeared that Cantona's career in England was over before it had begun, events took an undoubted turn for the better. Howard Wilkinson, the Leeds manager, was desperate for a striker after his regular centre-forward, Lee Chapman, sustained a broken arm in a collision with Manchester United's Gary Pallister during a 1–0 FA Cup defeat at Old Trafford. Wilkinson became aware that Cantona was in England and had quit Sheffield Wednesday. Moreover, he remembered being impressed by the player after watching him turn out for the French Under-21 team. 'I was desperately thinking of ways to supplement our push in the final third of the season,' Wilkinson told me during a meeting at the FA's Soho Square headquarters in London. However, he was also aware of Eric's reputation for being a hothead and decided to get references from his contacts in France. 'I phoned Gérard Houllier, I phoned Michel Platini, I phoned Glenn Hoddle, I phoned a friend of mine called Bobby Brown who had married a French girl and was working in France for a football club. And they all said the same thing. They confirmed that he was a good player but that he had had "problems" over the past five or six years in sustaining [his form] because of disagreements at various different clubs which had resulted in him generally downing tools and walking out.'

Wilkinson, a renowned disciplinarian, clearly believed he could handle a player of Cantona's temperament and on 31 January contacted Jean-Jacques Bertrand to arrange a meeting. As luck would have it, Eric was still in Sheffield. 'I lived in Sheffield,' Wilkinson told me, 'so I drove home and called in at the Swallow Hotel on my way. I was shown to Eric's room. I knocked on the door and went into the single room, which was almost cell-like. His agent, Jean-Jacques, was sitting in the chair. Eric was lying on the bed looking very dischuffed to say the least, with several days of growth on his face and looking as if the end of the world was nigh.'

The Leeds manager soon discovered that Cantona was definitely interested in playing at Elland Road. Although arrangements had yet to be made with Nîmes, the club that still held Cantona's registration, the three men there and then thrashed out the basics of a deal that would see Eric join Leeds on loan until the end of the 1991/92 campaign. Howard Wilkinson's team had a home game the following day, so the manager picked Cantona up in the morning and took him along to Elland Road. There he met the club chairman and chief executive, who, after brief negotiations with Bertrand, agreed the temporary transfer, the details of which were rubber-stamped by Nîmes a few days later.

The announcement of Eric Cantona's arrival at Leeds was made straight after the home game against Notts County, a match which produced a 3–0 victory for Leeds and featured a superb solo goal from David Batty as Wilkinson's men extended their unbeaten run to sixteen matches. Wilkinson, by his own admission, delighted in producing a new signing, none other than a French international striker, at the post-match press conference. 'It's always nice to create a surprise for my friends in the media,' he wrote later. Meanwhile, Eric was pleased that Wilkinson was prepared to show faith in him despite his self-confessed 'tumultuous past'. And his new manager promised Eric the 'passion of Elland Road would satisfy all my ambitions'.

After finishing fourth in the 1990/91 campaign, Leeds' first season back in the top flight, Howard Wilkinson's aim in 1991/92 was to gain a place in Europe, so he made a series of new signings in preparation for the team's assault on the league. In came Rod Wallace and his twin brother Ray for a combined fee of £1.7 million from Southampton. Tony Dorigo, the England left-back, was bought from Chelsea for £1.3 million, and Steve Hodge, another England international, arrived from Nottingham Forest to beef up Wilkinson's midfield options – although, sadly, he played little that season due to a calf injury.

The Leeds manager firmly believed there was no clear favourite to lift the title, even though Manchester United had got off to a flying start, winning eight and drawing four of their first twelve matches. It looked for all the world as if, under the management of Alex Ferguson, the Old Trafford club would finally win its first championship title for 25 years. That they did not is due partly to their own faltering form in the latter part of the season. Even so, Wilkinson's robust Leeds team deserve full credit for the spirit and determination that saw them win the day. The then Southampton manager, Ian Branfoot, was one of the first people to hail Leeds as potential champions after his side was soundly beaten 4–0 at the Dell on 28 August 1991. Rod Wallace played particularly well back in his old haunt and Gary Speed was also outstanding, scoring twice from midfield.

Despite Manchester United's awesome start to the campaign, Leeds were top of the table by a point come the end of October, although Ferguson's men had a game in hand. The Yorkshire team had also produced an excellent run of results at the beginning of the campaign, marching through the first ten matches without defeat. Things were still close come the new year, United topping the table after amassing 48 points from 21 matches, while Leeds were second with 46 from 23. The odds at that point certainly appeared stacked against a Leeds triumph. United already enjoyed a two-point lead and would have the chance to extend their superiority to eight points with their games in hand. Moreover, they were scoring freely.

In terms of the destination of the title, Leeds' defeat at the hands of their Manchester rivals at the quarter-finals stage of the Rumbelows League Cup was to prove a blessing in disguise. Although the Old Trafford club went on to win that competition, defeating Nottingham Forest 1–0 in the final, the fixture pile-up their success entailed was an important factor behind their failure to secure the title. Leeds, as the cliché goes, were happy to be able to concentrate on the League. However, in the aftermath of another cup defeat against United, Leeds' chances of claiming the title seemed to have been reduced dramatically by the injury to Lee Chapman, their leading marksman. Chapman's subsequent enforced absence led Howard Wilkinson to look for a stop-gap replacement who could fill the considerable void in attack. It was at that point that he became aware of Cantona's availability.

Cantona made his first appearance in a Leeds shirt as a second-half substitute during a 2–0 defeat at Oldham Athletic on 8 February 1992 – although at one point he was reluctant to come out of the changing-room because of the massed ranks of photographers, many of them from France, who were awaiting his arrival. He started the next game, a week later, against Everton at Elland Road. The match finished 1–1 and Eric struggled to make much of an impression; it would take him a while to grow accustomed to the hurly-burly of English football and, besides, he was not at his physical peak after a six-week lay-off. Cantona was dropped after the game, his disappointment clear for all to see. 'At times he looked almost suicidal as he moped around the dressing-room area,' Lee Chapman recalled. 'From my time in France [with Niort], I knew just how isolated he felt. Being dropped is bad enough, but when it is in a strange country, and you don't speak the language, it is considerably worse.'

During his time at Leeds, Eric roomed with Chapman, who spoke a little French. Along with Gary McAllister, in particular, Chapman made it his duty to welcome Eric to the club and show him around the area. As a result, Cantona soon settled. He was even happier when Isabelle and Raphael came over from France to join him. The family rented a modest semi-detached house near Roundhay Park, where Eric would take his son to play football on the way home from school.

Gary Speed, who despite his tender age enjoyed scintillating form that season, told me how the Leeds dressing-room helped Eric acclimatise to life in Yorkshire. 'I think we'd all seen pictures of him in France – you know, the bad boy. He came to the club, and although he spoke very little English everyone seemed to take to him straight-away, all the lads seemed to welcome him straightaway. I just remember he was a great talent.' Why was the Leeds dressing-room so happy to accommodate someone with such a bad reputation for not getting on with and even fighting his team-mates? Speed's response was straightforward: 'The way the Leeds dressing-room was then, they'd have welcomed anyone. That's one reason why we won the title, because of that [harmony in the dressing-room]. First of all he came over on his own and we socialised a lot – that was the way to get to know him. He used to come out with us a lot because his wife wasn't over then. The way the club was going then, we just tried our hardest to welcome him in and he seemed to thrive on that and it really showed on the pitch.'

Cantona returned to the fray against Luton Town on 29 February, and made an important impact. He came off the bench, almost immediately latched on to an aerial ball into the penalty area, and lobbed the advancing keeper, Steve Sutton. Unfortunately, this attempt looped just over the bar. Leeds went close again shortly afterwards as a Rod Wallace strike cannoned off the Luton crossbar, then, with the scoreline stuck at 0–0, the Frenchman had his first moment of glory. Gary McAllister picked up a clearance from the Luton box, controlling the ball brilliantly on the heavy pitch and taking out the entire Luton defence in the process before rounding the goalkeeper, only to be brought down. But Eric was on hand to hammer the ball into an unguarded net. He raised his arm in celebration, his index finger pointing to the heavens. Eric Cantona had arrived, and from the delight on his face it was clear that the moment genuinely mattered to him. 'Eric's face was a picture of joy as he turned away from scoring his first goal for the club,' Chapman remembered. 'What a contrast it made to his mood shortly before the kick-off. I ran to him and was greeted with a joyous interpretation of my name: "Shappee!"'

Subsequently, Eric got on the score sheet during a 3–0 victory at home over Chelsea. He produced an individual effort of supreme skill that certainly impressed his new team-mates. 'He scored a goal against Chelsea where he flicked the ball over three people's heads and volleyed it in the top corner,' Gary Speed recalled. That afternoon, for the first time, the Elland Road faithful sang the 'Ooh Aah Cantona' song, which would be his theme tune at Leeds and later at Old Trafford.

He spent three more matches on the bench after that, but following a humiliating 4–1 reverse at Queens Park Rangers on 11 March, Wilkinson put him back in the starting eleven for the visit of Wimbledon the following week. Cantona rewarded the manager's faith by scoring in a 5–1 victory, and that was enough to earn him a place in the team for the next four games, which included two draws, against Arsenal and West Ham United.

Then, on 4 April, Leeds suffered a major setback: they were hammered 4–0 at Manchester City. On the Monday after this thrashing at Maine Road, Wilkinson called his players together and told them that if they could secure four wins and a draw from their remaining five fixtures, he was confident they would beat off Manchester United's title challenge. The manager also decided to revert, for the most part, to the team he had relied on for most of the previous season, and which had achieved the best results in 1991/92. That side did not include Eric. Wilkinson's strategy also involved leaving out Gordon Strachan, the captain, from the team to face Liverpool at Anfield, the game from which he was determined to take at least a point. 'We won four of those games and we drew one [at Liverpool], which was championship form,' Wilkinson reflected. 'We took thirteen points from those five games whereas we had taken just six from the previous five [when Cantona appeared regularly in the starting line-up]. It was a remarkable turnaround in terms of performance.'

Remarkable, but closely run too. On 18 April, Manchester United still held the upper hand. They were top of the League with 75 points from 38 games; Leeds had 73 points and had played one game more. All the indicators suggested that the title was Old Trafford bound. But on Easter Monday United suffered a setback that proved to be a major turning point in the campaign. A crowd of 47,576 expectant fans crammed into Old Trafford, most of them hoping for the home win that would surely see United march on to win the title. But they were to be disappointed as they witnessed their team slump to the first of three consecutive defeats. United's opponents that day were Brian Clough's Nottingham Forest, who were determined to avenge their recent Rumbelows Cup final defeat. Forest recorded a 2–1 victory. In the words of Howard Wilkinson, Clough's men had done Leeds a 'massive favour'.

Later on the same day Leeds defeated Coventry thanks to goals from Chris Fairclough and Gary McAllister, and leapfrogged United into top spot. Just two days later Ferguson's men travelled to relegation-threatened West Ham United, where, not for the last time, the Upton Park side upset the United applecart, and with it their title aspirations. West Ham won 1–0, a result that left Leeds top of the table by a single point, both title contenders with two games left to play.

There was no respite for Manchester United. Less than a week after the West Ham game, on Sunday 26 April, they faced another crucial away game, this time against deadly rivals Liverpool, another team that would certainly not lie down and let Ferguson's men waltz their way to the win they so desperately needed. A trip to Anfield was the last thing they would have wished for. When Leeds had played there a few weeks earlier, some of their players had heard shouts from the Kop to the effect that Liverpool fans would rather Leeds claimed the title than Manchester United. Leeds also had a game on the day of the Liverpool–United clash, and this time they kicked off first, dismissing Sheffield United 3–2 in a Yorkshire derby at Bramall Lane that, according to Wilkinson, was full of 'ricochets, defensive howlers and own goals', but 'thankfully, luck was very definitely on our side'. At Anfield, United succumbed to a fired-up Liverpool by two goals to nil. The championship went to Leeds United. It was the first time Leeds had won the top division title for eighteen years. Remarkably, they secured the trophy just 22 days after being annihilated 4–0 at Maine Road.

After winning at Sheffield United, Eric Cantona, David Batty, Gary Speed and Gary McAllister headed to Lee

Chapman's house to watch the Liverpool–United game on television. Chapman allowed cameras from ITV's *The Match* programme into his house to film his and his team-mates' reaction to the result. However, the Leeds players were reluctant to celebrate and show too much emotion live on television. Chapman recalled: 'We knew the roles could have been reversed and it would have been wrong to gloat over United's demise.' It was an attitude that did them credit.

Whatever the debate surrounding the ludicrous schedule – five games in ten days – Manchester United were expected to follow at the end of the season, Leeds' record since the turn of the year had been the more impressive by far. Of their nineteen games, they won ten, drew six and lost three; over the same timespan United, in contrast, gained only seven victories, drew nine times and suffered five defeats.

Cantona was delighted to collect a championship winner's medal just a few months after touching down on English soil. He shared the joy and excitement of a city whose people were celebrating a famous victory. Eric's already iconic profile at Leeds United was confirmed when an 'Ooh Aah Cantona' single was released after the club had clinched the 1992 title. The single, which featured tired dance rhythms and the sort of clichéd piano part that was popular at the time, incorporated Cantona's famous line, pronounced when he was handed the mike at the title party in Leeds city centre: 'Why I love you – I don't know why – but I love you.'

The cult status rapidly bestowed upon Eric by the Elland Road faithful helped create something of a myth about the impact he made during his short spell at the club. According to the legend, it was Eric's arrival in Yorkshire that kick-started Leeds' campaign and saw them pip Manchester United to the title. 'It's a total myth,' Wilkinson asserted. 'Do you know how many games he played for us that season? He made six starts. In his six starts he scored one goal – that was the last goal against Wimbledon at home, and we won 5–1. He appeared nine times as sub and scored two goals in those, one at home against Luton, who were bottom of the League, and then we beat Chelsea at home 3-0, we murdered them, it could have been six, and he scored the last goal in that. So in nine sub appearances and six starts he scored three goals. The interesting thing about the six starts he had was that that was probably the time we dipped. We drew three, won two and lost one. The one we lost was the hammering we got at Man City. So in the consecutive games he played, by championship standards, we started to drop off the pace.

'If you're looking at leading lights in that championship season, you're looking at [Gary] Speed – I think he got double figures in goals – you're looking at Lee Chapman – I think he got 21 goals. Rod Wallace got fourteen. Strachan was player of the year according to the PFA. David Batty got into the England team. Gary McAllister got into the Scotland team. Tony Dorigo was on the fringe of the England team. Eric didn't get picked for France. So in terms of actual achievements, appearances and goals, there's no question that his influence was marginal compared with those other people.'

Even so, Gary Speed maintains that Cantona's sheer presence inspired everyone at the club during the final push towards the title. 'It was one of those [situations] where you knew it was going to be us and Man United for the title. It was pretty tense at that time and I remember Eric came in and he seemed to lift everyone, especially the fans. He didn't play that much of a part in the run-in really. People thought he won the title [for us], but that wasn't really the case. But I think at the time the thing that sticks out is the lift he gave the crowd and the lift he gave everyone around him because of his ability. He just happened to come at the right time, and I think that helped us eventually win the title.'

However important Eric's role in Leeds' success that year, one thing was for certain: the reaction back home to the Frenchman picking up a championship winner's medal in England was one of pride. Erik Bielderman recalled: 'It was a great, great, great period for Eric in the way the French media treated him. He was the king for everybody. Everybody was very proud to see a French player being the king of English football. It was something people hadn't believed would happen.'

That summer Eric did indeed travel to Sweden to play for his country in the European Championship. Although France disappointed at the tournament and were eliminated at the group stage, Cantona was enjoying his football again and was pleased he had made the move to England. And during the 1992/93 campaign, things were to improve.

6 The Crossing

*We weren't good enough to accommodate him and Man
United were. Man United had such good players around
him that when he went there it showed what an asset he
could be.*

GARY SPEED

Despite savouring the sweet taste of success in the late
spring of 1992, Howard Wilkinson was also aware that he
faced a dilemma concerning Eric Cantona. Leeds had
taken up their option to secure Eric's services on a
permanent basis, paying Nîmes around £1 million in the
process, but Wilkinson still harboured doubts as to Cantona's ability to adapt to the demands of English football.
While he had quickly recognised the Frenchman's undoubted talents right from his first training sessions at his
new club, Wilkinson doubted a foreign striker could have
a major impact in England, where a highly physical
approach and long-ball style were still favoured by most
teams – including, it could be argued, Leeds United.

It was a tricky situation. Should Wilkinson, as manager,
encourage Eric to adapt to the style of the Leeds team, or
construct team formation and style around the Frenchman's obvious skill and flair? In his autobiography,
Wilkinson opined that Leeds and Cantona could develop
each other's games in a symbiotic relationship. In short,
England could teach Eric discipline and the value of
teamwork and a strong team ethic, while the Frenchman's
touch and creativity would rub off on his team-mates.
That all sounded fine in theory, but in practice such
principles were soon discarded when Leeds produced a
string of poor performances that led to a crisis of
confidence.

At Elland Road, hopes for the 1992/93 season were high, and understandably so: the team had just lifted its first title in almost two decades. That level of success meant the prospect of players and manager measuring their capabilities against the Continent's elite in the European Cup. Wilkinson was aware of the need to bolster his squad if the side were to wage effective campaigns on both fronts, so he signed the experienced David Rocastle from Arsenal and Scott Sellars, a left-sided midfielder, from Blackburn Rovers.

Expectations were raised a notch when Leeds beat Liverpool 4–3 in August to win the Charity Shield. Cantona marked his first club appearance at Wembley with a scintillating hat-trick, which featured two right-foot strikes and a header. The Leeds players took a relaxed approach to the game, but the victory was a timely boost to squad morale ahead of the travails that lay in store. Yet the Charity Shield is a notoriously poor indicator of how a team will fare over the following nine months of domestic and European competition, as Leeds would soon discover.

In the summer of 1992 English football underwent a makeover that would change its appearance dramatically. A new era was dawning: England's top division was now called the Premier League. What is more, the men in charge of this new entity, the club chairmen, had negotiated a lucrative television deal with Sky, Rupert Murdoch's satellite TV company. This money would eventually swell the coffers of many clubs, not to mention the bank balances of the players, and with more televised live football than ever before, many more games would be played at times to suit football's massive TV audience rather than at the traditional time of 3 p.m. on a Saturday.

In the midst of all the razzmatazz and excitement, though, there were football matches to be played. Leeds started well enough. Cantona's pre-season performances had persuaded Wilkinson to put his faith in the Frenchman from the outset. He was in the starting line-up for a 2–1 home victory over Wimbledon on the opening day of the season, and a creditable 1–1 draw at Aston Villa followed. But a poor 4–1 defeat at relegation-destined

Middlesbrough was not a good omen, even if Leeds did go on to thrash Tottenham Hotspur 5–0 at Elland Road. Eric's performance in that match set headline writers searching for fresh hyperbole to describe a glorious hat-trick that included a spectacular volley of the type that became the Frenchman's trademark. He was unable to repeat that display during a 2–2 draw at Liverpool, but struck twice more as Leeds gained a 2–0 advantage at Oldham. Wilkinson's men let that lead slip, though, and Oldham rallied to earn a draw.

Leeds' away form was to be poor all season, as witnessed by a 2–0 defeat at Manchester United on 6 September, shortly after the Oldham débâcle. Wilkinson identified one of the factors behind the club's dramatic downturn in fortunes as the inability of his central defenders to adapt to the newly introduced rule that goalkeepers were unable to pick up back-passes. 'It had a remarkable effect on my two centre-halves who, all of a sudden, became quivering wrecks.'

The European Cup offered a glamorous distraction from the rigours of the domestic season, but Leeds' inability to perform away from Elland Road hardly instilled confidence that they could master the champions of other European leagues. Besides, English teams were still suffering badly as a result of their exclusion from European competition in the wake of the Heysel Stadium disaster. While the rest of the Continent had developed, English clubs had stood still. Leeds did eventually make it past a first-round tie with VfB Stuttgart of Germany, albeit in unusual circumstances. But the first leg in Germany on 16 September saw Eric Cantona do something that infuriated his manager.

It is an incident Wilkinson remembered well. 'We were doing very, very well until we conceded a bad goal which was very much down to Eric being unprofessional. He said he'd got a hamstring injury and we told him to come off, then he said he was all right, then the next thing he's asking for a ball off Tony Dorigo and he tries to hit this 75-yard cross-field pass with not much time to go in the first half [and with the score at 0–0]. It gets intercepted, the Stuttgart player goes past the full-back and bang, 1–0.'

In the end, Stuttgart cruised to a comfortable 3–0 victory, but back at Elland Road Leeds beat the Germans 4–1, Cantona contributing a goal and an assist. That result should have seen the English team eliminated on the away-goals rule until it emerged that Stuttgart had fielded more than the quota of overseas players allowed by UEFA rules at that time. A rematch was hurriedly arranged for a neutral venue, Barcelona's Nou Camp, and Leeds won 2–1. Carl Shutt scored the winner after replacing Cantona as a substitute.

That win set up a mouth-watering second-round tie with Glasgow Rangers, a clash that was dubbed the 'Battle of Britain'. The first leg at Ibrox on 21 October got off to a perfect start for Leeds as Gary McAllister smashed home a volley just a minute into the game. But Rangers were not to be outdone, and they eventually overcame Leeds thanks to an error by John Lukic, the Leeds goalkeeper, and the instinctive forward play of Ally McCoist. Once more Cantona managed to anger his manager, heading straight for the dressing-room after receiving a knock on the head and being replaced by Rod Wallace.

Howard Wilkinson claims that he only ever came to blows with Cantona over one issue: Eric's non-selection for the team. 'If he was left out, he found that very difficult and he might have a sulk for a while, and everyone would know he was having a sulk,' Wilkinson stated. Consequently, it is hardly surprising that Wilkinson's decision to drop Cantona for the next match, a Premier League tie at Queens Park Rangers on 24 October, triggered a chain of events that would see the Frenchman leave Elland Road for good.

'The night before I left him out at QPR,' Wilkinson explained, 'I had a long conversation with him and said, "Look, we're struggling, you've got certain qualities, but we are very much a team that has to have a pattern. People have to do jobs, we have to think in terms of what is the overall shape and strategy, and at the moment it is not possible to have the sort of consistent team and selection the manager would like." It pained me as much as it pained anybody because we'd gone from being a very good team to a team that was like a rollercoaster.' Besides, Wilkinson saw an opportunity to institute some sort of rotation policy with his strikers, Cantona, Chapman and Wallace, employing different pairings on a horses-for-courses basis. Although such a strategy was not common-place at the time, it made perfect sense considering Leeds were participating in four league and cup competitions in 1992/93.

On the morning of the QPR match, Wilkinson gathered his players together for light training in Hyde Park. Before the session began, however, he had the task of telling them who was in the team for the game that afternoon and who was not. 'I told them the team and he wasn't in it, he was on the bench, and he wasn't very happy – you could tell from his body language.'

When manager and team returned to the Royal Lancas-ter Hotel after that training session, Wilkinson insists he attempted to speak privately to Eric to smooth over the situation. Cantona, however, was having none of it. According to Wilkinson, he refused to listen to the manager's attempts to explain his decision. Wilkinson thought no more of the matter until Eric failed to show up for the pre-match team meeting shortly before they headed off to Loftus Road. The manager was keen to avoid further disruptions to the team's preparations and there-fore instructed Michael Hennigan, his assistant, to take Cantona his passport (which, for some reason that now escapes Wilkinson, the club held) and tell him to return for training the following Tuesday (the manager had already granted Eric a few days' leave in France at the player's request).

However, Gary Speed recalled a slightly different ver-sion of events, and still feels sympathy for the way Eric was told by Wilkinson to leave the squad and travel to France. 'I don't know why, but Howard Wil-kinson stood up in front of us and said, "Eric, here's your passport, off you go!" So he took his passport and had to stand up and walk out of the room. We didn't know what had gone on but at that time we just felt ever so sorry for him. Obviously something had gone on with Howard Wilkinson. He's an honest man, he wouldn't have done that out of nothing, so something must have happened. We had to just sit there and watch him go out. We wanted to say goodbye to Eric but no one did. We felt sorry for him, but I'm sure Howard Wilkinson had good reason.'

When the Tuesday came, Eric failed to report back to Leeds for training. Instead, he slapped in a transfer request to the club in the form of a fax from his agent and lawyer, Jean-Jacques Bertrand. According to Wilkinson, that communication simply stated that Cantona wanted to leave Elland Road, he wasn't coming back to the club again and he wanted a move to Arsenal, Liverpool or Manchester United. The Frenchman later claimed he was sick of getting conflicting signals from his manager. 'One moment he would tell me that he wants me to know that I owe everything to him, that I am only a Frenchman lost in the English League, and other times he would say to me that without me the team is nothing and that I am the essential part,' Cantona wrote.

Eric did play for Leeds again, scoring in the second-leg 2–1 European Cup defeat at the hands of Rangers at Elland Road and appearing in a 4–0 thrashing of Manchester City in the Premiership, but his days at Leeds were clearly numbered. The club was listening to reasonable offers. They would rather have sold him to an Italian or Spanish club than to their fierce rivals on the other side of the Pennines, but no bids were forthcoming from the Continent.

So, like other clubs before them, Leeds had gambled on Eric's fiery reputation and been disappointed. Moreover, the club was afraid it would not recoup any of the £1 million outlay it had had to cough up to acquire the player's services in the first place. In 1992, £1 million was still considered a tidy sum. Clubs in the newly formed Premiership had yet to fully feel the benefits of the massive injection of cash from the sale of television rights from which they would benefit in the years to come. Besides, Leeds' financial situation had further complications. 'Our problem was that we had come a very long way in a very short time [from the old Second Division to the old First Division title and European football in the space of just four seasons] and we were skint. We didn't tell anybody we were skint, but we were skint. Cantona was on good money, and we'd just paid £1 million for him. And at that time, despite his little cameos, there was nothing to show that he was anything other than what his history had suggested, which was a very talented player who had a problem putting it together week in, week out and settling down to the nitty-gritty,' Wilkinson explained, though he neglected to mention the fact that Cantona had scored eleven goals in twenty games in all competitions the season he was sold.

While Wilkinson admits that he could do without people constantly reminding him that he sold Manchester United, Leeds' greatest rivals, the catalyst for their astonishing success of the 1990s for £1.2 million, he is adamant that he took the right decision in the autumn of 1992, given the circumstances. 'Even with twenty-twenty hindsight, if you lay down the facts then there is no evidence to suggest I should or could have done anything other than what I did.'

It is clear that manager and player didn't always see eye to eye, yet Wilkinson claims stories of bust-ups between the two have been exaggerated – 'I actually found him a very personable and, at times, amusing bloke' – though he added cryptically: 'His life off the pitch was sometimes colourful and required assistance.' He then stressed: 'I can't dish too much dirt, I can't tell you of too much aggravation. Once you cut away all the myth and all the dressing up and all the manufactured stories, he was fairly straightforward.'

Although Gary Speed says that Eric socialised a fair amount at Leeds, he also recognises that the Frenchman was 'definitely a loner'. 'He socialised and he seemed to enjoy that when he first came, but you'd never know where he was or what he was doing. I don't think you'd ever pin him down. You couldn't say, "Eric, come out for a drink, mate!" Sometimes he was just there. He was certainly a very independent man. He was his own person.' And that person was clearly one with whom it was good to play football. Although Cantona was at Leeds not even for a whole season, he certainly left a lasting impression on other players at the club. 'He was obviously very talented,' Speed continued. 'To me, being a midfielder, he always seemed to be available. Our type of play was a bit more direct than Man United's at the time and he seemed to add a different dimension to us. The one thing I can remember more than anything really is his ability in training. He didn't really play that many games for us, although some of the games he did play in, his contributions were outstanding.'

Yet despite these glimpses of what could be, Leeds, as a team, were never able to create the sort of conditions in which Cantona could really flourish. This is a fact Gary Speed openly acknowledged. 'Eric was off the cuff and, if you like, he was a bit of a luxury, and Leeds got found out the next year [1992/93] with that because we were that kind of side where everybody had to be working as hard as one another to be successful. The year after [winning the title] when Eric was in the team and things weren't going well, we weren't good enough to accommodate him and Man United were. Man United had such good players around him that when he went there it showed what an asset he could be. They built the team around Eric, and the results were there to see because he was absolutely phenomenal for Man United.'

Although his brief fling with Leeds turned sour, Cantona has always acknowledged a debt of gratitude to the club, its fans and Wilkinson himself for affording him the opportunity to stay in football. 'I have forgotten nothing about Leeds,' he wrote. 'I have forgotten nothing about you, the supporters, who came in thousands to acclaim the team after we had won the title. I will never forget your applause or your generosity, which I found dazzling.'

The story of how Eric Cantona came to join Manchester United is a strange one. On a wet Wednesday afternoon in late November 1992, Alex Ferguson, the Manchester United manager, and Martin Edwards, the club chairman, sat in the latter's office and discussed players they might bring in to Old Trafford to beef up their attempts to win the title for the first time since 1967. The immediate priority was to find a replacement for the unfortunate Dion Dublin, who had recently suffered a bad leg fracture in a game against Crystal Palace.

When it became clear that Dublin, who had arrived that summer from Cambridge United for £1 million, would be sidelined for some time, Ferguson had turned to David Hirst as an alternative. But his £3.5 million bid for the striker was unceremoniously rebuffed by Sheffield Wednesday manager Trevor Francis. Ferguson and his chairman were pondering the possibility of a bid for Everton's Peter Beardsley when Edwards received a telephone call on his private line. It was Bill Fotherby, the Leeds United chief executive. At Howard Wilkinson's behest, Fotherby was enquiring about the availability of Denis Irwin, the Ireland full-back. As Edwards told Fotherby that Irwin was definitely not for sale, a thought suddenly crossed Ferguson's mind. 'Ask him about Cantona' he scrawled on a piece of paper on the chairman's desk. Edwards read the message and shifted the phone conversation to the subject of the Frenchman. To the surprise of both men, Fotherby indicated that a deal was a strong possibility, once Wilkinson gave the go-ahead. This he duly did. Only half an hour had elapsed before Fotherby was back on the phone to thrash out the minutiae of the deal with Edwards.

Edwards was keen to know what had prompted Ferguson's interest in Eric Cantona. The Scot recounted how Gary Pallister and Steve Bruce, his trusted centre-halves, had told him that the Frenchman had caused them myriad problems during their 2–0 defeat of Leeds earlier in the campaign. Moreover, the new French national team boss Gérard Houllier had given his countryman wholehearted, glowing references when he and Ferguson had discussed him.

The following day, 26 November, after a brief meeting between the two interested parties – Cantona and Bertrand on the one hand, Ferguson and Edwards on the other – a press conference was hastily arranged. There, Eric was unveiled as Manchester United's new £1 million signing. When asked in a television interview how a fiery Frenchman and a cantankerous Scot would get on, Ferguson responded: 'The French and the Scots have great old alliances, if you know your history, and I'm hoping this is part of a new alliance.' At the press conference to announce his transfer, Eric made a prescient remark: 'I've learnt many things from the English game and there is still a lot for me to learn, but the day when I stop learning, that's the day when I will retire from the game in general.'

Alex Ferguson's signing of Eric Cantona caused a mass raising of eyebrows, not least within the Manchester United squad. Lee Sharpe, the winger, has very clear recollections of how, where and when he heard that Eric had signed for the Old Trafford club. 'I was actually doing an autograph session for my boot sponsors in Leeds at the time, funnily enough. I got in the car, and whoever it was from the sponsors was taking me round to where I had parked my car, and they said: "Have you heard Eric Cantona's signed for your lot?" I said: "Yeah, right, absolutely no chance." So he turned the radio on and there it was: Eric had signed for just over £1 million.

'It was a total shock. He'd done well for Leeds and we thought there was no way they would sell him to us, especially for £1 million. But he just hit it off [with everyone] straightaway. I don't think it took him long to start playing well, to win the fans over and to win the players over. Obviously we knew he was a good player anyway, but we were all like, "Oh God, he's a bit of a madman this one, don't argue with him, he might try and knock your lights out." ' Sharpe recalled that when the news broke that Cantona had signed for United, the media was full of stories about some of the more unsavoury incidents he had been involved in during his time in French football. 'We were like, "This bloke's a total nutter, what are we doing? And he comes to Man United, fits in, blends in and causes not one bit of trouble with the lads. The lads all love him, he produces great football, so where's the problem?" '

The Frenchman was certainly assured of a warm welcome from Manchester United fans, many of whom shared Bruce and Pallister's admiration for the way he had performed at Old Trafford that September. Andy Mitten, editor of the *United We Stand* fanzine, remembered: 'When he visited Old Trafford with Leeds and pulled off a stunning overhead kick that nearly resulted in a goal, he was applauded by those around me in K Stand. To applaud an opposition player was a rarity, to applaud a Leeds United player was unheard of in my time.' Mitten recognised that many football fans delight in signing their rivals' top players, thus depriving opposition supporters of their former favourites. 'Cantona really did come out of the blue, and before we knew it he was wearing a hideous away kit of the same colour in an Old Trafford photo call. Many United fans were happy that the signing had pissed Leeds fans off too. He had been a central figure in their championship-winning team that had taken advantage of Manchester United's deficiencies a few months earlier. It was scant consolation, but it was some consolation.'

In France there was widespread delight that the French international had secured a transfer to a club of Manchester United's prestige. 'It was seen as a great move,' Erik Bielderman remarked. 'Obviously to go to Manchester United was a tremendous transfer and everybody was happy to see him operating for the best team in England. They had more well-known players than Leeds and everybody was excited to see Eric as the leading man of what was to become a great team.'

However, Ferguson's swoop for Cantona and his confidence in the Frenchman's ability provoked a mixed reaction among football writers and pundits in England. Duncan McKenzie, writing in the now defunct *Today* newspaper, hit the nail on the head when he stated: 'The transfer is a great coup for Alex Ferguson and, at £1 million, has got to be classed as a bargain.' And in the *Daily Star*, George Best, a former Manchester United number seven, recognised what Eric could bring to Old Trafford: 'Cantona is one of the best players in the League, if not the most exciting in the country.' But not everyone thought it was such a brilliant move. 'In my opinion,' barked Emlyn Hughes in his *Daily*

Mirror column, the former Liverpool player failing to recognise the likely impact of the superior technique with which the Frenchman was blessed, 'he's a flashy foreigner. He'll score goals for United . . . when they are two up.' And John Giles, billed by the *Daily Express* as 'the man the players read', opined: 'He is a great entertainer. But there has never been any mention of Cantona being a great player. And I don't think he is.'

Hughes, Giles and the other detractors would be proved wrong in the most dramatic and spectacular style imaginable. At long last club and player had found the perfect symbiosis for which each had been yearning for many years. Each was to be eternally grateful for what the other brought them.

7 Breaking into Heaven

Of course there were lots of games when it didn't happen for Eric and you thought 'Oh my God, he's been terrible', but that's what happens with ball players that are trying to create; sometimes it doesn't work for you. But even in the games it didn't work for him, he ended up scoring and he grabs the headlines and gets a nine out of ten. That is the great player he was.

LEE SHARPE

For anyone who started watching English league football in the mid-1990s, it must have been impossible to imagine that Manchester United had failed to win the country's top division for two and a half decades. When Eric Cantona arrived at Old Trafford in November 1992, he joined a club whose last title-winning party had taken place in 1967. Not since the days of Bobby Charlton, Denis Law and George Best had the country's most famous club celebrated a championship victory. There had been a few near misses, notably in 1979/80 and 1991/92, and a fair share of FA Cup triumphs, not to mention Cup Winners Cup glory in 1991. Yet the all-important trophy continued to elude United. Moreover, the inability to produce a title-winning team had become a millstone around the neck of every manager since Sir Matt Busby. 'I think quite a few people wondered if there was a curse on the club in terms of the title,' Mark Hughes wrote when he cast his mind back to the end of the 1991/92 season.

Happily, the programme of reconstruction and youth development initiated by Alex Ferguson when he was appointed manager in November 1986 was about to bear fruit. However, the signs at the time of the Cantona transfer were not good. United were sixth in the

Premiership, nine points adrift of the pace-setters, Norwich City. Unusually for a club whose entire heritage is based on the principle of scintillating attacking play, the team just couldn't score goals. Granted, Ferguson had put together the best defence in the country, but at the other end United had managed just eighteen goals in seventeen games before the dawning of the Cantona era.

The player who had received the most criticism was Welsh striker Mark Hughes. Although he had already notched up seven Premier League goals that season, many detractors insisted it was impossible to find a strike partner who could complement his robust style of play. It was a burden that had begun to weigh heavy on Hughes's shoulders, as he recalled in his autobiography: 'The idea went round at one stage of my career that Mark Hughes was difficult to play with, and following my return from Spain and Germany there were people suggesting that Manchester United would have to get rid of me because it had become impossible to find a man I could hit it off with up front.'

Cantona was aware of United's profligacy in front of goal but was convinced that he could help turn the situation on its head. He recognised that there was the potential to bring back the glory days of Bobby Charlton et al his father had told him about. And, more recently and more practically, he had seen United overcome Barcelona 2–1 in Rotterdam to clinch the Cup Winners Cup. Many of the players in that team were still at the club, and Eric saw that with the addition of his craft, his vision and his goals, happier times were most definitely on the horizon.

Moreover, he understood the very special demands of playing for Manchester United and the traditions and history that still inspire generations of the club's players and fans. The wounds inflicted on Manchester United on 6 February 1958 still affect many people at Old Trafford extremely deeply (of course it does not help that fans of some rival teams insist on pulling the scab off the wound by singing sickening taunts about the air crash during matches). 'Here at Old Trafford, everyone remembers this with great emotion,' Cantona wrote of the tragedy in which 21 people, United players, club officials and journalists among them, lost their lives. 'The directors of the club told me about it as soon as I arrived at the club. But I already knew. The city will never forget it.'

Undoubtedly the Frenchman's clear grasp of the significance of the deep-seated pain caused by that tragedy helped him form the enduring bond with Old Trafford that made him one of the true greats in Manchester United's history. And, of course, there will always be enormous reverence for him at the club because his performances in a United shirt helped transform a good team into one that dominated English football for the rest of the 1990s and beyond.

It took Alex Ferguson just one training session at the Cliff to realise that he had recruited a genuinely special talent. As the rest of the squad headed off for a hot shower, Cantona made a request of his new manager: he required the assistance of two players to help him 'practise'. Ferguson was taken aback but delighted that his new player was showing such an appetite for training, and he immediately instructed three youngsters to join him back on the training field. One was a goalkeeper; the other two spent the next half hour delivering crosses so that Eric could practise his volleying. Word soon spread around the dressing-room that Cantona had taken this unusual step, and the following day several players stayed behind to join in Eric's self-imposed practice regime. Every United training session since has ended with what would once have been regarded as extra practice.

In his autobiography, Alex Ferguson acknowledges that he learnt a great deal about effective training methods from that one incident. It made him realise that his sessions did not contain enough technical practice because there was so much else to get through. 'Many people have justifiably acclaimed Cantona as a catalyst who had a crucial impact on our successes while he was with the club, but nothing he did in matches meant more than the way he opened my eyes to the indispensability of practice. Practice makes players.'

Cantona first took to the field of play in a Manchester United shirt when the club's cross-town rivals, Manchester City, visited Old Trafford on 6 December 1992. Although Eric, a second-half substitute for Ryan Giggs, did not trouble the scorers in a 2–1 victory, there were signs of the impact he would make in the future. His manager was already convinced. 'Tall and straight-backed, with the trademark upturned collar, he conveyed a regal authority, and the place was in a frenzy every time he touched the ball. I was struck at once by his insistence on making the easy pass whenever possible, a characteristic that showed itself as a great strength of his game in his time with us.'

Crucially, Mark Hughes too recognised straightaway that his partnership with Cantona would flourish. 'It's always difficult hitting the pace when you come on as a sub, especially in a derby, and I suppose overall Eric didn't do a lot. But there was one moment early in the second half when he suddenly got clear down the right to knock in a great cross. I wasn't expecting it, and I'm afraid I made a mess of my attempt to score with a header. At the same time I thought the fellow can certainly play a bit, and if he carries on like that I'll score more than I miss.'

Six days later, Eric was in the starting line-up for the first time as United took on title rivals Norwich City at Old Trafford. His impact on proceedings was limited, but United emerged with a valuable 1–0 victory thanks to Mark Hughes's effort. Cantona did not have to wait long for his first goal in a United shirt. Six days before Christmas Ferguson's team travelled to Chelsea, and it was at Stamford Bridge that the Frenchman broke his duck. Lee Sharpe launched a deep cross from the left flank and Mike Phelan managed to head the ball back from beyond the far post towards an unmarked Eric. The striker swivelled and volleyed home past Kevin Hitchcock, the Chelsea goalkeeper. 'He knows how to celebrate all right, and he knows how to finish,' enthused Clive Tyldesley on the television commentary. The moment was doubly significant: not only had Eric got his first goal for United, he had also helped them salvage a point from a game that might otherwise have been lost. He would perform similar heroics time and again as United strode to four championships in his five-year stay at Old Trafford.

Next up, on Boxing Day, was a visit to Sheffield Wednesday. With twenty minutes left on the clock United appeared down and out as the Yorkshire team led by three goals to nil, but an astonishing turnaround ensued as Brian McClair scored twice and Eric grabbed a late, late equaliser. Admittedly there was an element of luck involved in his goal: he lost control of the ball just five yards from the Wednesday goal, but it was held up in the muddy goal mouth and Eric reacted quicker than Chris Woods, sliding in and poking the ball home. 'It was this reversal of the situation which clearly illustrated our determination never to believe that we were beaten, even when all the evidence seemed to point that way,' Cantona stated. 'It was to be one of the keys to our successes.' Again, this never-say-die attitude not only brought success in 1992/93, it helped United overcome many of the hurdles that lay between them and glory even after the Frenchman's departure.

Two days after the draw at Hillsborough, Coventry City were mauled 5–0 at Old Trafford, Eric coolly slotting a spot-kick past Jonathan Gould. Penalty-taking was to prove one of his many fortes during his Old Trafford career. Mark Hughes, Ryan Giggs, Lee Sharpe and Denis Irwin were also on the score sheet that day.

However, it was in the next fixture, the visit of Tottenham Hotspur on 9 January 1993, that United really started to display all the self-belief whose emergence had coincided with Cantona's arrival. In a spectacular 4–1 success, Eric twice combined brilliantly with Denis Irwin as the pair registered a goal apiece. The two goals provided the perfect snapshot of the range of his abilities. First, he towered above the Spurs defence to head Irwin's deep cross into the top left-hand corner of the net from his position on the right edge of the six-yard box. Then he produced a subtlety of touch not seen at Old Trafford since George Best's time to send Irwin through on goal. The Irishman played a square pass to Eric, who was stationed some ten yards outside the penalty area. Instinctively, Eric flicked the ball with the outside of his right boot back into Irwin's path, lifting the ball over the advancing defenders. The full-back latched on to the pass and rifled the ball home from the inside left position. 'The return ball from Cantona was one of the passes of the season,' drooled John Motson on BBC television. 'This man is playing a game of his own.'

Cantona's sublime skill was once more in evidence during a 2–0 home win over Nottingham Forest towards the end of January. As Steve Bruce brought the ball over the halfway line, he indicated to his team-mates that nobody was offering themselves for a short pass. Then he looked up and spotted the Frenchman hovering around the edge of the Forest penalty area. Bruce's long pass was not quite perfect, forcing Eric to retreat a couple of yards to collect it. Nevertheless, he cushioned the ball perfectly into the run of Mark Hughes, who volleyed home in typically emphatic fashion from twenty yards. It was proof enough that the two strikers would perform well in tandem.

Indeed, Hughes would later reflect upon how the influence of Cantona helped his own career to blossom. 'So thank you very much indeed, Eric Cantona, a player who, in my view, has given United in general a new dimension and me in particular a first-class partner. We may not speak the same language, but I think I can safely say that from time to time we make the ball talk louder than words. It's not really for me to say how well I am playing these days, but I think, without being unduly immodest, that I have played my part in our run of success. I certainly feel as if I have made a reasonable contribution, and I know that the Frenchman has changed my footballing life.'

The quality of Eric's performances and his ability to lift the team as a whole meant he was soon the focus of great affection from Manchester United's massive army of supporters. The club shop did a roaring trade in Cantona memorabilia. Some fans even started wearing Eric masks to games, and the Old Trafford faithful began to sing 'Ooh

Aah Cantona' to the tune of the Marseillaise as Can-
tomania took a firm grip. The player himself, who
received fan mail from as far away as south-east Asia and
the United States, was amazed by the extent to which the
team wooed supporters all over the world.

On the playing front, Eric's next contribution, on 6
February, was to provide a goal and an assist in a 2–1
defeat of Sheffield United at Old Trafford. His task after
that was an unenviable one: to run a gauntlet of hate on
his return to Elland Road. Relations between the supporters of Manchester United and Leeds are sour at the
best of times, but the defection of Eric Cantona to Old
Trafford meant the atmosphere within the stadium was
particularly unsavoury that day. 'The papers often talk in
exaggerated terms about certain grounds being a cauldron
of hate, but Elland Road on this occasion was a really
mean place,' Mark Hughes reflected. 'Clearly, they regarded him as a traitor and they were out to show that
they hated him.'

Ironically, the attitude of the Leeds fans was in stark
contrast to that of many of Eric's former team-mates. Gary
Speed, for one, was disappointed not to have a proper
opportunity to catch up with the Frenchman. 'It was
strange, really. Obviously when he did come back he got
lots of stick from the crowd and he was a volatile
character. It was like you'd never known him as an
individual, it was like he was a stranger again. Every time
he got the ball the crowd booed him, so obviously that
must have got to him and he wasn't in the mood where
you could say, "Hello, Eric, how's it going?" So it was very
strange after that. He had a [farewell] game at Manchester
United and he did invite me back to play in that, so I think
he was just a victim of circumstance with the Leeds fans
being so harsh. But I did get invited back for that game so
he obviously remembers me as a friend.'

Cantona found himself embroiled in controversy after
the goalless draw when it was alleged that he had spat at
a fan. In his defence, Eric told an FA disciplinary
committee that he had indeed spat, but at a wall, and out
of frustration. He was fined £1,000 for his actions. At the

same hearing he received a two-match suspension for exceeding the 21 disciplinary points mark, even if most of them had accrued during his spell with Leeds.

United continued their good form and Cantona's influence grew and grew. His next goalscoring exploits were in a 3–0 home win over Middlesbrough at the end of February. A fortnight later, following a victory at Liverpool and a surprising defeat at Oldham, United faced Aston Villa at Old Trafford in what was billed as a title showdown. Things started badly for the Reds as Villa took a 1–0 lead through a Steve Staunton net-buster, but the man who was so often to be the team saviour created a goal for Mark Hughes, and that meant the points were shared.

All the while Cantona's enthusiastic approach to training and the ability he displayed were having a positive impact on the rest of the squad. 'Professional footballers are not easily impressed because they see good footballers all the time, but I tell you, our Frenchman has opened our eyes a good many times,' Mark Hughes wrote. 'Very often we simply stop playing and clap in admiration. It's amazing what he can do with the ball, especially when he ties someone up in knots with one of his little juggling stunts.' According to Hughes, the rest of the squad were able to improve the technical side of their game simply by watching Eric practise and trying to emulate the more skilful, patient approach he had brought with him from the Continent. However, Alex Ferguson was concerned that the rest of the players might try too hard to copy the French master. 'In one team talk he said, "All these flicks and things, leave them to Eric because he can do them and you can't." We all burst out laughing, but he had a point.'

United's next task, on 20 March, was to negotiate a derby match at Maine Road, without doubt a potential banana skin for their title aspirations. The team's performance was mediocre, but Cantona grabbed a crucial goal to secure a point. Lee Sharpe remembered that goal and the subsequent celebrations clearly: 'I've gone down the left wing and crossed one in and he's headed it in. And he came running over to me by the Man United fans and we grabbed the sides of each other's heads and were just shouting at each other. I've got a photo of that some-where; I'll always remember that.'

After a goalless home draw with Arsenal, Cantona, Sharpe and co. embarked on a run of five consecutive victories through April that effectively wrapped up the inaugural Premiership with two games to spare. Eric was a scorer as United mowed down Norwich City's title hopes, then came an extraordinary match against Shef-field Wednesday in which United appeared to be heading for defeat until the redoubtable Steve Bruce headed two late goals, an equaliser and a winner, the latter deep into stoppage time. Brian Kidd, the United assistant manager, was overcome with emotion and ran on to the pitch to kiss the Old Trafford turf. Cantona was again on target as Chelsea were brushed aside 3–0 at Old Trafford.

Manchester United's excellent form heaped pressure on Aston Villa, their only remaining championship rivals. So much so that come Sunday, 2 May, three games before the end of Villa's season, they had to beat Oldham Athletic or the title would be delivered to United. Alex Ferguson took himself off for an afternoon on the golf course instead of watching the Boundary Park clash on television. He advised his players to follow suit, but most of them simply could not focus on anything else. They knew how close they were to glory. Mark Hughes recalled the tension of that afternoon: 'I must admit I was nervous, and drifted in and out of the living room. I spent a lot of time in the kitchen making cups of tea and then we all came back in front of the television for the last five minutes. I told the kids that in a few minutes I might be giving them the biggest hugs they had ever had in their lives. I don't think they really understood, but they knew something special was in the air, and when the final whistle went for Oldham's victory we were all in tears, me especially.'

It was an unlikely defeat inflicted by a Nick Henry goal, but one for which everyone at Old Trafford was extremely grateful. United had finally ended their 26-year quest for the league title without even kicking a ball, and the players held an impromptu celebration party at Steve Bruce's house. Lee Sharpe had spent much of the early part of the evening trying to get through to his team-mates on the telephone without realising that they were all enjoying the centre-half's hospitality already. Sharpe described the scene when he arrived: 'I drove around, stone cold sober, and the lads had been there for hours drinking champagne. Eric was there letting his hair down and joining in with the team.' Memories of that party caused Sharpe to reflect on Cantona's nature and behaviour within the dressing-room. 'I don't think we saw him as aloof. You see an arrogance in him, I think that's impossible not to see with the way he plays, but we never really saw that in the dressing-room or when he was socialising with us. He never said a lot. I don't think he was overconfident about his English but he understood everything that was going on and joined in the laughs and said the odd thing. The lads totally accepted him.'

When Eric had arrived at the title party, Queen's 'We Are the Champions' was blaring out of the stereo (the clichéd nature of the celebrations can perhaps be excused in hindsight, given the significance of the players' achievements that season). He was certainly ecstatic to have collected a third consecutive championship winner's medal, after previous successes at Marseille and Leeds, especially since he had experienced so many difficult times in the previous eighteen months. He has admitted that he didn't sleep too well when he returned from the celebrations at Bruce's house; he was too excited about the following day's festivities, which would be witnessed not just by 40,445 delighted United fans but also by Michel Platini and Gérard Houllier, the men who had instigated his move to England. 'I had only one thing on my mind, and I could not forget it: to rejoin my team-mates at Old Trafford knowing that this day was going to give me the greatest sunshine of my career.'

The following day, a bank holiday Monday, Blackburn Rovers were the guests at Manchester United's title party. The script dictated a United victory and the players duly obliged by beating their hangovers and Rovers 3–1. Late in the game Gary Pallister, the only player not to have scored that season, stepped up and drove home a low twenty-yard free kick to put the result beyond doubt. Afterwards, Sir Matt Busby looked on with pride as Bryan Robson and Steve Bruce, club captain and stand-in captain, raised the Premiership trophy together.

Alex Ferguson already had a strong team at his disposal when he signed Eric Cantona. Peter Schmeichel was rapidly emerging as the best last line of defence in the world. In front of him was a defence that boasted an excellent blend of strength, pace, experience and courage with Gary Pallister and Steve Bruce at centre-half and Paul Parker and Denis Irwin playing as full-backs. In midfield, the duo of Paul Ince and Brian McClair provided ample bite for United to win possession and then control it. And on the wings the team was blessed with the pace and skill of Ryan Giggs and Lee Sharpe. Up front, Mark Hughes combined strength and aggression with an ability to score crucial goals.

And then there was Cantona. Quite simply he was the magic ingredient, the extra element that transformed a good team into a brilliant one with his range of passing, his creative eye, his ability to free himself of his marker and his knack of producing goals just when his side needed them most and expected them least. The Cantona record for 1992/93 confirms the validity of this assertion: Eric scored 20 goals in the season, nearly half of them for United; he had a hand in 22 of the 46 goals scored in the Premier League after his arrival at Old Trafford, contributing thirteen assists and nine goals; Hughes and Cantona started 20 games together and produced a return of 39 goals between them; and United lost just one of the 22 games in which he played.

Throughout the campaign it had appeared that the battle for the title would go right down to the wire, but the team's ability to extract points when they really needed them, often thanks to Eric's timely interventions, meant that by the season's end a ten-point chasm existed between the champions and Aston Villa in second place.

Lee Sharpe, who played alongside Cantona for four seasons before working under Howard Wilkinson at Leeds, summarised how Eric was able to thrive at Old Trafford: 'Having played under Howard Wilkinson as well, he does like everyone working his socks off and out-working the other team. Whereas at [Manchester] United we were more organised in two banks of four. The midfield protected the defenders and the defenders kept a rigid four and we had Eric floating about anywhere he wanted to. And then you had Mark Hughes who was a danger to any centre-half that got on the ball. It worked well for us. Of course there were lots of games when it didn't happen for Eric and you thought "Oh my God, he's been terrible", but that's what happens with ball players that are trying to create; sometimes it doesn't work for you. But even in the games it didn't work for him, he ended up scoring and he grabs the headlines and gets a nine out of ten. That is the great player he was.'

Amid the euphoria that greeted United's 1993 title triumph, another emotion was in evidence: relief. At last the players of the modern Manchester United had learnt to live with the ghosts of the past and the high expectations they had to meet. Clayton Blackmore, a member of the title-winning squad, recalled on MUTV: 'For the players it was a massive relief. You're always living in the shadow of people like George Best, living legends. They're the ones who made the club so big all around the world.'

Now United had a new legend, and his name was Cantona.

8 Destiny Calling

*There are those who represent something extraordinary,
something sublime. Not just as a result of individual
performances on the pitch, but because they are blessed
with the talent to inspire and pull everyone else together.
Eric Cantona belonged in this category.*

PETER SCHMEICHEL

When his squad returned for pre-season training in the summer of 1993, Alex Ferguson called them together for a pep talk. He congratulated them all on their achievements the previous season and said he hoped they had all enjoyed their summer break. However, he also expressed doubts as to the hunger of certain unnamed players for the coming campaign. He told them there was an envelope in his drawer which contained a piece of paper on which the names of three players were written. These, he claimed, were the people about whom he harboured doubts. It was typical of the psychology employed by Ferguson as he sought to motivate his troops and nip any possible hint of complacency in the bud. But Brian McClair, the Scottish midfielder, remembered that everyone in the squad was determined to taste success again. He told MUTV: 'Having had the night when we actually won the title, we wanted to do that again. So we were feeling quite confident.'

Ferguson had made one extremely significant new addition to the team during the close season. The purchase of Irish midfielder Roy Keane from Nottingham Forest for a British record £3.7 million was to prove a smart investment. The United manager had been on the 22-year-old's trail for three years and had finally got his man, beating off the challenge of Blackburn Rovers, in particular, for Keane's signature. The Irishman's energy and purpose meant he would fit in perfectly alongside Paul Ince in the country's most menacing central midfield partnership. Keane's pedigree and drive, both in evidence during his first appearance at Old Trafford for Nottingham Forest when he piled into a fierce challenge on Bryan Robson straight after kick-off, made him an excellent signing and an instant hit with the fans.

Keane was a long-term replacement for Robson, whose appearances were becoming more and more rare as the many injuries he had sustained during his glittering career began to take their toll. Moreover, the former Forest player formed a crucial part of the ever-voracious Ferguson's ambitious master plan. The manager was desperate to dominate the domestic scene and emulate the success of his mentor and compatriot, Sir Matt Busby, by bringing the European Cup to Old Trafford.

Although they would have to wait a few years for glory on that stage, Ferguson's men certainly set about the 1993/94 Premiership campaign with efficiency and gusto. After beating Arsenal 5–4 on penalties in the Charity Shield, Manchester United hit the ground running. The programme presented them with a difficult trip to Norwich City, one of the previous season's title contenders, on the opening day of the campaign, 15 August. United, without Cantona, who sustained a knee injury in the Charity Shield, but now with the extra bite and verve of Roy Keane in midfield, re-established their superiority over the Canaries with a 2–0 victory courtesy of goals from Bryan Robson and Ryan Giggs, the team's oldest and youngest members respectively.

United in fact won five of their first six Premier League games despite Cantona's absence for the first four encounters. Three days after the game at Carrow Road, Sheffield United were soundly beaten, 3–0, at Old Trafford; a 1–1 draw with Newcastle United then ensued at the same venue on 21 August. Only in England could a side start the season with four games in the first eight days but, for once, the intensity seemed to suit Ferguson's eager team as they beat Aston Villa 2–1 away just 48 hours after the Newcastle clash.

At the end of August United travelled to Southampton for a traditionally awkward fixture at the Dell. Cantona was now back to full fitness and immediately started to reproduce his goalscoring exploits of the previous season as the team clinched a 3–1 victory. The Frenchman's goal demonstrated that the close season had done nothing to dull his sense of awareness, perfect touch and lethal execution. As a loose ball broke to him on the edge of the Southampton penalty area, Cantona spotted that the goalkeeper, Tim Flowers, had strayed from his line. Without hesitation or the need to take an extra touch of the ball, Eric chipped it deliciously over Flowers and into the far corner of the net. He ran towards Gary Pallister and jumped into the defender's arms in celebration. The King was back in business.

There then followed a comfortable 3–0 home win over West Ham during which Eric scored from the penalty spot. And although they suffered a 1–0 reverse at Chelsea ten days later, Cantona quickly got the team back on track when Arsenal visited Old Trafford on 19 September. Such is the intensity of the traditional rivalry between United and the North Londoners that the pair usually produce the tightest games; often one moment of luck or individual brilliance dictates which side will emerge victorious. It was thanks to the sheer brilliance of an Eric Cantona free kick that the home side collected the points that day.

The goal arrived from a set-piece that was as simple in its conception as it was devastating in its execution. The ball was placed in a central position, 25 yards from David Seaman's goal. The England custodian had plenty of men in his wall, but no one could do anything to stop the thunderbolt unleashed by Cantona as he smashed Paul Ince's lay-off goalwards. 'Well, it's just teed up for Cantona. Ohhh! On the biggest stage, he is the master performer,' raved Martin Tyler on Sky television as every one of Eric's team-mates bar Schmeichel (he only comes up to try to score goals, not celebrate them) rushed to salute the Frenchman.

Cantona's ability to grab such crucial goals and to create openings for team-mates meant his impact within the dressing-room simply grew and grew. He was now the focal point of United's attacking thrusts, and in times of need the rest of the team looked to him for guidance. Lee Sharpe reflected: 'I think just to see his name on the team sheet is an inspiration. It doesn't matter how he performs, it's just knowing you've got him there. He was always looking for the ball, always trying to get on the ball. As a wide player myself, I would knock the ball into Sparky [Mark Hughes] or into the midfield and then Eric would get on it and you could make a run knowing that he was going to find you. It was great for someone like me. I remember times when I would knock the ball into him and start running and he knocked it down the line and it was right in my path and just out of the reach of the full-back. He was just ready for you to play one or two touch. His passing was exquisite at times.'

Swindon Town were the next to perish at the Theatre of Dreams. Cantona was on target again in a 4–2 win, this time with a cool finish when one-on-one with the goal-keeper, a situation in which he never seemed to miss. He then created goals for Mark Hughes and Ryan Giggs as the side strode to a 3–2 win at Sheffield Wednesday on 2 October. Ferguson's men were on a roll, winning each of their next three Premier League fixtures, against Everton, Tottenham and Queens Park Rangers.

The game against the latter featured another Cantona masterpiece, on this occasion a solo effort. Eight minutes into the second half, with United trailing 1–0 despite home advantage, Paul Ince's firmly headed clearance reached the Frenchman on the halfway line. In an instant he had flicked the ball cleverly round an advancing defender and was racing forward in search of the QPR jugular. Although Ryan Giggs and Mark Hughes provided options either side of him, he had spotted a clear shooting opportunity. He struck his shot low and true from 25 yards; the ball fizzed beyond the keeper's despairing dive and clipped off the inside of the far post before nestling in the back of the net. Hughes later struck the winner but, as ever, it was Cantona who had set the team on its way.

* * *

Manchester United's first European Cup tie since the 1968/69 season, when they were eliminated 2–1 on aggregate by the mighty AC Milan, saw Cantona and co. visit Kispest Honved of Hungary, for whom the great Ferenc Puskas had played in the 1950s. Just 9,000 spectators witnessed the Reds' (they actually played in green and yellow shirts) 3–2 victory at the Joszef Bozsik Stadium on 15 September 1993. Roy Keane added to his growing reputation by netting twice, while Cantona grabbed the third with an expert finish after good work from Ryan Giggs on the left wing and a slip in the opposition defence. A fortnight later United finished the job with a 2–1 victory at Old Trafford in which Steve Bruce was twice on target.

Round two pitted the team against the then relatively unknown talents of Galatasaray, the champions of Turkey, who would produce one or two shocks to the Old Trafford system. United were expected to experience few difficulties in securing a passage through to the next stage of the competition, but they had not counted on the resilience of the Turks. Moreover, the 3–3 scoreline was an indication of how much clubs from emerging footballing nations had caught up with English teams during their ban from European competition. The fans were grateful to Eric for another exquisitely taken goal, otherwise the scoreline might have been even more embarrassing. Roy Keane chipped a ball deep into the Galatasaray penalty area which Eric met with a perfectly timed volley on the run.

Gary Pallister described the match for MUTV. 'We went 2–0 up against Galatasaray at Old Trafford and we thought: "This is easy." They weren't supposed to be a tough team, Galatasaray, at the time; they certainly had no reputation as being a top team, one that we should have feared. We got lulled into a false sense of security, and before we knew it we were 3–2 down, and it was only a last-gasp equaliser from Eric that got us a 3–3 draw.' Pallister also recalled what appeared to be Turkish fans running on to the pitch and burning a flag in some sort of demonstration during the match. Peter Schmeichel got hold of one of them and physically ejected him from the pitch, an action the team would live to regret.

Even Alex Ferguson, famed for coming from a background as unforgiving as the streets of Govan, had witnessed nothing like the vicious abuse to which the United party was subjected during their stay on the banks of the Bosporus. Hundreds of incensed Galatasaray fans greeted them at the airport with angry and offensive banners and chants, and the night before the game the players' sleep was interrupted. 'We had boats sailing down the river every hour or every couple of hours,' Lee Sharpe recalled. 'They had supporters partying on them and singing "Galatasaray, Galatasaray" and honking horns all through the night. They were all shouting over to the hotel, making signs and blowing horns and just generally trying to keep us awake during the night.'

Things were even worse inside the Ali Sam Yen Stadium, and there was certainly no sympathy – nor, indeed, any protection – from the local police, who appeared to be nothing but unruly thugs in uniform. The following is Lee Sharpe's description of the Istanbul experience: 'That was probably the most hostile game I've ever played in. We got there two hours before the kick-off, to go and have a look at the pitch, to get accustomed to the place. When we got there both sides of the ground were packed. There were flares, there were flags, there were horns, they were singing from side to side, over the ground, giving us abuse. There were armed military people there, police. We weren't very well protected; the coach got bricked as we were coming into the ground. You just felt it was a dangerous place to be. And after the game, I don't think we got particularly well protected when we were leaving.'

For the game itself, Alex Ferguson left out Mark Hughes, packed five players – Robson, Keane, Ince, Giggs and Sharpe – into midfield and left Eric Cantona to lead the line in the hope that the Frenchman might produce the one moment of magic that would secure his team's place in the next round. He was to try a similar tactic away at Juventus in the 1996/97 Champions League campaign. Sadly, on neither occasion did it work. Cantona is no lone striker. He did not thrive on having the ball played into him and having to hold up play while support arrived. His game was all about collecting the ball in space, facing goal, and looking to feed others ahead of him. Eric struggled to make his usual impact as he ploughed a lone furrow for most of a frustrating match. United simply could not make the breakthrough, and a fractious encounter, which involved ample gamesmanship from the home team, saw United eliminated on the away-goals rule.

The United players and staff were furious at the level of play-acting and time-wasting employed by the Turkish players and they were absolutely livid with the referee for allowing such tactics to go unpunished. At the final whistle Cantona approached Kurt Rothlisberger, the Swiss referee, and formed his forefinger and thumb into the shape of a zero to indicate what he thought of the official's performance. What Eric didn't realise was that as he turned and walked away, the referee decided to brandish a red card in his direction.

As the United players headed for the tunnel, they were surrounded by Turkish police and a fracas ensued. Cantona received a blow to the back of the head from a police truncheon, while Bryan Robson later had to have stitches in his gashed hand. 'Of course I was upset at being knocked out of the European Cup, at the spoiling tactics of the opponents, at the fact that no stoppage time was added, and by being given the red card after the game had ended,' Eric angrily recollected. 'But above all I had been hit from behind by that shit of a Turkish policeman. Maybe we'll bump into each other again some time.' Alex Ferguson certainly shared Cantona's assessment of the Swiss referee's performance that evening, maintaining in his autobiography that Rothlisberger 'seemed to offer the Turkish team every assistance'.

There are so many different versions of what happened as the Manchester United players left the pitch at the Ali Sam Yen Stadium that night that it is difficult to establish the truth of the matter. One UEFA official insists that

Cantona was to blame for the incident with the police. 'He did not get hit, he pushed a policeman. I was present at that match, I was a witness myself. The police were more or less blocking the entrance to the tunnel leading to the dressing-room area, but Cantona came down and he clearly pushed one of the policemen down the stairs, and you cannot do that. He was lucky that he did not get arrested. I know that a policeman was pushed and that he fell down the stairs; I cannot say whether he was accidentally pushed by Cantona.' However, he does admit that he did not see what had happened to trigger such a reaction from Cantona.

The injuries sustained by the United players at the hands of the Turkish police were small beer compared with the enormous damage inflicted on United's next continental campaign by the suspension imposed upon Eric by UEFA. European football's ruling body banned the Frenchman from playing in the first four matches of the following season (1994/95). In fact, the Swiss referee had demanded much greater punishment, especially after Cantona told French journalists that the official must have been bribed to perform the way he did. Still, it was a sentence that would have a disastrous impact on United's hopes of European glory that term.

Ironically, Rothlisberger later received a lifetime ban from UEFA after it emerged that he had offered to influence another referee to make decisions in favour of Grasshopper Zurich in a European tie with Auxerre in October 1996. Rothlisberger, by then retired, had suggested to Erich Vogel, the general manager of the Swiss club, that this could be done in return for 'financial compensation'. Vogel informed UEFA, who launched an investigation into the allegations. However, it is important to stress that there is no concrete suggestion, and certainly no evidence, of any impropriety surrounding Manchester United's tie against Galatasaray.

United promptly took the frustration of this European exit out on their domestic rivals. With Eric in inspirational form, they entered a purple patch that would not see them lose another Premier League match for some four months. In the 16 games following their return from Turkey, they gained nine victories and seven draws before succumbing to Chelsea at Old Trafford on 5 March 1994.

And along the way there were, of course, plenty of thrills and spills. One thing Manchester United have rarely been accused of down the years is being boring. Four days after the agony of Istanbul, on 7 November, United faced another stern test: a Manchester derby at Maine Road. City enjoyed themselves for much of the match, Niall Quinn, the Irish centre-forward, giving them a two-goal lead.

Cue an Eric Cantona-inspired comeback. Seven minutes after half-time a mistake in the City defence threw United a lifeline as an attempted back-pass fell straight into Cantona's path. The Frenchman did not err; he slid the ball beneath the body of Tony Coton and into the far corner of the net. The revival continued eleven minutes from time as Eric collected a loose ball halfway inside the City half, juggled with it as he moved forward and flicked a pass to Roy Keane, who, in turn, fed Mark Hughes. The Welshman found compatriot Ryan Giggs, who instantly swept the ball from right to left into the penalty area. His cross was perfect, in the no-man's land between goalkeeper and defenders, and Cantona pounced to stroke the ball home. The recovery was completed by Keane, whose late run into the penalty area enabled him to volley home Denis Irwin's teasing centre. Eric, like the rest of the team, delighted in the fact and the manner of that victory. 'I score two goals to draw us level. I run to the fans massed behind a goal to celebrate. They sense that we will win and they're happy because it is worse to lose to City than anyone else. They are right, and Roy Keane scores the winner with two minutes to go. We had proved that we could recover from the disappointments of Europe.'

That comeback may not quite rank alongside the one that led to United's 1999 European Cup triumph over Bayern Munich at the Nou Camp in Barcelona. Nevertheless, to execute such an astonishing turnaround against your city rivals is always sweet. Cantona seemed to enjoy playing against Manchester City. The Frenchman's record during his time at Old Trafford shows that he scored in every game he started against the Maine Road club, and he was never on the losing side as United won six of the seven derbies in which he appeared. Moreover, his return was eight goals past four different City keepers.

Following the drama of the derby-day comeback, United beat Wimbledon and drew with Ipswich Town, both at Old Trafford, before Eric was again on target, with a header, in a 1–0 win over Coventry City at Highfield Road. That made it 31 wins in 42 outings since Eric's signing a year earlier. And three days after a home draw with Norwich City on 4 December, United visited Sheffield United. The fans who made the journey were ready for more great deeds from Cantona, and their hero did not disappoint. After helping to clear a corner, the Frenchman combined brilliantly with Lee Sharpe and Ryan Giggs to launch a lightning counter-attack which saw Eric run half the length of the field with the ball at his feet before slamming it left-footed into the Sheffield net. The team from Manchester won the game 3–0.

The week before Christmas, after a 1–1 draw at New-castle, Alex Ferguson's men entertained their fellow title contenders, Aston Villa. Yet again, Cantona led the way with two calm finishes in a crucial 3–1 victory. The team then collected four more points before the turn of the year as a 1–1 home draw with Blackburn Rovers, destined to be United's closest title challengers that season, was followed by the 5–2 demolition of Oldham Athletic at Boundary Park, during which Eric converted a penalty with custom-ary aplomb.

The longer Eric stayed at Old Trafford, the happier he was becoming with life there. He enjoyed an excellent relationship with Alex Ferguson and was on more than one occasion grateful for the club's commitment to protecting its players. At one point, the manager caught wind of the fact that some tabloid journalists were tailing his star player in the hope of uncovering evidence of some sort of tryst. Rumours had been rife during Can-tona's days at Elland Road that he had been romantically involved with the wife of a team-mate, an accusation Eric always strenuously denied and one Howard Wilkinson described to me as 'bullshit'. Once he became aware of this latest campaign to tarnish his reputation, Cantona had some fun giving the journalists, who were tracking him in a Mini Austin, the run around the streets of Manchester and Leeds before finally losing them.

However, incidents of an unsavoury nature were relatively few and far between during this period, and Eric continued to feel at home in Manchester. He was a popular figure in the dressing-room, and the individuality that had seen him clash with previous coaches and team-mates merely inspired a keen sense of affection at Old Trafford. Lee Sharpe gave an insight into the atmosphere within the United squad during that time: 'Me and Keaney used to hammer Brucey about the way he used to dress, and Eric used to burst out laughing. Then Eric would come in in something like a big woolly cardigan, a pair of jeans and a pair of cowboy boots, and Brucey used to say: "Hang on a minute, just because he's like ooh aah Cantona doesn't mean he can get away with it." And we used to say: "Yeah, but he looks cool, Brucey, he carries it off." ' Although none of the real jokers in the squad dared play pranks on Eric as they might have done with other players, he was still very much part of the camaraderie that existed between the players. 'We sort of took the mickey out of him from time to time if he made a mistake. He was truly one of the lads really. He had this mad reputation before, but he was one of the lads.'

But Eric liked poetry, art and hunting – what did the other lads in the dressing-room make of that? 'It was all part and parcel of his persona,' Sharpe insisted. 'They saw him as a one-off and a bit eccentric, different, and they just accepted it. Steve Bruce had a testimonial dinner and Eric had brought in one of his paintings to auction. It was quite a simple painting with blocks of colour, and Brucey was taking the mickey out of him saying it was like painting by numbers, and Eric was laughing and saying, "Yeah, yeah, whatever." But it still goes and fetches about £3,000 or £4,000 in the auction. He accepted the lads giving him a bit of stick. I think it made him feel part of things and one of the lads.'

Above all, Cantona developed a genuine feeling of warmth and respect for Alex Ferguson, describing him thus: 'He is the boss. He is a lover of football, someone who would be watching boys playing in the rain if he did not happen to be the manager of the biggest club in Britain.' And Eric always enjoyed training and benefited from his excellent rapport with Brian Kidd, the United coach. 'When I'm driving to Manchester to train, I look forward with eager anticipation to the sessions of Brian Kidd, our coach. I'm happy because, at some clubs, the training sessions have not been of any interest. But there are coaches like Kiddo who make you want to train and he gives you a lift, he motivates you. What a joy it is to train under him with the ball all the time for physical and technical work, passing, shooting and small games.'

Time and again in the months and years to follow, Cantona would be grateful for the support of his manager and team-mates; he would realise that he owed his survival as a footballer to everyone at Old Trafford. However, this relationship was not a one-way street. At that point in its history, Manchester United needed Eric Cantona too.

9 The Double and Strife

One love, we don't need another love
One love, one heart and one soul
We can have it all
Easy peasy.

'ONE LOVE', THE STONE ROSES

There have been few dull moments in Manchester United's history, and certainly none during Eric Cantona's colourful and sometimes controversial career. The second half of the 1993/94 season was to produce some of the highest and lowest points of the Frenchman's stay at Old Trafford. On the field, 1994 started with draws against two of the team's fiercest rivals. A goalless home stalemate with Leeds United on New Year's Day was followed by an extraordinary match at Liverpool three days later. This time it was United who marched into a commanding lead, only to see the opposition launch a spectacular comeback. Alex Ferguson's men raced to a three-goal advantage as Steve Bruce, Denis Irwin and Ryan Giggs all beat Bruce Grobbelaar in the Liverpool goal. But the Anfield side were not to be outdone that day and eventually stole a draw, with Nigel Clough to the fore.

There was to be no respite for the United players during the remainder of the campaign as they battled hard in search of glory on three fronts (it would, of course, have been four but for their surprise European Cup exit to Galatasaray). Early January was a particularly busy period as attention switched first to the FA Cup third round. United negotiated their way through a difficult tie at Sheffield United thanks to Mark Hughes, who scored the only goal of the game. Just three days later Portsmouth were the visitors to Old Trafford for a League Cup quarter-final, which ended 2–2. Ryan Giggs and Eric Cantona scored the United goals, the latter with a typically powerful header to direct Paul Parker's cross home from six yards. Although the south coast side fought hard throughout, they would eventually succumb to Brian McClair's goal in the return match at Fratton Park.

Meanwhile, Manchester United's fifth game in a fortnight was a Premier League encounter at Tottenham Hotspur, which produced a 1–0 victory for the away side. The team then had the luxury of a week without a match, but it was a period tinged with great sadness as on 20 January Sir Matt Busby, the man whose courage, vision and stoical endeavour created the 1968 European Cup-winning side of Best, Law and Charlton from the ashes of the Munich air disaster, passed away at the age of 84. Old Trafford mourned.

All the United players were deeply affected by the loss of such a pivotal figure in the club's history, and were determined to produce a performance of which Sir Matt would have been proud when Everton visited Old Trafford that weekend. Although there were times when they almost tried too hard, United played with style and panache, Giggs scoring the only goal of the game with a classy header to convert Roy Keane's pinpoint cross. The goal celebrations were modest; respect was the order of that day.

Fittingly, the hearse carrying the great man's mortal remains drove past the Theatre of Dreams on the way to the funeral the following week. There was a huge turnout as many United fans paid their last respects to the man who had brought happiness to so many and instilled great footballing traditions at Old Trafford. Eric Cantona had been a Manchester United player for little more than a year, yet he shared the grief of those who had been inspired by Busby's paternal influence over the previous five decades. 'Nobody can ever write or speak about Manchester United without mentioning his name,' Cantona eulogised. 'You sense and feel that his blood runs through every vein of the club's body. His name is engraved on the hearts of all of those who love beautiful football. His kindness, courage, gentility and resilience serve as an inspiration and example to everybody.' Above all, Eric recognised the significance of the approach Busby had imbued at United: winning alone was not enough; winning with style, flair and imagination was what mattered. 'His legacy of playing with style – win, lose or draw – will be preserved. His ideals, principles and beliefs will not be forgotten. I am pleased that I played in front of him, and that he lived to see United champions once more.'

The team's good form continued as they travelled to Norwich City for the fourth round of the FA Cup. A 2–0 success saw Cantona register the first of many FA Cup goals for United. The Frenchman intercepted Rob Newman's over-ambitious cross-field pass, controlling the ball twice with his head and once with his thigh before flicking it nonchalantly past Bryan Gunn, the Norwich keeper. It was clear Eric and United would thrive in the competition.

Queens Park Rangers were the next League opponents to succumb to the Red machine, despite home advantage. Cantona again proved his worth as a striker, rising above his marker to head home Denis Irwin's cross at the far post as United secured a 3–2 victory. On 13 February, Cantona and co. were back in League Cup action as they overcame Sheffield Wednesday 1–0 at Old Trafford in the first leg of their semi-final. Despite that narrow margin and the absence of the injured Cantona, they then romped to a 4–1 triumph in the return match at the beginning of March to book a place in the final against Aston Villa.

The FA Cup also continued to bring success as United sailed through a seemingly difficult fifth-round clash with Wimbledon at Selhurst Park. Denis Irwin and Paul Ince were both worthy scorers that night, but it was a strike from Cantona that will live longest in the memory. Denis Irwin swung a long ball from left to right into the Wimbledon area. The centre was cleared but only to the fringes of the area where Eric lurked after finding himself both time and space. With one touch on the instep, the ball was fully under control and awaiting the powerful volley that duly arrived. Eric had set the ball up perfectly for himself and delivered a net-busting strike with a devastating swing of his dexterous right foot. It was quite simply one of his best goals in a United shirt and one of the most spectacular of his career. He knew it, too, and ran straight to the United bench to celebrate. It was a goal that certainly brought a rapturous response from Sky television's commentary team. Andy Gray raved: 'It's all about the magic of Eric Cantona. Watch the way he just backs away. He takes one touch to set it up, and what about the quality of the volley? One to admire, time and time again!'

After their exploits in both cup competitions, United's Premiership form suffered a minor blip which coincided with Eric's being forced to sit on the sidelines for a couple of games. He had picked up an injury during a 2–2 draw at West Ham on 25 February, causing him to miss the 1–0 reverse at home to Chelsea the following week, as well as the League Cup semi-final second leg against Sheffield Wednesday. The Chelsea defeat was the team's first in 34 matches, and their first at home for nearly one and a half years.

Although everyone at Old Trafford was disappointed to see such a fantastic sequence of results broken, they soon cheered up when Eric and, inevitably, winning ways returned: Charlton Athletic were beaten 3–1 at Old Trafford in the FA Cup quarter-final on 12 March and Sheffield Wednesday were routed 5–0 in the League four days later as a crowd of 43,669 witnessed a Cantona masterclass. Again it was the sheer range of his abilities that was so thrilling.

First, he fulfilled the role of playmaker as he picked up possession halfway inside his own half before chipping an expert pass over the Wednesday defence for the lightning-quick Ryan Giggs to burst on to and slide the ball home for the opening goal. Provider then turned scorer as Eric made space for himself, received Paul Ince's through-ball and slotted a goal past the hapless Kevin Pressman. And the Frenchman claimed the fifth goal of the match as he finished off a move he had started, and which involved four other players. Several sequences of controlled possession ended with Eric dropping his left shoulder to fool the Wednesday defence and allowing the ball to come across his body on the edge of the area before rifling it into the corner of the net with a powerful left-foot drive. Not only had United turned on the style, the win took them seven points clear of Blackburn Rovers, their closest challengers for the Premiership title.

United's season was heading inexorably towards glory with Eric Cantona orchestrating on-field proceedings with a surgeon's precision and the flair of a great composer. Sadly, however, he was then involved in two incidents which would remove some of the gloss from his 1993/94 achievements and help change public perception of him for ever. He received two red cards in the space of just four days; the first was fully justified, the second, it must be said, a touch unfortunate.

On 19 March, Cantona and his team-mates travelled to the County Ground for an apparently straightforward encounter with relegation-destined Swindon Town. Despite the fact that they were having a poor season, Swindon frustrated the champions and the game ended in a 2–2 draw. Eric's dismissal came after he was challenged by John Moncur as he released a pass to Roy Keane. With the Swindon man's legs wrapped around his own from behind and an arm attempting to pull him down – yes, it was a clear foul, but certainly nothing more sinister than that – Cantona unleashed a stamp that was simply indefensible, an act of violence for which there were no mitigating circumstances.

Moreover, although he admitted he was in the wrong, the attitude Eric conveyed in his autobiography was never likely to attract much sympathy from his detractors. 'Against Swindon I could have no complaints with the referee's decision, although I'm certain that my rubber studs would have caused little discomfort to John Moncur. Ironically, he told me that he had voted for me in the PFA Player of the Year award, due to be announced soon after.' Ironic, perhaps, but one thing was certain: Eric did himself no favours seeking to belittle the significance of the incident by emphasising the lack of damage likely to be caused by his choice of footwear. In that instance, intent was all-important.

His subsequent dismissal at Arsenal on 22 March in another 2–2 draw was highly controversial. After receiving a booking earlier in the match, Cantona collided with Arsenal's Tony Adams, but referee Vic Callow took the view that the Frenchman had committed a late tackle on the Arsenal defender and punished him with a second yellow card – which, of course, meant he had to leave the field. The referee may have had his opinion swayed by the nature of the challenge for which he had awarded the first card: a review of the slow-motion replay revealed what certainly appeared to be a two-footed lunge on Ian Selley, even if there was no real contact made. Perhaps the referee thought two wrongs – Cantona's tackle and his mistake in punishing it with just a yellow – somehow combined to make a right.

This time Eric certainly did not accept his punishment willingly. 'It was a travesty of justice,' he recalled. 'Players close to the incident were outraged, for I had simply jumped over Adams to avoid a clash, conscious of the fact that I had already been cautioned and that a second sending-off would mean that I missed several games. I was astonished to see the referee waving a red card at me, but I walked straight off while my team-mates protested and the travelling United fans howled at the referee. The television pictures, shown so often, were to prove that I should not have been sent off. Both Paul Merson and Tony Adams were generous enough to say to the press that the decision was wrong.'

Although Eric left the field quietly after receiving his marching orders, he had plenty to tell French journalists after the match. Naturally he was furious about what he saw as a serious error by the match official, but the FA did not take kindly to the fact that his opinion was plastered all over the English papers the following day after being translated from the French. According to Cantona, the FA's attitude was indicative of a clash of cultures; the type of remarks he had made would have been acceptable in

France. 'In France,' he argued, 'we are allowed to make such observations about the referees, and all I was saying was that he should have been man enough to admit that he had made a mistake. Such an admission would have enhanced his reputation.' The men in blazers did not agree and rebuked him for his remarks at a disciplinary hearing, during which punishment for his two red cards was meted out.

Cantona was further infuriated by the FA's attitude because it seemed they were not concerned about the referee's mistake, which had caused matters to escalate in the first place. Worse still, the penalty they imposed was a five-match ban, a suspension that could hardly have come at a worse time for United as they looked to step up their pursuit of all three domestic trophies.

Broadly speaking, the demons that had haunted Eric during other periods of his career had not descended during his spell at Manchester United before those mad few days in mid-March. But there had been one hint of the trouble to come, a clash with Norwich City's Jeremy Goss which had indicated that Eric's simmering temper could be brought to the boil again without warning. The incident had taken place during the FA Cup fourth-round tie between the two clubs at the end of January. As Eric broke quickly down the right wing, Goss busted a gut to keep up and limit any danger to the Norwich goal. The pair tangled and Goss fouled Cantona, but it was a clumsy challenge rather than one born of genuine malice and no real harm appeared to have been done. But that was not the way the Frenchman saw things. He felt aggrieved that his attacking foray had been halted illegally and retaliated by aiming a spiteful kick at Goss. The Norwich player, to his credit, did not indulge in histrionics after he was struck, probably saving Cantona from a dismissal. Alex Ferguson was certainly not happy about the incident but decided to hold his peace. That was not the case, though, after Eric's stamp on John Moncur, an act which caused the manager to lose his temper with his star player for the first time, although he did then take Eric's side over the second sending-off at Arsenal.

Support for Eric within the United dressing-room never waned. In later years, Gary Pallister explained on MUTV why Cantona always received the backing of the rest of the squad: 'I think sometimes Eric felt as though he wasn't getting the protection from referees that he thought he should be getting, and he can be a volatile player, as can a lot of players who are in that top echelon. I think it was just frustration at times with Eric. He wondered why he didn't get protected, so he'd have a kick back. He probably didn't do it as cleverly as a lot of players and seemed to get caught a lot more often.'

The Frenchman's suspension did not come into force until after United's home win over Liverpool in the Premiership on 30 March. Three days earlier their hopes of completing the domestic Treble had been dashed by a 3–1 League Cup final defeat at the hands of Aston Villa. Although United dominated periods of the game, Villa took their chances well and had their cause helped by the awarding of a penalty and subsequent dismissal of Andrei Kanchelskis.

Thereafter Eric missed a 2–0 defeat at Blackburn Rovers, a result that could have spelt serious trouble for United's title hopes, a 3–2 home victory over Oldham Athletic and a 1–0 reverse at Wimbledon, all in the Premiership – two defeats and a narrow victory in three games during a critical phase of the campaign. Ferguson was discovering just how much his side missed Cantona's influence. Symbolic of the way in which United struggled without their talisman was the way the team misfired against soon-to-be-relegated Oldham when the two sides met for their FA Cup semi-final at Wembley. The under-dogs held a 1–0 lead into the dying seconds of the clash, then Mark Hughes produced a trademark volley which rescued United. Goals from Denis Irwin, Andrei Kanchel-skis, Ryan Giggs and Bryan Robson duly saw United storm to a 4–1 victory in the replay at Maine Road. They would play Chelsea in the final a month later.

The impact of Cantona's absence was further empha-sised by United's results after his return. Of the remaining five Premiership fixtures, they notched up four consecutive victories before drawing the fifth with the title already secured. In the seventh match since his comeback, they lifted the FA Cup. Eric scored five times in the seven appearances that followed his ban.

His first game back was a derby against Manchester City at Old Trafford on 23 April. The Frenchman gave further evidence of his penchant for putting City to the sword by scoring both United goals in a 2–0 win. The first, after 35 minutes, was a tap-in after the pace of Kanchelskis had demolished the City rearguard. The second, just a few minutes later, was the archetypal Cantona finish. Andy Dibble, the City keeper, rushed out to meet the unmarked Eric in the inside left channel. Dibble did what keepers are taught to do and stood tall for as long as possible, but he lost the battle of nerves and committed himself. As he did so, Eric simply toe-poked the ball under him. The Frenchman's cool demeanour gave the impression that scoring such a goal was as easy as cutting a slice of Camembert. And, to him, it was.

Four days later United travelled to Elland Road where they secured a 2–0 victory which Alex Ferguson hailed as their best all-round performance of the season. However, in the following match they were surprised to find themselves trailing 1–0 away to Ipswich Town until Eric intervened, heading the equaliser from Kanchelskis's cross. Giggs then scored the winner, and United were confirmed as champions the following evening after Blackburn failed to beat Coventry City.

During United's penultimate home game of the season, the 2–0 defeat of Southampton on 4 May, Cantona again worked his magic to create an opening for Mark Hughes to smash home a typically unstoppable shot from twenty yards. Andrei Kanchelskis was also on target as the Reds celebrated a second consecutive championship success. The official trophy presentation took place after the 0–0 draw with Coventry City four days later. A special ovation was reserved for Bryan Robson, who was shortly to leave Old Trafford for Middlesbrough after thirteen years of the most dedicated service imaginable. Even so, the club's supporters now had an ideal replacement as the focal point for adulation, albeit one who provided more subtle inspiration than the barnstorming approach of Robson.

While he had been serving his five-match suspension, Eric Cantona had been voted PFA Player of the Year, thus becoming the first foreign player to receive the award. Such recognition from his fellow professionals sparked enormous pride in Eric, and the gratitude he expressed in his autobiography gives a clear insight into the more modest side to his personality. 'I owe this honour to my colleagues at Old Trafford and to the role I have been allowed to play in the team. It suits me to have the freedom to create, invent and to drift unnoticed into positions from which I can make or score goals. I am grateful to Alex Ferguson and Brian Kidd for devising those tactics, and to all my team-mates who contribute so much to my own personal success. Not all managers allow their players such freedom to express themselves fully on the pitch, nor are they able to ensure that it fits the team plan at the same time.' Cantona's is an extremely honest appraisal of the situation: he clearly recognises that without the help of others at Manchester United he would never have fulfilled his rich potential. Such comments betray a marked difference in attitude to the defensiveness he displayed at other times in his career, perhaps when things were not going so well.

The Frenchman now had a hat-trick of championship winner's medals to his name, but the season was not yet over. On 14 May several important new additions were to be made to both the history of Manchester United and that of English football. Never before had a Frenchman played in an FA Cup final. Chelsea, their opponents at Wembley, were the only team to have beaten United twice that season and the only side against whom the Reds had failed to score. Glenn Hoddle's Stamford Bridge outfit now stood between Ferguson's men and the club's first ever League and FA Cup Double.

Surprisingly, United were slow out of the blocks in the first half. Chelsea, in contrast, showed that they weren't there simply to make up the numbers at another United party by playing the better football, and even hitting the crossbar. However, Cantona and co. soon turned things round in the second period. Not only was Eric the first Frenchman to play in England's showcase final, he also became the first to score in one, converting not one but two penalties past Dmitri Kharine. As Eric strode forward to take the first penalty, awarded after a foul on Denis Irwin, Dennis Wise, the Chelsea captain, attempted to distract him. Eric ignored his offer of a £100 wager on the outcome of the spot-kick and, detecting Kharine's movement to his right, instinctively slotted the ball to the keeper's left. The Russian was completely outfoxed for a second time when he assumed Cantona would not put another penalty in the same place. He did. Goals from Mark Hughes and Brian McClair ensured a rout, and United collected the League and FA Cup Double for the first time in their history.

Eric was delighted to have close family members at the final and the subsequent celebrations: his wife Isabelle, their son Raphael, his father and his two brothers were all in attendance. He certainly enjoyed the revelry that followed the final and the triumphant return to Manchester to parade the trophies around the streets of the city. 'To be a part of such a unique triumph for a club like Manchester United is a wonderful feeling,' he wrote.

Cantona had scored four goals in five FA Cup appearances. Moreover, his two goals in the final had made both fans and the media in his homeland proud of their footballing export. 'The FA Cup final is one of the most highly regarded games in France,' Erik Bielderman explained. 'It's always live on French TV. So, obviously, to see Eric winning and Eric scoring was something very important, and it was also a chance to see him live on the TV.'

Despite walking the disciplinary tightrope, especially in the month of March, Cantona's on-field achievements clearly marked him out as a top-quality footballer without whom Manchester United might not have scaled the heights they reached in 1993/94. He did not play as an out-and-out striker, yet the Frenchman was still the club's top scorer with 25 goals in all competitions. 'He was a joy for a lot of people to watch,' Gary Pallister said. 'He was a joy for the players to play alongside and I think Eric appreciated the side that he came into as well. The side was 95 per cent complete, it just needed that spark, and Eric certainly provided it.'

Alongside him Mark Hughes also flourished, notching up 21 goals. Paul Parker, the United right-back, described the value of the Cantona–Hughes partnership on MUTV: 'He [Cantona] scored some great goals, he made some great goals. He did unbelievable things on the edge of the box for us. He was someone to pass it in to. We had Sparky [Hughes]. Sparky was all strength and we'd wait for him to hold three players off and someone would make a run. Eric – people were always scared to get close to him because they were scared of Eric taking the mickey out of them. Eric had that ability, he earned that respect.'

For his part, Eric continued to be full of praise for all his team-mates that season, singling out the goalscoring contributions of midfielders Ryan Giggs, Roy Keane, Paul Ince, Lee Sharpe and Andrei Kanchelskis as one of the key ingredients of United's success. And not only had Eric enjoyed a great season with these players on the field, he had continued to integrate well with them in a social context. Lee Sharpe recalled that once every couple of months, if the team had a free weekend coming up, the players would meet for lunch followed by drinks, normally at Bryan Robson's local pub. 'It would be beers all round, and we'd all be sat round this table with bottles of beer and Eric would turn up and have a bottle of champagne in an ice bucket. He was always different, but always accepted. I think it was just coming to the end of the lads' get-togethers. I don't think they're so common now. They were definitely a lot more common in the eighties, and then in the early to mid-nineties we were just seeing the last of them. It did us good, we won the League on it. I don't think the manager was over keen, but as long as we didn't have a game coming up and we had the next day off, he was reasonably accepting of them. Eric was part of it. He'd stay out with the lads and enjoy himself, have a good time.'

* * *

Despite France's failure to qualify for the World Cup that summer, Eric still travelled to the United States to watch the tournament since he was contracted to provide commentary on French television. It was a role he was looking forward to with great enthusiasm and one he would find enjoyable, even if there was the inevitable fracas along the way. It wouldn't have been very Eric had there not been one, after all.

The Frenchman was involved in an argument with a security guard while trying to get to his commentary position for the third-place play-off match between Sweden and Bulgaria at the Pasadena Rose Bowl. He was not the only member of the media to be frustrated by the long queues to get into the press box and the personal searches carried out by FBI officers that day. In hindsight, given the atrocious events of 11 September 2001, nobody should really have complained; in 1994, however, it would have annoyed anyone.

Martin Tyler revealed that he too experienced difficulties with the arbitrary nature of security at the game. 'I bumped into him [Cantona] at the World Cup finals in America in 1994. He'd had a bit of a run-in with the authorities there because of the way the security was overblown. I was commentating for an Australian channel, SBS, and I was doing the third-place game the day before the final, and a lot of the broadcasters who had booked it had gone home because their countries had gone out, so there was bags of space.' Tyler's allocated seat was next to a fellow British broadcaster who was relatively inexperienced at the time. Concerned that his presence might distract his colleague, Tyler moved to a seat in the row behind. 'It was totally empty. Then the security guy came and asked for my ticket and said, "No, you've got to sit there." So I explained, and he said, "If you don't go and sit there, I'll take your accreditation away and you won't be able to come into the final." I can imagine that sort of thing upset Eric.'

It wasn't all furrowed brows. Tyler also recalled sharing a joke with the Frenchman. 'I remember bumping into him and saying, "Gosh, you're working for the media!"

with heavy irony. And he went [adopts deeper voice and French accent], "J-J-Just this once!" He recognised the wryness of my remark. Always in the tunnel a nod, and I'm sure if I bump into him anywhere on our travels now it'll be, "How're you doing?" He was always very reserved and you knew not to prolong the conversation, but he always acknowledged you.'

10 Spills, Thrills and Bellyaches

Everything in the garden was lovely. Eric was happy at United and we were happy that he wanted to stay for the rest of his career. Nobody could have foreseen the horrors that were about to descend on us.

ALEX FERGUSON

It was a bad omen for Manchester United's 1994/95 season in general and Eric Cantona's in particular when the Frenchman received his marching orders for a studs-up challenge on the Rangers defender Steve Pressley at a pre-season tournament in Glasgow. If you were to piece together the previous flashpoints of his career – the red cards, the abuse of match officials, the fights with team-mates and the outbursts at coaches – you could construct a narrative piece entitled 'Chronicle of Selhurst Park Foretold'.

However, while there was little doubt that Eric's volatile nature meant there was a disaster waiting to happen, only with enormous hindsight could anyone have envisaged the catastrophic twist events would take. Even from those moments where the red mist clearly descended in front of Eric's eyes, nobody could have predicted the incident which took place at 8.57 p.m. on 25 January 1995 during a largely uneventful 1–1 draw with Crystal Palace at Selhurst Park.

All told, the season was not to be a happy one for Manchester United. Before the campaign had even kicked off, Eric was embroiled in further controversy when an advert for Nike in which he appeared was banned from British television by the Broadcasting Advertising Clearance Centre. The ad featured Cantona recounting how he had once called the French national team manager a 'shit bag'. The *Sun* deemed the story worthy of its front page on 13 August, and Brian Woolnough, the journalist who penned the article, referred to the Frenchman as 'soccer wild man Eric Cantona'. Such an epithet provides ample evidence, if evidence is indeed required, of the exaggerated level of media attention being directed at the flamboyant French star. To appear in such an advertisement may not have been the height of diplomacy on Eric's part, but it hardly made for earth-shattering news.

In the Charity Shield, the traditional curtain-raiser to the new season, it was business as usual from the outset: United cruised to a 2–0 victory over Blackburn Rovers, their opponents by dint of the fact that they had finished second in the League the previous season. Cantona slotted home a penalty with his usual aplomb, and central defender David May, who had transferred allegiance from Ewood Park to Old Trafford for a fee of £1.2 million over the summer, was roundly booed by the Blackburn fans. Everything was as expected and it all boded well – but, as has already been identified in these pages, the outcome of the Charity Shield tends to be an unreliable indicator of how the participants will fare over the coming campaign. More especially, it offers little real evidence as to the ultimate destiny of silverware in May the following year. Blackburn were again to be Manchester United's main championship rivals, but this time Kenny Dalglish's team would steal their crown in dramatic and, for United, near disastrous circumstances.

The season started well enough for Cantona, once he was allowed back on the field of play. He scored his first goal in a 3–0 home win over Wimbledon on the last day of August, powering home a header after some wing wizardry and a pinpoint cross from Ryan Giggs. United had already picked up wins against Queens Park Rangers and Tottenham Hotspur, as well as a draw at Nottingham Forest, while Eric served a three-match suspension for his dismissal in the Glasgow tournament. However, the Frenchman's penalty in the fifth game of the campaign at Elland Road, coolly despatched despite the deafening attempts of the Leeds United fans to distract him, was not enough to prevent a 2–1 reverse.

In the run-up to the Leeds clash, an article in the *Today* newspaper emphasised the level of pressure Cantona now had to endure. The piece revealed that after Leeds had sold him to Manchester United Eric had received hate mail, had had fireworks pushed through his letterbox and missiles thrown at the windows of his house (the Cantona family had remained in Leeds for almost two years after the transfer; Isabelle, his wife, taught at Leeds University and, besides, the family had generally been happy there), as well as having his car tyres slashed.

There is a flawed theory that footballers should learn to tolerate abuse and insults because of the vast sums of money they earn. 'I could put up with that for twenty grand a week,' runs the argument. But the same is not generally considered to be the case with, for instance, film stars or captains of industry, who are also extremely well remunerated for their services. However much someone may appear to be rolling in cash, there can surely be few greater pressures on a man than when he feels his family is under threat. Human nature dictates that he will adopt a defensive stance in a variety of circumstances as a result. Perhaps with hindsight it is possible to detect a growing sense that Eric was being backed further and further into a corner.

Another insight into Eric's love–hate relationship with the English football-watching public came from the most unlikely of sources. Bernard Manning, the comedian who is blue both in terms of his material and his support of Manchester City, appeared in a newspaper article apparently outraged that a picture of Cantona had been slapped on the billboard opposite his house. The shot in question came from the Nike advert which suggested that 1966 had been a good year for English football because that was when Eric was born. Manning was photographed by the hoarding, a red card in his left-hand, his right gesturing as if to enforce a sending-off. And Manning was quoted as saying: 'I should imagine the advert will be there for months. It's just as well I secretly think he's a fabulous player.'

That is the key. Manning, like so many others, would have given the right arm he had thrust out in the picture to have a player like Cantona at his club. Through all the vitriol and resentment directed at Eric during his time in England, opposition fans still struggled to hide their admiration for his ability as a footballer. So it was simple: if he was on your side, you loved him; if he was against you, you pilloried him for whatever reason while secretly wishing he played for you.

The Leeds defeat marked the start of a spell of patchy form for United. Although they overcame Liverpool 2–0 at Old Trafford on 17 September, Eric creating the second goal for Brian McClair, the Frenchman was once more involved in controversy which saw the tabloid news-papers sharpening their knives. ERIC'S BECOMING A NASTY B*****D screamed the headline to John Fashanu's column in the *Sun* the following Tuesday. Under the title 'Fash, His Weekly Bash, Only in The Sun', which itself requires no further comment, the Wimbledon player recommen-ded Eric visit his martial arts guru to learn self-discipline. The suggestion came in the wake of ugly scenes during that United–Liverpool clash in which Eric retaliated with a crude and dangerous tackle from behind on Neil Ruddock after appearing to be elbowed in the face by him. Cantona received a booking for his troubles; Ruddock escaped any form of sanction despite being reported to the Football Association after the match.

The *Sun*'s coverage of the affair was typically distorted. Firstly, a whole page was dedicated to severe criticism of Cantona for his role in the incident, while RUDDOCK FACES FA RAP OVER ELBOW received just a couple of column inches. Had the roles been reversed and it was the Frenchman who had been accused of using an elbow, doubtless that would have been the bigger story. Sadly, balance is not something for which Britain's tabloids are noted.

The attitude conveyed by the *Sun* was counter-produc-tive on two fronts. For a start, it almost encouraged anti-Cantona vitriol at matches while also affording Man-chester United an excuse to adopt the club's famous siege mentality instead of dealing with the actual issue. A player of Cantona's huge ability and fragile temperament will always attract wind-up tactics from some opponents as they attempt to lure him into a situation where he gets himself dismissed. David Beckham certainly found that out after his clash with the Argentinian midfielder Diego Simeone in the 1998 World Cup. United surely needed to attempt to calm down an increasingly hotheaded Eric before he did something deeply regrettable. This, for whatever reason, they were unable to do, until after Selhurst Park.

Unsurprisingly, Neil Ruddock made no mention in his autobiography of the incident where he at least appeared to elbow Cantona (the jacket sports a photograph of Razor himself thrusting a finger up each of his nostrils). He did, however, claim that Cantona attempted to elbow him during the match. According to Ruddock, the Frenchman took umbrage because, throughout the game, the Liverpool defender insisted on walking up to him and turning his collar down, as part of a bet with a comedian called Willie Miller. He also asserted that Eric suggested the two of them continue their debate in the tunnel afterwards, but that they did not meet again until the post-match drinks. 'I felt a tap on my shoulder and turned round to find Monsieur Cantona standing right behind me. My first thought was that he wanted to continue where we'd left off on the field, but instead he produced a pint of lager and as he handed it to me he gave me a little wink and walked off.'

Cantona may have experienced problems with opposition players and fans, referees and the media, but there was one group of people with whom his popularity simply soared with each majestically taken goal, each clash with authority, each extravagant flick, each 'ooh' and each 'aah': the Manchester United supporters. 'He was very good with the fans,' Lee Sharpe acknowledged. 'Some days we would have 1,500 or 2,000 fans at the training ground in the summer or school holidays and he was probably the one who signed the most autographs for people.' This is a view to which Andy Mitten, editor of the fanzine *United We Stand*, also subscribes. When asked how Cantona treated United fans, he responded: 'With respect. He would applaud fans after the game as enthusiastically as Beckham and Gary Neville do now. That he chose to live in a three-bed semi in Boothstown, a pleasant suburb but by no means the most salubrious in Manchester, endeared him to fans too. That he turned up in genuine Manchester boozers instead of the plastic phoney bars normally associated with footballers all added to his appeal. And he did things with a football that no other players did.'

Eric clearly appreciated the fans' adulation and enjoyed his relationship with them. He revealed how important it was to him to reciprocate their affection when he said, 'It's not a case of signing autographs so that people will think I'm a nice guy, but rather I don't want them to have a bad experience. I don't want to hurt them by letting them down.'

Sandwiched between those troublesome Leeds and Liverpool games was the opening game of United's European Champions League offensive. Alex Ferguson was hamstrung by two key issues when it came to selection policy in Europe. First of all, Eric Cantona was banned for the first four games of the campaign after his dismissal in Turkey the previous season. Moreover, under UEFA restrictions which were enforced for that year alone the manager could only field five non-English players in his team. That meant having to choose any five from first-team regulars Peter Schmeichel, Denis Irwin, Roy Keane, Andrei Kanchelskis, Ryan Giggs, Mark Hughes, Brian McClair and, when he returned from suspension, Cantona. It was certainly a conundrum for the manager.

Initially, though, neither issue appeared to be an insurmountable problem as the team got off to a good start by beating IFK Gothenberg 4–2 at Old Trafford. Before the match Eric expressed his confidence that the team would be in a strong position to qualify for the next stage of the competition by the time he returned in the fifth game of the group stage. And in typical fashion, he insisted that he did not regret his outburst in Istanbul the previous season. 'I don't regret it because it has happened.

Champion: Eric raises the trophy to the heavens as he celebrates winning the championship after just four months at Leeds United, May 1992.

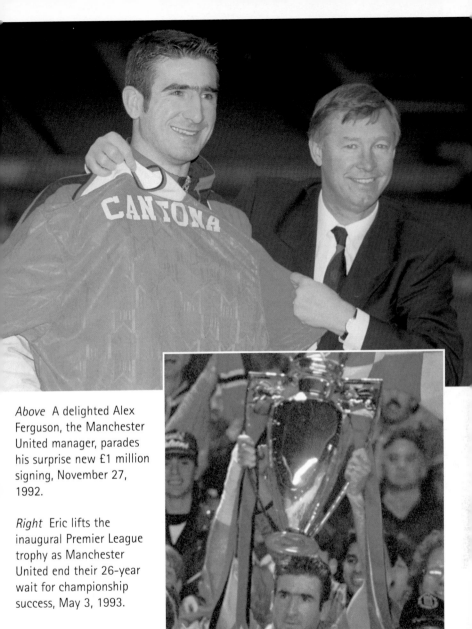

Above A delighted Alex Ferguson, the Manchester United manager, parades his surprise new £1 million signing, November 27, 1992.

Right Eric lifts the inaugural Premier League trophy as Manchester United end their 26-year wait for championship success, May 3, 1993.

Left Getting shirty! Eric explains his side of the story to referee Roger Gifford, August 1992.

Left Representing his country, October 1994. Cantona scored 20 goals in 45 appearances for France but some observers regard his international career as a failure.

Right Eric celebrates after converting a crucial penalty against Liverpool at the end of his nine-month suspension, Old Trafford, October 1, 1995. He thus began a one-man crusade to bring the Premier League title and FA Cup Double back to Old Trafford.

Below Eric plunges into the crowd to deliver his infamous kung fu kick, Selhurst Park, January 25, 1995.

Eric demonstrates his flawless technique as he strikes home another vicious volley, a crucial equaliser against Sheffield Wednesday at Old Trafford, December 9, 1995.

Above Two young English fans deliver their verdict on France coach Aime Jacquet's decision not to include David Ginola and Eric Cantona in his squad for Euro 96, as France take on Romania at St James's Park.

Left The Frenchman strikes a typically haughty pose as he leads Manchester United to a 4-0 Charity Shield victory over title rivals Newcastle, August 11, 1996.

Above Cantona shares David Beckham's delight at the Englishman's winning goal against Liverpool, October 12, 1996. Beckham would inherit Eric's number seven shirt and the attention of the media.

Left The United skipper performs his duties before a 2-1 defeat to Chelsea at Old Trafford during United's autumn blip, November 2, 1996.

Cool as ever, Eric watches a practice session for the Spanish Grand Prix from the garage of the Arrows team, May 1999.

He may have put on a pound or two but Eric shows that he has lost none of his ball skills as he warms up for the Sega Dreamcast Beach Football Challenge, July 2000.

You have to live with the consequences of your actions, and that's what I'm doing,' he was quoted as saying in the *Daily Star*. 'But it's possible to realise that you've made mistakes in your life, and perhaps I made one. Of course I feel frustrated at not being able to play. Of course I'd love to be out there.'

A fortnight later Eric did not travel with the rest of the team to Istanbul (United had once again been pitted against Galatasaray). Given the incident in which he had been embroiled the previous year, the club decided it would be more diplomatic to leave him at home. Those who did make the trip saw the team emerge with what seemed to be a valuable point from a 0–0 draw.

Hopes of progressing in the competition were still high when Lee Sharpe's late back-heeled goal earned United a 2–2 draw at home to Barcelona. After that, however, the wheels fell off United's European bandwagon as they suffered back-to-back away defeats. First they were humiliated 4–0 by Barcelona at the Nou Camp, the Catalan team's crack strike partnership, the Brazilian Romario and the Bulgarian Hristo Stoichkov, torturing the United defence all night. The suspended Cantona could only watch on in horror from his position in the stands; next to him was Peter Schmeichel who had been replaced by the young English goalkeeper Gary Walsh as Ferguson employed three overseas outfield players.

Some sections of the media began to round on Eric after the Barcelona débâcle, blaming his absence, at least in part, for the disastrous outcome. LOOK WHERE YOU WERE WHEN WE NEEDED YOU, ERIC screamed the headline to an article in the *Today* newspaper. And quotes from Paul Ince, one of Cantona's closest friends at Old Trafford, summed up how much the team had missed the Frenchman and how the rest of the players looked to him for inspiration. 'Eric may think he owes Manchester United something for not being there when we needed him and go out and really do the business in Gothenberg. He knows it was his own fault he was not with us in Barcelona and maybe now he might think the result might have been different if he had been playing. That is irrelevant now, but what is important is that Eric is desperate to get back into Europe – and even more so after seeing what happened to us in Spain.'

If what had happened in Barcelona was bad, worse was to come in the shape of a 3–1 reverse in Sweden which signalled the end of their European quest. They would not get the chance to prove themselves among the Continent's elite for another two years. United went into the game in the knowledge that a draw followed by victory over Galatasaray two weeks later should see them through to the quarter-final stage of the tournament. UNITED LOOK TO CANTONA IN HOUR OF NEED a headline in the *Independent* reminded the Frenchman. But Eric was unable to exert any real influence on proceedings as the team's collective anxiety showed and they failed to impose themselves on the match. David May, a centre-half pressed into service at right-back, endured a particularly torrid night at the hands of a young, lightning-quick left-winger, Jesper Blomqvist. It was the youngster who opened the scoring.

Ironically, some four and a half years later May and Blomqvist would stand side by side celebrating Manchester United's 1999 European Cup triumph at, of all places, the Nou Camp in Barcelona. But in December 1994 the 4–0 drubbing of Galatasaray was scant consolation for Eric Cantona and the rest of the Manchester United team as they bowed out of Europe at the first hurdle. There was one small crumb of comfort to be had that night: a goal on his European debut for one David Beckham. And at least the Old Trafford faithful had not lost their sense of humour. On United's first, infamous visit to Istanbul, some Galatasaray fans had unfurled a banner which read WELCOME TO THE HELL. In contrast, a group of United supporters produced one which described the aura around the Theatre of Dreams on big European nights: WELCOME TO HEAVEN it proclaimed to the small pocket of Turkish fans within Old Trafford.

Eric was naturally disconsolate after another European failure. At the end of the previous season he had written: 'Watching AC Milan play against Barcelona in the European Cup final, we have seen the standards we must aim for. And we will. The club and the people of Manchester deserve that honour.' Sadly, he was destined never to get his hands on a European Cup winner's medal.

After that Premiership victory over Liverpool in mid-September, United suffered a surprise 3–2 reverse at Ipswich Town, who were to be relegated that season. Eric contributed a goal, as did a very young Paul Scholes, but it was not enough even to rescue a point. Back at home the following week, United beat Everton 2–0, but the trend of winning at home and losing away continued as they lost 1–0 at Sheffield Wednesday on 8 October. A week later, at home, Ferguson's men were victorious again as Eric scored the only goal of the game, taking advantage of Alvin Martin's inability to clear the ball from the West Ham United area and tapping in from close range.

Ferguson's team finally broke their run of poor away form when they visited Ewood Park on 23 October for what was to be a controversial clash with Blackburn Rovers. United emerged 4–2 winners, although the home side complained vehemently about the debatable sending-off of Henning Berg, the Norwegian defender who would one day sign for United. Eric, his hair soaked after a downpour, converted a penalty with typical ease, while Andrei Kanchelskis bagged a brace and Mark Hughes was also on target. On the same day as that success, it emerged in the press that the Football Association had recruited Eric, as well as Germany's Jurgen Klinsmann and England's David Platt, to help launch ticket sales for the Euro 96 tournament. The Frenchman clearly had his uses for English football outside Manchester United after all.

The win at Blackburn was the second of six consecutive victories as United began to find the sort of form that had lifted them to the top of the pile in the two previous campaigns. Newcastle United were beaten 2–0 at Old Trafford at the end of October, followed by a 2–1 victory at Aston Villa. And on 19 November Crystal Palace were brushed aside 3–0, Eric finding the target with a close-range header. United were deprived of the services of five key players for the Palace clash and Alex Ferguson was forced to field a number of youngsters, including right-back Gary Neville. 'Cantona was supreme,' purred Paul Walker in the *Daily Star* the following Monday as, for once, the English tabloids sided with the Manchester United player after suggestions from across the Channel that he might be dropped from the France team. 'The crazy French don't believe he can lead and motivate their young side, but he did just that for United's boys. Coaxing, guiding, creating, Cantona did it all.'

But it was the Manchester derby, nestled between the games against Villa and Palace, in which United produced one of their outstanding displays of the season, and during which Eric simply excelled. City held United at bay in the opening exchanges before Eric broke the deadlock with a breathtaking goal that would serve notice of the final outcome – a 5–0 hammering for City in front of an ecstatic Old Trafford crowd. Andrei Kanchelskis found himself in possession on the halfway line, in his right wing position, shooting towards what is now Old Trafford's West Stand. As the Ukrainian looked up, he spotted Eric making a run towards the goal that would surely catch the City rearguard unawares. Typically, he had found himself space, but when the Frenchman received Kanchelskis's thirty-yard pass, he still had plenty to do. He was moving forward rapidly but had to check slightly to take the ball down, which he did with an exquisite piece of control to cushion the ball with the outside of his right shin into his path so that he could strike it with his left foot, almost without breaking stride. He hammered the ball home with such verve and venom that although the shot passed within his reach, Simon Tracey in the City goal was powerless to stop it. Eric then spent the rest of the night torturing City by setting up Kanchelskis for all three goals of his hat-trick. Mark Hughes was also on target with a finish of delicacy and precision, yet, in reality, the night of 10 November belonged to Eric Cantona.

After a goalless draw at Arsenal, Eric led United back to winning ways on 3 December with the only goal of the home game against Norwich City, finishing a delicious move which he had helped set in train. However, after the following match, a 3–2 win at Queens Park Rangers, United's form hit a patch of inconsistency. Cantona scored the United goal, heading home a Ryan Giggs corner, in an unexpected 2–1 home defeat at the hands of Nottingham Forest on 17 December. He was on the score sheet again nine days later, this time from the penalty spot, as his team won 3–2 at Chelsea on Boxing Day. They then drew at home to Leicester City and away to Southampton before the turn of the year.

The first game of 1995 saw Alex Ferguson's team get back on track by overcoming Coventry City 2–1 at home. Eric added another goal to his tally through a spot-kick, which was described thus by Sky's Martin Tyler: 'There have been so many penalties around Coventry, for and against, in recent games and very few of them have gone in, but this is Eric Cantona, penalty-taker supreme. This for two-nil, Manchester United. There it is!' And his co-commentator, Andy Gray, chipped in with, 'Was there any other outcome?'

Six days later United started their defence of the FA Cup with a tricky third-round tie away to Sheffield United. A howling gale and an equally inhospitable home crowd conspired to make the going tough for the holders, but Ferguson's teams have never lacked courage and application, qualities which saw them eventually overcome the Sheffield side with second-half goals from the dynamic striking duo of Mark Hughes and Eric Cantona. The Frenchman's effort was a triumph for sublime skill over hostile conditions. Typically, the whole move started with a strong headed clearance from Steve Bruce, the leader of the United back line. The ball looped in Eric's direction and he allowed it to fall over his shoulder before first killing it on his right instep and then releasing it to Mark Hughes with a quick flick of the inside of his left boot. In turn, Hughes fed Ryan Giggs down the left flank. The Sheffield defenders were caught out of position and Giggs swept the ball back across the field to Cantona, who collected it just outside the penalty area, to the right of centre. As the Frenchman took a touch, he looked up to see that the Sheffield goalkeeper had strayed from his line. Without hesitating, he produced the deftest of chips to leave the keeper stranded. The ball found its way into the back of the net via the crossbar. It was the hallmark of a true genius, but it was also to be Eric's last contribution to United's 1995 FA Cup campaign.

During the first week of January it had emerged that Eric Cantona was in the process of negotiating a new contract with Manchester United. The *Daily Star* reported that those who held the purse strings at Old Trafford had agreed to pay their master performer £2.5 million in a four-year deal that would effectively tie him to the club until the end of his career. Meanwhile, the *Sunday Express* asserted that Eric was stalling on a new contract while he sought assurances that Alex Ferguson would be allowed the funds to recruit another top-quality defender.

Whatever the truth of those claims, Eric had decided to stay at United, even if it was another few months before he actually put pen to paper. Moreover, Ferguson was indeed given money to spend in the transfer market, although he did not buy a defender. Instead, he chose to bolster his attacking options by signing Andy Cole from Newcastle United on 12 January. Cole, who had amassed an astounding 55 goals in 70 League games during his spell on Tyneside, cost United a British record £6 million, plus Keith Gillespie, the young Northern Ireland winger, valued at £1 million. Ferguson viewed Cole as a long-term replacement for Mark Hughes, now 31, and an ideal partner for Eric Cantona.

Ironically, the fixture calendar dictated that Manchester United's next Premiership match was away at Newcastle United. The two clubs sensibly agreed that neither Cole nor Gillespie should be selected, especially since the former could well have expected an ugly reception from sections of the home crowd who viewed him as a traitor for leaving St James's Park to join the champions. As it was, Mark Hughes, the man whom Cole had been bought to replace, scored for the Manchester team in a 1–1 draw, although in doing so he sustained a knee injury that would keep him sidelined for the following four Premier League matches.

A point from the St James's Park clash was far from disastrous for Alex Ferguson's men given Newcastle United's growing reputation under Kevin Keegan. As reigning champions, United approached the following Sunday's match with confidence. Blackburn Rovers were there for the taking in a game United had to win if they were to keep in touch with the clear leaders of the title race. It was a tight yet exciting encounter. Blackburn lacked United's overall flair, but they had grown into a strong, well-drilled unit under the tutelage of Kenny Dalglish. It would take a touch of magic to break them down. Cue Eric Cantona, the master magician. The Frenchman fed Ryan Giggs in the inside left position and the youngster recovered after initially losing possession to Henning Berg to swing a measured cross into the penalty area in the direction of Cantona, who had continued his run. The striker stooped slightly to get power and accuracy into his header as he sprinted, at an angle, beyond the far post. Tim Flowers, then one of the best goalkeepers in the Premiership, was left helpless despite being well positioned to deal with the header. The ball flew into the very top corner of the net, almost grazing the angle of post and crossbar as it did so. United held on to win 1–0, and it seemed that Eric had set them back on the road for a historic hat-trick of title wins.

The future looked bright, and Cantona was upbeat as he gave an interview to Steve Curry of the *Daily Express*, sitting in the bar of the Four Seasons Hotel in Manchester. He opined that Andy Cole would turn out to be a bargain buy despite the fact that he had found the going tough during his debut. 'We talk too much about money and not enough about quality. If Andy Cole has cost £7 million [with Gillespie] it is because he is one of the best players in the country,' he told Curry. 'What was important was the result. We had to win the game, not just for the points but for the psychological advantage that winning has given us.' Eric was clearly relishing the title race ahead and the opportunity it afforded him to repeat the successes of the previous campaign.

But Cantona's winner against Blackburn was to be his last goal that season. The following day, 23 January, Eric's agent, Jean-Jacques Bertrand, met with Martin Edwards, the United chairman, to discuss the details of his client's new contract. Alex Ferguson recalled the feeling of security that enveloped the club at that time: 'Everything in the garden was lovely. Eric was happy at United and we were happy that he wanted to stay for the rest of his career. Nobody could have foreseen the horrors that were about to descend on us.'

11 Fall from Grace

When the rainy season comes I hang my head
For all the things I have seen and done and said
And then I wonder why I hold my head up high
And feel the rain.

'RAINY SEASON', RODDY FRAME

'Eric Cantona's talent is undoubted, his temperament well known, but tonight he finally went over the top, into the crowd, fighting, having been sent off. It's likely to mean big trouble for him and for Manchester United.' That was how Des Lynam opened the BBC's *Match of the Day* programme on Wednesday, 25 January 1995. He was certainly not wrong.

Just a few minutes into the second period of United's fixture earlier that night against Crystal Palace at Selhurst Park, Peter Schmeichel had launched a clearance from his own penalty area into the home team's half. Lee Sharpe and Eric Cantona of Manchester United and Richard Shaw, the Crystal Palace defender, pursued the ball as it sailed over their heads, down United's left flank. As they did so, Cantona kicked out at Shaw, who fell to the ground. The linesman, who was right up with play, waved his flag immediately and Alan Wilkie, the referee, blew his whistle to halt proceedings.

Several players, including Palace's Gareth Southgate and Chris Coleman, as well as Andy Cole and Denis Irwin of United, soon arrived on the scene. They were followed by the referee, who brandished a red card in Eric's direction. On seeing this, the Frenchman turned away in a gesture of incredulity before placing his hands on his hips and walking towards the touchline as Irwin and Cole took turns to remonstrate with Wilkie. United were wearing all black, as they were on each occasion Cantona was dismissed in the Premiership.

Alan Wilkie later explained his reasons for giving Cantona his marching orders in an interview published by *FourFourTwo* magazine. 'There was no doubt in my mind that violent contact had been made and no doubt that Cantona had kicked or attempted to kick an opponent,' the official said. 'To his credit, Cantona showed no protest. The look on his face told me he knew exactly what he'd done.'

Cantona looked to the bench but he received no sympathy from that quarter since the manager was incensed that he had got himself dismissed again. 'I was in a rage over Eric's stupidity. Not for the first time, his explosive temperament had embarrassed him and the club and tarnished his brilliance as a footballer.' But in hindsight the fiery Scot was even more critical of the performance of the referee. He claimed that the Crystal Palace defenders had committed dangerous tackles on his players and that he had complained about this to the referee during the half-time interval, as well as warning Cantona to keep away from Richard Shaw and to avoid getting embroiled in a physical battle. 'I don't know Alan Wilkie and I'm sure he is a decent man, but to my mind he is a poor referee. His inability to stamp out the disgraceful tackles from Crystal Palace's two central defenders, Richard Shaw and Chris Coleman, made subsequent trouble unavoidable.'

Lee Sharpe was another person to feel Eric had received precious little protection from the referee that night. 'I think he was getting wound up all through the game. Whoever was marking him was pulling and trying to kick him. I think he had been wound up and he sort of snapped and lost his temper.' David Meek, who was reporting on the game for the *Manchester Evening News*, agreed: 'My view was that the referee could have exercised a bit more control a little bit earlier and that the game was beginning to get out of hand with over-severe tackling. But when Eric blew up, so to speak, I felt the referee had no option but to send him off. Eric retaliated, and it is often the guy who retaliates who cops it.'

Richard Shaw insisted that he and his fellow defenders had simply gone about their normal business that night and that there were certainly no special plans to antagonise the Frenchman. 'A lot of people seem to think there's a lot more to it than there was. All I can say is, and this is the God's honest truth, there were no instructions, nothing. It was just a normal game. The incident [when Cantona assaulted Matthew Simmons, a Crystal Palace fan] happened and the fact of the matter is that I was miles away from it and some people obviously think I was instrumental in it and I don't really know why. I was on the pitch and it was me he fouled, but nothing could be further from the truth. I totally, totally respect him as a person, I have no trouble with him. As a player, I thought he was magnificent. He was a great, great player, and even now I would pay to go and watch him play because he was that good, he really was.'

About halfway through his fifty-yard walk to the tunnel, Cantona stopped. The words of a man in the crowd, whom seconds earlier a steward had attempted to calm down, caught his attention. He was wearing a leather jacket, white shirt and Crystal Palace tie; his hair was closely cropped. He was one Matthew Simmons, and he had run down eleven flights of steps to get to the front by the advertising hoardings. From there he unleashed a string of abusive expletives at the Frenchman. Cantona flew at him, right foot first, to deliver the soon-to-be infamous kung-fu kick. After the initial impact, Eric fell on to the barrier but was quickly back on his feet as the two men traded punches.

As the Frenchman was restrained by Norman Davies, the United kit man, and the steward, several players from either side rushed over, most of them to make the peace. United's giant goalkeeper Peter Schmeichel helped bundle Eric back off in the direction of the tunnel, quickly followed by Norman Davies, who finally escorted him to the refuge of the changing-room. Once there, the Frenchman said nothing. He eventually had a shower and Davies got him a cup of tea.

Back on the pitch, David May put United ahead before Gareth Southgate levelled for the home side. An otherwise forgettable football match ended 1–1, a poor result for United's title charge but a reasonable one for Palace's hopes of surviving the threat of relegation.

After the final whistle, the atmosphere in the away changing-room was understandably flat. Although Lee Sharpe clearly remembered Eric apologising to the rest of the team for his outburst, the incident remained one the Frenchman was reluctant to discuss at length. Sharpe recalled: 'It was one of those things you don't like to talk about in the dressing-room. It was like the less we spoke about it, the quicker it would go away. We were expecting to win and it wasn't a good atmosphere afterwards. I think the manager just said, "Eric, you can't go round doing things like that." [Of course, Alex Ferguson hadn't actually seen what had happened at that point].'

Shortly after the match it emerged that the police were to launch an investigation into the affair, possibly with a view to levelling criminal charges at Cantona. When the Frenchman got home that night he received a less than cordial reception from Isabelle, his wife. However, few people at United appear to have been aware of the full gravity of the situation until the team and the club's officials arrived back in Manchester. Alex Ferguson only realised what had actually happened when, unable to sleep in the early hours of the morning, he crept downstairs to watch the highlights of the game on a tape recorded by his son Jason. Naturally, he was horrified when he saw what Eric had done.

Under pressure from leading figures at the Football Association, including chief executive Graham Kelly and director of public affairs David Davies, Manchester United acted swiftly to make it clear they were treating the matter with the utmost concern. Between them Alex Ferguson, chairman Martin Edwards, Maurice Watkins (a United director and a solicitor) and Sir Roland Smith, chairman of Manchester United plc, decided to suspend Eric until the end of the season and fine him two weeks' wages, which, when you included bonuses, amounted to about £20,000. Cantona gave his consent to the punishment, a necessary step in order to avoid any potential legal wrangling over, for instance, restriction of trade. The following day, Friday, 27 January, Manchester United called a press conference at which the club delivered its verdict. In a statement, Watkins said: 'In reaching this decision, which the player fully accepts, Manchester United has had regard to its responsibilities both to the club itself and the game as a whole.' However, no apology was forthcoming from either the club or the player at that time.

Meanwhile, the country's tabloid newspapers went into overdrive to see who could make the most mileage out of the crisis and sell the most copies off the back of it. The *Sun* scooped its rivals by securing exclusive rights to Matthew Simmons's version of events after reportedly paying the twenty-year-old self-employed glazier from Thornton Heath, Surrey, between £20,000 and £80,000 for his story. It was cheque-book journalism at its worst. CANTONA'S BOOT STUDS SLAMMED INTO MY HEART screamed the headline in a deliberate attempt to exaggerate the damage inflicted by the Frenchman's kung-fu kick. In reality, a police statement had already revealed that Simmons had suffered no more than minor bruising.

It was all fairly typical of the distorted reporting of the time. 'There was a lot of hysterical stuff in the media,' David Meek maintained. 'Some wanted him banned from the country, sent home to France in disgrace, suspended indefinitely from English football.' He believed the root cause of the bile being spouted by some sections of the media was an element of xenophobia that exists within certain tabloid newspapers. 'There was an element of racism there. There was the typical reaction that the newspapers exaggerate both ways: they over-glorify and they over-denigrate. They went to extremes because that's the way tabloid newspapers have gone to sensationalise and sell newspapers.' Meek's point is a good one. There is something deeply disturbing about the fact that the nation's press and public were, in general, more damning in their condemnation of Eric Cantona's attack on some-one who had provoked him with vile abuse than they were of, for instance, Paul Gascoigne's assault on his wife Sheryl a few years later.

Not to be outdone by its rivals, the *Daily Star* ran its own exclusive after discovering that Simmons apparently had a conviction for his part in the brutal robbery of a garage. The newspaper had unearthed the service station's cashier, who claimed Simmons tried to smash him over the head with a two-foot spanner. Other papers uncovered evidence of past connections with extreme right-wing groups and the fact that he had been banned from Selhurst Park the previous season for his part in a pitch invasion during a match against Watford. There were also allegations on a Radio Five Live phone-in that Simmons had spat at a father and his children when, earlier in the match, the father had asked him to tone down his language after becoming sick of his constant loud abuse of players and match officials.

The way in which the Selhurst Park affair descended into a battle to see who could sell the most newspapers somehow mirrored the media-driven trial of O.J. Simpson, which was in full swing at that time. Yet as details concerning the true character of Matthew Simmons emerged, some of the country's more discerning sportswriters began to recognise that Cantona was far from being the only villain of this particular piece. For instance, Richard Williams wrote in the *Independent on Sunday*: 'You didn't have to look very long and hard at Mr Matthew Simmons of Thornton Heath to conclude that Eric Cantona's only mistake was to stop hitting him. The more we discovered about Mr Simmons, the more Cantona's assault looks like the instinctive expression of a flawless moral judgement.' Touché!

Eric Cantona had rarely enjoyed more than fragile popularity in his native France, and this latest folly won him few friends and lost him plenty. It was already common knowledge that the relationship between Cantona and Claude Simonet, the president of the French Football Federation, was far from harmonious. From the outset, the latter made it clear that the events at Selhurst Park meant that Eric had played his last game for his country. 'I am stunned at such behaviour, which is against all sporting ethics. The FFF will probably take draconian measures when the time comes,' he said. As ever, French football's governing body seemed determined to act as judge and jury and hand out Eric's sentence before his case had even been heard.

With the benefit of several years of hindsight, Erik Bielderman was able to put the impact of the whole affair into a broader context for me: 'Everybody was shocked, everybody was upset. Everybody thought at that time that it was the end of Eric's story in England and maybe the end of Eric's story for good. We thought at that time that he might go to Japan or the United States to play, that that was the end of the high-profile Cantona. There wasn't too much support for him because at that time England had just come back into Europe after the hooligan problems [of the 1980s] and it wasn't the right way for a player to encourage peace in English stadiums because if you go into the stands to fight, you can't tell the hooligans not to fight one another.' Japan and the United States were not mentioned in the English media at that time as speculation grew as to where Eric might find himself playing football in the future. Most observers here believed Internazionale of Milan or Barcelona were more likely destinations.

As the furore continued, Eric escaped on holiday with Isabelle, now pregnant with their second child, and their son Raphael. They headed to Guadeloupe in the French West Indies. Cantona was public enemy number one, and the stress was beginning to take its toll. 'It was impossible to escape from the press and all the pressure,' he revealed on the video *Cantona Speaks*. However, controversy was to follow the Cantonas abroad as Eric became embroiled in an unsavoury altercation with Terry Lloyd, a respected television reporter, and his ITN camera crew. Although versions of events differ, it is clear that Cantona became incensed by the presence of Lloyd and his crew, especially since he believed they were filming his pregnant wife while the family relaxed on the beach. Lloyd was assaulted, and an X-ray later confirmed that he had sustained fractures to his ribs. He alleges that these were caused by Cantona attacking him. A case of Eric losing control of his temper again, or a camera crew paying the price for invading the privacy of a celebrated footballer and his family at a time of high stress? The actual truth of the matter probably lies somewhere between the two. Anyway, the local police decided it was the latter and confiscated the camera crew's film on the back of French privacy laws.

On Eric's return to England he was charged with common assault by South Norwood police in connection with the Selhurst Park incident. Then, on Friday, 24 February, he attended the FA's disciplinary hearing into the matter at a hotel in St Albans, Hertfordshire. The upshot of that was that the ban already imposed by the player's club was extended until 30 September. He was also fined £10,000 after the FA found him guilty of misconduct and bringing the game into disrepute. In making the announcement of the FA's sentence, Graham Kelly confirmed that Cantona had expressed his regret. Maurice Watkins also insisted in a press conference that the player had apologised in private. No public apology was forthcoming, however.

The judicial case was to be heard at Croydon magistrates court on Thursday, 23 March. Paul Ince, the United midfielder, was also in the dock that day since he too was charged with common assault in connection with events at Crystal Palace, although he was acquitted after pleading not guilty. The two players prepared for the hearing by indulging in a night out in London, during which they also ran into, among others, Paul Gascoigne and the film star Mel Gibson. They did not arrive back at the Croydon hotel until just before dawn on the day they were due in court.

Cantona's statement, read out in court by his barrister, Mr David Poole, claimed of Simmons: 'His face appeared to be contorted with hatred or rage and he was making an obscene gesture. He was shouting in abusive, insulting and racist or nationalistic terms.' Cantona also said that while the referee's decision to send him off was correct, he had been 'repeatedly and painfully fouled in the course of the match'. Cantona was 'hurt and insulted' by the abuse hurled at him by Matthew Simmons as well as 'frustrated' at getting himself sent off.

Ridiculously, Simmons claimed he had only shouted 'Off, off, off! Go on, Cantona, have an early shower.' But a witness who was in the crowd that night remembered a slightly different version, claiming that Simmons had in fact bawled 'You fucking cheating French cunt. Fuck off back to France, you motherfucker. French bastard. Wanker.'

Astoundingly, Mrs Jane Pearch, chairman of Croydon magistrates, sentenced Cantona, who had obviously pleaded guilty, to two weeks in prison. Matthew Simmons, who had been charged with threatening behaviour, received a £500 fine and a year's ban from Selhurst Park. Ever since 25 January the public and media had demanded that Cantona should not receive special treatment on the basis that he was a famous footballer, that he be treated like any member of the public. The magistrates went to the opposite extreme and sought to make an example of him.

Martin Edwards, the Manchester United chairman, was livid that such a harsh sentence had been meted out and even stated in a newspaper interview that if the club had known how austere the punishments were going to be from the FA and the court, it would not have imposed such a lengthy ban on Eric itself. 'I feel very sorry for Eric because he has been punished three ways, really.' As Cantona was being sentenced, Alex Ferguson was receiving his CBE at Buckingham Palace. It was a day of mixed emotions for the United manager.

The media circus again descended on Croydon eight days later when it was time for the Frenchman's appeal to be heard. Judge Ian Davies sensibly commuted the sentence to a period of 120 hours' community service, coaching youngsters to play football. During the press conference that followed the hearing, Eric made a cryptic comment which would be quoted time and time again as journalists and psychologists, professional and otherwise, sought desperately to interpret its meaning: 'When the seagulls follow the trawler, it is because they think sardines will be thrown into the sea. Thank you very much.' Were the seagulls the newspapermen and paparazzi who trailed his every move? Who knows. One thing is certain: despite his evident nervousness when delivering that statement, he must have taken enormous satisfaction from the fuss his words have created ever since.

Now that a punishment had been found that would fit the crime, Eric could start getting on with his life again. He clearly benefited from the positive type of rehabilitation the community service afforded him, especially since it was also a humbling experience. The Frenchman coached young boys and girls from all sections of society, including several handicapped children. They came from a football club made up of kids from a Salford housing estate, picked at random from the thousands who asked to be coached by Cantona. 'The community service with the children was a very good experience and I enjoyed it very much. I hope I helped them to become better footballers. I don't know if they enjoyed it, but I enjoyed it very much and it helped me too. So it wasn't like a punishment, it was like a gift,' Eric later wrote of these sessions, which took place in the afternoons after training with Manchester United.

The 1994/95 campaign was the only one of Eric Cantona's five seasons at Old Trafford in which Manchester United failed to win the Premiership – and, indeed, any other trophy. The team's inability to clinch a potential second Double in as many years was no coincidence, given the absence of its talisman. United finished second in the League, just a point behind Blackburn Rovers, and might even have won it had they shown greater poise and enjoyed a little more luck in front of goal against West Ham United in a last-day decider. The following Saturday, despite ninety minutes of constant endeavour, they succumbed 1–0 to Everton in the FA Cup final and the misery was complete.

Alex Ferguson has always been adamant that with Cantona in the side for those crucial last few months of the campaign his team would at least have secured a third consecutive Premiership crown. 'I think it's summed up in the three games we had in a row at home [between 15 March and 17 April]. We drew 0–0 with Chelsea, 0–0 with Tottenham and 0–0 with Leeds United. Having only lost the League by the one point, no one's going to tell me or even attempt to convince me that he would not have made one goal or scored a goal in one of those three games,' he reasoned on the *Cantona Speaks* video.

The manager's view is one that is also endorsed by the players. Lee Sharpe told me: 'One man doesn't make a team, but I think he was definitely very influential at the time, and when it does come down to the wire and you're looking for that little bit extra, he was that for us and we maybe lacked that.' And most sections of the media concurred. 'Eric made a very good team into a great team, and when he wasn't there they just reverted to being a very good team, but not one that was really going to win much without him. He was a match-winner, there's no doubt,' David Meek remarked.

At the end of the FA Cup final television cameras caught a shot of Cantona, Andy Cole and David May, none of whom, for different reasons, had been available or were selected to play in the match. As they got to their feet, their dark suits matched the expression of disappointment and helplessness on each of their faces. 'And Manchester United have ended with nothing,' exclaimed Barry Davies, the BBC commentator.

You don't have to be involved in football for long before you realise that fans of the beautiful game can be a fickle breed. However, the backing of Manchester United supporters for Eric Cantona during his ban from football was unstinting. It is testimony to his popularity and outstanding achievements at the club that he continued to be viewed with the highest regard and held in deep affection by all at Old Trafford, even as they saw their dreams of a second Double fail to materialise. In other circumstances, Eric might well have provided an easy scapegoat since his absence definitely contributed to United's lack of silverware.

Andy Mitten summed up why the Frenchman remained so popular in spite of actions that had clearly caused the football club enormous difficulties. 'Would you turn against someone who had brought so much happiness to so many lives because of one indiscretion? We owed it to Cantona to stick up for him because nobody else would. We wanted to repay what he had given us. At first it may have seemed like United fans were trying to defend the indefensible, but so much hyperbolic crap was written about the incident that he actually became quite easy to defend. When clueless politicians whose knowledge of football was minimal started bleating about how it was a "national disgrace" they left themselves as open to ridicule as Cantona did by assaulting a Croydon no-mark.'

Lee Sharpe compared the situation with that of Roy Keane, another Old Trafford favourite who has found himself on the receiving end of an FA suspension from time to time. 'Supporters like someone who shows a bit of aggression and passion. They love Keaney, and I don't think there's too many that'll turn against Keaney when he gets sent off. They may not be too happy at the time, but a couple of weeks down the line when he's winning tackles and running the midfield again, he's back in their hearts. And I think that's the way Eric was.'

While nobody could possibly condone Eric Cantona's assault on Matthew Simmons, in the years that followed the events of 25 January 1995 there have been suggestions of sympathy for the Frenchman from other professional footballers who have grown weary of the abuse they are expected to endure from some fans. Gary Speed revealed to me how many players viewed the situation: 'I think the reaction was that obviously he shouldn't have done it, but [a lot of people thought] "I hope he gave the fan a good hiding" – that was from the players, especially the people who knew him. Obviously he shouldn't have done it, it was a terrible thing that happened, but people felt a bit of sympathy for him because there are people who come to matches and sometimes they get away with murder. Obviously we didn't condone what he'd done – it was awful – but there was a hint of sympathy for him.'

Since Selhurst Park, Ned Kelly, United's chief security officer and a former member of the SAS, has accompanied

Manchester United players who have been sent off from the moment they leave the pitch until they are safely back in the dressing-room. Eric Cantona's story might have been very different had such a policy been in operation that January. And the writing of this book would certainly have been a very different experience.

Whatever the rights and wrongs – and they were mainly wrongs – of the Selhurst Park affair, not even the Frenchman's greatest dissenters could dispute the fact that Cantona had been sorely missed by Manchester United. When he returned, he would make amends in the most wonderful and dramatic fashion.

12 Second Coming

Get me back on board, pull me up with grace
Get me back on board, let me be embraced
Cos I'm always, always trying to be
The archetypal free.

'BACK ON BOARD', RODDY FRAME

The summer of 1995 saw a period of change at Old Trafford, with Mark Hughes, Andrei Kanchelskis and, perhaps most significantly, Paul Ince all banging the exit door behind them. Hughes joined Chelsea since the Stamford Bridge club had offered him a better contract and more first-team opportunities. Kanchelskis was sold to Everton in ignominious circumstances, and Ince was offloaded to Internazionale in Italy's Serie A, a move he had always dreamt of making.

One man Alex Ferguson was desperate to hold on to, despite his troubles the previous campaign and his ongoing suspension, was Eric Cantona. The Frenchman had been aware of interest from Internazionale himself since before January, when the Italian giants had sent a high-level delegation to England in an attempt to persuade United to sell Cantona and Ince as a replacement for Dutch duo Dennis Bergkamp and Wim Jonk, who were, at the time, enjoying mixed fortunes at the San Siro. Although United initially refused to countenance the sale of these two key players, Inter did not give up easily and eventually signed Ince. They almost got their hands on Eric Cantona, too.

Despite the fact that when Inter came calling Eric was 29, had just a year left on his contract and was in trouble right up to his neck in England, United were desperate to retain the services of the man whose mercurial presence had helped transform a team of title contenders into title winners. So the club set about negotiating a new contract with the Frenchman, but the going was tough. Cantona did not feel as welcome in England as once he had. He felt he received inadequate protection from referees, the FA had banned him from all football until the end of September, and a magistrate had attempted to have him incarcerated. Moreover, if he did stay at Old Trafford, he would surely have to face a barrage of abuse at away grounds up and down the country, particularly from fans whose traditional hatred of Manchester United is well known. Anfield, Elland Road and Upton Park in particular would undoubtedly test his nerve to the full. Then there were the players from other teams. Plenty of them had indulged in ritual Cantona-baiting of both a physical and verbal nature in the past. Now, given recent history, such people would barely give him a moment's peace on the pitch, or so the theory went. And off it the press would scrutinise his every move, waiting to pounce as soon as he stepped out of line in the slightest way.

It was against a backdrop of such obvious and under-standable concerns that Martin Edwards and Alex Ferguson sought to convince the Frenchman that he still had a future in English football. It was no easy task. However, Eric was extremely touched by the enthusiasm of the children he coached during his spell of community service, so much so that it appears to have renewed his faith in human nature. Furthermore, the way United fans continued to sing his name and register their support for their fallen idol in myriad ways reminded him of the affection in which he was held at Old Trafford. These two elements made him remember why he had enjoyed the majority of his time in England so much.

When Eric sat down to discuss a new deal with Martin Edwards, on Monday, 24 April, rumours were rife that the Frenchman had already agreed to take up Inter's offer. Both parties at the meeting already knew that the Italians were prepared to offer United around £5.5 million for their star player and that they were promising Eric double the salary his present club could afford. It looked as if

Edwards would have to break the legendary Old Trafford wage structure. The discussions lasted an astounding eleven hours, and the only concrete decision reached was that at the end of the week Eric would announce his decision as to whether he was staying at United or seeking a new life in Milan.

A press conference was arranged for the Friday morning, and Old Trafford held its breath while its favourite adopted son pondered his future. The tabloids played out the usual will-he-won't-he drama that week, but by the Thursday Alex Ferguson had clearly received indications that Cantona was going to give him some good news. 'I'm optimistic,' he said, 'and if we get the right decision tomorrow it will be terrific for us, the best news we have had at United for a long time.' But not even the manager was absolutely certain of the upshot of Eric's reflections until the Frenchman strode into his office just before 10 a.m. on the Friday and confirmed his intention to remain at United for another three years. His verdict was certainly heartening for Ferguson, who said at the ensuing press conference: 'This is a giant step towards winning things. We have never had a complaint from Eric about his punishment, he never said a word. He has handled it all so well.'

In front of the media, Eric was more at ease than he had been for several months. He admitted that he had briefly considered joining Internazionale but that Old Trafford still had a complete monopoly on his footballing loyalties. He added: 'I am happy to spend the rest of my career at Old Trafford. We are bigger than the people who have been so hard and so wrong sometimes. I can forget everything now, even the criticism, because I know we can win everything.' He even ended proceedings with a joke, excusing himself on the basis that he was due at training in preparation for his next game in . . . He paused for a moment, grinned and pretended to look into the distance, before adding, 'October.' It was a rare glimpse of the warm, humorous man behind the ever-so-serious veneer.

Eric's decision to stay in England and confront the situation in which he had landed himself marked a turning point in his career. Hitherto, when the going had got tough, Eric had got a transfer to another club. On this occasion, however, he stayed put, determined to repay the faith shown in him at Manchester United by helping to catapult the team to new glories. Eric had already hinted that the time for running had passed, when, two years earlier, he said on the video *Ooh Aah Cantona*: 'My solution was to say to myself that I was passing through. This way, when things got difficult, I would say to myself, "You're just passing through." ' Perhaps he had matured and finally learnt from his mistakes. Whatever the case, his decision to commit his future to United was met with relieved delight by everyone involved with the club. Even so, just a few months later Cantona appeared once again to be on his way out of Old Trafford.

Despite the sale of three star names over the summer of 1995, Alex Ferguson was confident that his group of young players, including Philip and Gary Neville, Nicky Butt, Paul Scholes and David Beckham, would develop quickly and fully enough to bolster the existing first-team squad without the need for further forays into the transfer market. Butt, he reasoned, would replace Paul Ince and play alongside Roy Keane in the centre of midfield; Scholes could play in a variety of attacking roles to supplement his first-choice strike partnership, which would be Eric Cantona and Andy Cole when the former returned from suspension; meanwhile, Beckham would prove to be Andrei Kanchelskis's long-term replacement on the right flank. But the manager believed that Cantona's presence was crucial to knit together the youngsters with the more experienced players such as Steve Bruce, Gary Pallister, Denis Irwin and Peter Schmeichel. It was, therefore, imperative that Cantona stayed at Old Trafford.

Under the terms of Eric's suspension, he was not allowed to play in any organised match, including charity friendlies. However, he was allowed to train as normal and participate in games that were deemed part of United's training programme. Ferguson therefore arranged a number of matches against local teams such as

Oldham, Rochdale and Bury which would take place at the Cliff training ground. The manager felt that such games would help the Frenchman get in as good a condition as possible ahead of his return to competitive action at the start of October, and the club believed them to be permissible given the parameters laid down by the ban. However, after details of the first such training game appeared in the press, Lancaster Gate informed Old Trafford that the FA defined such outings as friendly matches, thus proscribing Eric's involvement in them.

Cantona, already frustrated by a lengthy period of inaction, could remain patient no longer and decided to leave, with Alex Ferguson's blessing, for France. Once again it appeared that the Frenchman's love affair with Old Trafford was over. But a conversation with his wife Cathy convinced Ferguson, who had begun to view Cantona's departure as inevitable given the pressure he was under, that all was not yet lost. Cathy had expressed surprise at how easily her normally obstinate husband had allowed Eric to return to his homeland. So Ferguson followed Eric to Paris, determined to persuade him once and for all that he could recover his lost sense of achievement and fulfilment at Old Trafford.

Once in the French capital, the United manager had to avoid the many members of the English press who had gathered there in their editors' eagerness to get to the bottom of the story, which Ferguson himself had inadvertently allowed to leak. Jean-Jacques Bertrand arranged for Ferguson to be smuggled out of the back door of his hotel before being rushed on the back of a Harley Davidson to meet Cantona for dinner. Eric clearly knew the restaurateur well since he agreed to close his premises that night and serve dinner exclusively to the small Cantona party. Over the course of the evening, Ferguson was able to allay Eric's fears about what lay ahead for him in England, and he duly consented to return to Old Trafford. Ferguson has since described that evening thus: 'I pride myself on having an excellent recollection of teams, goalscorers and dates, and it impressed me that he was in the same league when it came to remembering outstanding occasions back in the fifties and sixties. Those hours spent in Eric's company in that largely deserted restaurant added up to one of the more worthwhile acts I have performed in this stupid job of mine.'

The manager's deliberate use of understatement should not be ignored since Cantona was a crucial part of his plans. However, it still seems remarkable that Alex Ferguson, a manager who has not always been famed for his powers of forgiveness, was prepared to dash across the Channel in pursuit of an errant player. Remarkable, that is, until you consider the evidence. Despite the Frenchman's brushes with authority, he had never undermined the manager – unlike Paul Ince, a player whom Ferguson had reluctantly deemed transferable. In his autobiography, Peter Schmeichel made it clear that Ince had to be sold to avoid disharmony spreading through the ranks at Old Trafford. 'I felt he was, to put it mildly, self-centred and arrogant, and his potentially adverse influence on young players in particular was something that I know worried Alex Ferguson.' The Danish goalkeeper, like his manager, was sickened by Ince's insistence on referring to himself as the 'Guv'nor'. References to the nickname appeared on his boots and the numberplate of his car, much to the annoyance of Ferguson, who, according to Schmeichel, once spouted, 'I'll show him who the fucking Guv is!'

Moreover, Lee Sharpe emphasised that the manager viewed the Cantona situation as a massive challenge from the moment he decided to sign him. 'He obviously knew about his reputation and knew he was a loose cannon and played on the edge a little bit, and maybe felt it was a personal battle for him [Ferguson] to control him [Cantona] and get the best out of him. And there's no two ways about it, he definitely got the best out of him. I think that was one last push to show how much he cared about and respected him, that he went after him [to France] and told him he still wanted him.'

Although Ferguson would probably bristle at the suggestion, it is clear, from an outsider's point of view at least, that Eric Cantona was given a certain amount of leeway both on and off the field. However, Sharpe insisted that rather than this creating ill feeling within the camp, the rest of the squad were usually able to see the funny side, relating the following anecdote in order to illustrate his point: 'I remember turning up one year to a town hall reception after we'd won the League or the Cup. Because it was the Lord Mayor and everything, everyone had to wear conservative-looking suits – grey suits, black suits, navy blue suits. I turned up, because it was like eighty degrees, in this olive-coloured silk suit and the manager started ripping me to shreds. Then Eric turns up with a black suit on and white shirt with no tie and a pair of red Nike trainers on. So I'm like, "Well, he can do it." I wasn't being horrible to Eric, I was just jesting, really, and the manager just walked off because he had no argument.' Nevertheless, Sharpe was quick to realise why the manager was prepared to offer Cantona the extra level of flexibility he craved. 'We understood that Eric got away with it, I suppose. At the end of the day his performances allowed him to do it as well. If he'd have come in and not been the best and struggled, then I think it would have been different. But because he came and set the place alight, I don't think anybody could really argue with him.'

David Meek contended that the rest of the squad accepted Ferguson's touch of leniency with the Frenchman since he was such a model professional in many ways. 'Players get resentful if there's one law for one and one law for the other if the guy who is being made an exception doesn't warrant it. But I think they held Eric in such regard that they were prepared to make allowances. They didn't see him being made a favourite, so to speak, and they accepted that he was different in so many ways, apart from the fact of being French, in the quality he brought. So they were quite happy to accept Eric without resentment if, indeed, he tended to flout some of the club disciplines that they had to conform to. Footballers are not stupid, and they know when a player is flouting something serious. If he was late for training, if he was not putting 100 per cent into training, if he was disappearing early, they would resent that if the manager covered that up, but, in the important things, Cantona set an example.'

Sharpe recalled that during training the rest of the squad could sense Eric's frustration at not being allowed to play competitive football for such a long period of time. 'There was a lot of media speculation that he wouldn't stay, that as soon as the ban was up he would go. But we never really got that feeling from him. He seemed to enjoy training. I don't think we ever felt he was aloof, but sometimes because of the language barrier it was a bit difficult asking questions like, "What's happening? Are you going to go?" They were questions that never really got asked. I was only 23 or 24 at the time anyway, so I was hardly an experienced pro to go up to him and start getting into the ins and outs of whether he was staying and how he felt about the place.'

On the other hand, Sharpe admitted that he did have the inside track on Ince's plans to leave Old Trafford. 'I knew that Incey was going because we used to play a lot of golf together and he told me that he'd been speaking to Inter Milan and that United had accepted an offer. There was loads of media [coverage] about Andrei [Kanchelskis] wanting to leave. He showed that he was unhappy because he was sub a lot of the time or he was getting brought off. He didn't speak good English at all but you could tell from his body language that he wasn't happy. So you do get a feeling for these things.'

Despite Eric's absence, the young United team's early-season form was good, even if it did get off to the worst possible start. The 3–1 defeat at Aston Villa on 19 August caused *Match of the Day* pundit Alan Hansen to pontificate on how United would be unable to win silverware that season 'with kids'. But the youngsters gave notice that they were rapidly coming of age by winning all of their next five Premier League matches, against West Ham United, Wimbledon, Blackburn Rovers, Everton and Bolton Wanderers. The seventh outing of the campaign was a goalless draw at Sheffield Wednesday on 23 September. United had won five and drawn one of their first seven fixtures, a record bettered only by the Premiership's pacesetters and long-term title contenders, Kevin Keegan's Newcastle United. There were embarrassing set-backs of course, in the UEFA Cup, against Rotor Volgograd, and in the League Cup at the hands of York City, but Ferguson's young players by and large repaid their manager's faith in them.

Through a quirk of the fixture calendar, Manchester United were pitted against their great rivals Liverpool at Old Trafford in a game originally scheduled for Saturday 30 September, the day Eric Cantona was due to make his comeback. Naturally, the match was switched to the following day so that it could be broadcast live on Sky TV. In the build-up to his eagerly awaited return, Eric appeared in a television advert aimed at promoting racial tolerance at football grounds. The advertisement cut cleverly between Eric and Les Ferdinand, the Newcastle striker, as they uttered the words: 'What do you see, a black man, a Frenchman or a footballer? Is it OK to shout racial abuse at me just because I am on the football pitch? Some people say we have to accept abuse as part of the game. Why? I know that violence is not acceptable in sport. So why should we accept hatred? Why argue about differences? I'd rather play football.'

The Frenchman also starred in an advert for Nike, his preferred boot manufacturer, which some saw as making light of the seriousness of the incident at Selhurst Park. Others, however, simply saw it for what it was: Eric Cantona announcing to the world that he was back, that he was stronger than ever and that, crucially, Selhurst Park could be consigned to history. 'Hello,' he said. 'I want to make an apology. I made some terrible mistakes. Last year, in a certain 5–0 victory, I only scored one goal. Against Newcastle I put a shot three inches wide of the post and at Wembley I failed to complete a hat-trick. I realise this behaviour was unacceptable and I promise not to make such mistakes again. Thank you.'

Unknown to most people in England, many of whom always assumed Eric to be a rather humourless character, his keen sense of irony was also in evidence when he featured in a French TV advert. He posed in a trawler as a sardine fisherman and showed off a mock video collection featuring row upon row of, you've guessed it, tapes about sardines. What is more, they had a footballing theme, with titles like 'Sardines in the back of the net' and 'Physical training for sardines'.

Some Manchester United fans were so keen to show their appreciation of Cantona ahead of his comeback that they placed advertisements in a national newspaper and on billboards with the message 'We'll never forget that night at Selhurst Park (when you buried that amazing volley against Wimbledon)'. Lee Sharpe explained why Eric was made to feel so welcome on his return. 'They [the fans] understand that playing on the edge is their game and that's the way to get the best out of them, and it means that once or twice when there's a hiccup, the fans are willing to let that go and forget about it to get the best out of them and see them wear their hearts on their sleeves for the club.'

Nike launched its own poster campaign, using the line 'He's been punished for his mistakes – now it's someone else's turn.' Alongside it was an image of Eric in full United kit, about to walk out of a dark tunnel, past a recently opened barred door and into the light. Attempts to use similar images with other footballers would have been simply risible, but somehow with Cantona they seemed like nothing out of the ordinary. Of course, Eric Cantona was a marketing department's dream: he was an instantly recognisable figure; he was admired, often grudgingly, by football fans nationwide; many women found him attractive; plenty of blokes admitted he was, well, pretty cool; and come October 1995, whether they loved him or loathed him, members of the public were fascinated by his every move.

The hype and expectation surrounding Cantona's comeback were simply immense. On that Sunday afternoon French *tricolores* were unfurled at Old Trafford and Eric's name was sung with extra gusto as United fans prepared to welcome him back. Pictured in the tunnel as the teams began to file on to the pitch, Eric struck a typical pose: he puffed out his chest, stood up straight and tall and, with his collar upturned in customary fashion, strode out to accept the standing ovation that awaited him.

It did not take Eric long to make a positive impression. In the opening minutes of the match Andy Cole's pass found him unmarked on the left-hand edge of the Liverpool penalty area. The volume rose and fans behind the goal got to their feet in eager anticipation. Cantona's floated cross fell to Nicky Butt. One touch and the ball looped up invitingly for the midfielder; a second, and he had lifted it over the advancing David James in Liverpool's goal. Most of the United players sprinted over to Butt to offer congratulations, but Ryan Giggs, Butt's best friend at Old Trafford, looked instead for the goal's provider. The Welshman hugged Cantona before Gary Pallister arrived on the scene to lock the Frenchman in the sort of embrace normally reserved for loved ones you have not seen for years. With twenty minutes of the match remaining, however, United trailed 2–1. But then Giggs won a penalty, and up stepped Eric to strike the ball home from twelve yards. Spot-kicks had always been his forte.

He may have created one goal and scored a second, yet Eric's overall performance attracted mixed reviews in the media. 'The game went on around him and occasionally he deigned to join in, reminding everyone of what the fuss was all about, with a deft flick or a casual piece of control,' was Andrew Longmore's assessment in *The Times*. Yet for Martin Tyler, who commentated on the game for television, Cantona's comeback lives long in the memory. 'The whole feeling that he'd been down to the depths and now was going to touch the heights – you didn't know that, but when you look back on it you think it was an extraordinary recovery from a period in his life which would have definitely dented lesser men.'

Two days after the match, the *Daily Mirror* published an interview with Joël, Eric's brother. The younger Cantona had attended the match alongside Albert, their father, and both men were delighted with his performance. Moreover, Joël gave an insight into what his brother had gone through and how he had emerged a stronger character for it. 'It's been a nightmare eight months for Eric. The worst period of his life. But he's come through it because of his character. Now neither Eric or myself want to speak about the past. That period has gone and must be forgotten for ever. We must look forward to the future.'

That same day, 3 October, Eric appeared in the side that crashed out of the League Cup 4–3 on aggregate after a 3–1 victory at York City. He then played for the reserve team against their Leeds United counterparts in front of a huge crowd of 21,500, most of whom turned up at Old Trafford that evening just to catch a glimpse of the returning hero. Unfortunately, however, he sustained a minor knee injury which saw him miss the 1–0 home win over Manchester City on 14 October. A week later, though, he was fit again and played a full role at the heart of a stunning performance in which United's superior passing and movement saw them run out 4–1 winners at Chelsea.

Bryan Robson's Middlesbrough were the next visitors to Old Trafford and were beaten 2–0, Eric's vision helping to create the second goal for Andy Cole. United then produced an accomplished display at Arsenal on 4 November but came away with no points after Denis Irwin's error let in Dennis Bergkamp to score the only goal of the game. But it was back to winning ways a fortnight later as Southampton were thrashed 4–1 at the Theatre of Dreams, Eric with a hand in two of the goals. A midweek trip to Coventry City provided another goalfest, the only surprise in the 4–0 romp being that Eric did not get on to the score sheet. In fact, despite being involved in much of the team's best play, Eric struck only once in the first seven matches after his return. That goal tally soon doubled, however, as he both won and converted a penalty in the 1–1 draw at Nottingham Forest at the end of November.

Unfortunately, December was a shockingly bad month for United as the side mustered just three points from the fifteen available, thus handing the initiative to Newcastle United in the title race. It all began with a 1–1 draw at home to Chelsea in which Eric received his only caution of the season, for a foul. Alex Ferguson's squad was beginning to show serious signs of wear and tear as injuries and suspensions piled up. Goalkeeper Peter Schmeichel and the team's central-defence duo of Gary Pallister and Steve Bruce all spent prolonged spells on the treatment table, while Roy Keane and Nicky Butt both served out bans.

On a happier note, Eric rediscovered his goalscoring form with a brace in a 2–2 home draw at Sheffield Wednesday on 9 December. The first was a delicate finish to complete an exquisite move involving snappy passing from Sharpe, Scholes and Cole. The second provided an example of the Frenchman's flawless volleying technique as he arched his body and swivelled to hammer home from the edge of the area. However, he was powerless to prevent subsequent comprehensive reverses in the hostile atmospheres that greeted United at Liverpool and Leeds. During the latter he received a cut to the head that required stitches after an accidental clash.

So United were ten points adrift of runaway Premiership leaders Newcastle when the two sides clashed at Old Trafford two days after Christmas. Kevin Keegan's side, with Peter Beardsley, Les Ferdinand and David Ginola to the fore, had been turning in breathtaking performances all season. Eric and his team-mates simply had to win to shoehorn themselves back into the title race, and win they did, courtesy of stunning strikes from Andy Cole and Roy Keane. Just to prove that every silver lining has a cloud, however, centre-half David May sustained an injury that would keep him out of action for several weeks. With Bruce and Pallister also still out, Alex Ferguson was desperate to find another central defender. Quite by chance, one of Eric's mates, William Prunier, a centre-half by trade, was available, and he came to Old Trafford on a trial basis. He appeared just twice as United conceded five goals in two matches, then returned to France. But he did help set up Andy Cole's goal in a 2–1 success over QPR three days after the Newcastle match.

Although Eric had yet to reproduce his very best form, his performances in the first two months since his return from an eight-month absence displayed remarkably few signs of rustiness. He had clearly kept himself in good shape, both mentally and physically, to meet the challenges ahead. Just as he had when inspiring Montpellier's cup run in 1990, Cantona reacted to his punishment and the problems he had caused for his club by launching a virtual crusade to recover lost honour and propel the side to greater glory. The Frenchman had always been noted for his sense of rebellion, but this time he had a cause.

13 Fields of Gold

I think they've got problems. You just can't win anything with kids.

ALAN HANSEN

Manchester United's makeshift defence suffered a traumatic evening at Tottenham Hotspur on New Year's Day as the team crashed to a 4–1 defeat. It was certainly a bad way to start 1996, but it turned out to be their penultimate defeat of the season as they embarked on a run of consistent form that would culminate in glory on two fronts.

Five days after the White Hart Lane débâcle Cantona served first notice of what was to be a recurring theme throughout the rest of the campaign as he began a trend of scoring vital goals that clinched a United victory or saw them avoid defeat. With ten minutes of their FA Cup third-round clash with Sunderland remaining, Alex Ferguson's men were staring at an early exit from the competition, trailing 2–1. That was until Lee Sharpe swung a free kick from the United right to Sunderland's far post, where Eric got in front of his marker and forced home a powerful header.

United were held to a goalless home draw by Aston Villa on 13 January despite a string of attempts from Andy Cole, then came the replay with Sunderland. Although United's injury worries had eased with the return of Peter Schmeichel and Steve Bruce in particular, the team had to come from behind to keep their FA Cup aspirations alive at Roker Park. Second-half strikes from Paul Scholes and Andy Cole finally put an end to Sunderland's resistance.

The next League fixture took them to West Ham and one of the grounds where Eric could expect a particularly vitriolic reception from a highly vocal home crowd. However, he displayed a new-found calmness to rise above the taunts and scored the only goal of the match, firing Ryan Giggs's low cross into the roof of the net with his left foot from a seemingly impossible angle. What is more, he even acted as peacemaker in an altercation between Nicky Butt and Julian Dicks, the West Ham left-back. Eric's cool approach provided a striking contrast with the frayed tempers around him and offered compelling evidence that he was now in control of the demons that had haunted him in the past.

The next test for his temperament was an FA Cup tie at Reading. United fans who attended the game were surprised by the hostile nature of the atmosphere that greeted them and suspected that many of the spectators in the home stands were, in fact, supporters of other Premiership clubs. During the match Eric was jeered and even had a piece of fruit thrown at him from a section of the home crowd. The Frenchman picked it up and, for a moment, the United players and fans feared the worst, before Eric calmly and gently lobbed the object back whence it had come. And when he completed United's 3–0 victory with a tap-in to add to goals by Ryan Giggs and, unusually, Paul Parker, Eric put his fingers to his ears, thereby signalling that the Reading fans had been silenced.

On 3 February he returned to Selhurst Park for the first time since that catastrophic night the previous year as United took on Wimbledon in the League. If the Frenchman had feared any ghosts in south-west London, they were soon exorcised by his orchestration of a fine 4–2 victory. He scored United's third goal with a stooping header to meet David Beckham's cross after the two had combined to fool the Wimbledon defence with a move of great precision. Eric rushed straight to hug a section of United fans behind the goal, although stewards soon moved to break up the celebrations (if only they had been so alert the previous season!). After scoring his second goal from the penalty spot, he started to head for the crowd again before catching the eye of a steward, raising a hand in acknowledgement and turning around to search out his team-mates instead. Another lesson had been learnt. The following Saturday, United completed a League double over Blackburn Rovers, whose defence of the title turned out to be less than spirited, courtesy of Lee Sharpe's tap-in after fine combination play between Cantona and Andy Cole had seen the latter rattle a post.

United's 1996 FA Cup campaign continued with a mouth-watering derby at home to Manchester City on 18 February. On this occasion, the red half of Manchester had reason to be grateful to referee Alan Wilkie who awarded a dubious penalty after spotting a foul on Eric at a corner. The City players, understandably, were furious, but Cantona ignored the commotion around him to slot home a penalty with an apparent lack of anxiety that most people would struggle to achieve when playing in their back garden. He always enjoyed the challenge of taking penalties, and wrote later: 'Out there in the middle on your own, there remains that small but persistent element of risk. You know it should be straightforward to score, though in reality it's not at all easy – and that's what gives you a buzz. The risk involved means the penalty represents an ephemeral but exciting challenge.' United controlled the match thereafter and Lee Sharpe grabbed a late winner as the side progressed to the next round of the competition.

Everton, the team who had denied United FA Cup glory the previous season, were the next visitors to Old Trafford in the Premiership. Typical Cantona artistry saw him collect the ball midway inside the visitors' half and release a perfectly measured pass into the path of the marauding Roy Keane, who swept home past Neville Southall to open the scoring. And the Frenchman was also involved in the counter-attack that led to the Ryan Giggs goal which wrapped up victory and secured three more crucial points for Alex Ferguson's men. Four days later, on 25 February, United underlined their resurgence in form with a crushing 6–0 win at Bolton Wanderers, thus making a mockery of predictions that such a local derby would prove a banana skin for the would-be champions. Remarkably,

Eric did not feature on the score sheet that day and was replaced by Paul Scholes, who netted twice. But the Frenchman's purple patch would start soon afterwards.

By the end of February, United had reduced Newcastle's advantage at the top of the table to just four points, but, since the Magpies had a game in hand, it was essential the Manchester side take maximum points from the teams' meeting on 4 March. The match was billed as a title showdown in the media and several newspapers set it up as a head to head between Eric and his compatriot David Ginola, fully aware that the two men had not been on speaking terms for over two years. The *Sunday Express* even quoted Michel Platini's opinion of the two men he had managed at international level. He clearly admired both players but saw greater value in Cantona's extra flexibility, arguing that he could play two roles, that of a striker or that of a midfield playmaker, with equal ease. Ginola, on the other hand, while highly talented, had greater limitations in so far as he could only really function in wide positions. 'The playmaker is a role that will suit him because he sees the game so clearly,' Platini asserted of Cantona with the foresight of the most perspicacious clairvoyant. 'Great players do not have to be at the centre of things every second of the game, their influence can come in fleeting moments, but those fleeting moments are the most important.'

The clash of the two Uniteds also drew great attention in France; the game was in fact broadcast on national television. According to Ginola, the TV station was obsessed with whether or not the two men would shake hands at the final whistle. 'The cameras followed our every move to see what would happen. In the event, we avoided each other.' Ginola also claimed that Eric was put out by the Newcastle man's desire to shine as brightly in England as he did. 'I'm convinced he resented me coming to play in England. Until I arrived in Newcastle in 1995 he had been the only French star in the English game. But I stole his limelight. Football came between our friendship. Football drove us apart. Eric was idolised at Manchester United and always wanted to be the king in England, but

I wanted the same, so there was an inevitable clash.' The suggestion that Ginola's performances at Newcastle deflected public attention away from Cantona is quite preposterous: the latter won four Premiership titles and two FA Cups during his time at Old Trafford; Ginola claimed no medals during his two-year spell in the north-east and was sold to Tottenham Hotspur in 1997.

Not only was this encounter with Newcastle to be a massive turning point in the battle for the championship, in many respects it was a microcosm of the Manchester team's season. The main qualities that would see United pip Kevin Keegan's exciting side to the title were in full evidence that Monday night in the north-east. Peter Schmeichel, rightly heralded as the world's foremost goalkeeper at the time, repelled a barrage of Newcastle pressure throughout the first half as the home side mounted wave upon wave of attack; Steve Bruce stood steady as a rock in the heart of defence, defying the ageing process that would see him leave Old Trafford at the end of the campaign; Roy Keane was his usual committed, combative self in central midfield; the younger players – Philip and Gary Neville, Nicky Butt and Ryan Giggs – were full of energy and purpose. But it was Monsieur Cantona, as ever, who ultimately decided the outcome. Six minutes into a more even second half Eric, who had been relatively uninvolved in proceedings hitherto, met Phil Neville's looping far-post centre with a majestic volley that travelled low, hard and true back across the goal and into the Newcastle net. Again, it was the Frenchman's finely honed technique that allowed him to execute the shot with such control and accuracy.

The 1–0 victory provided a blueprint for much of the rest of the season: remain parsimonious in defence and competitive in midfield, and Eric will grab the vital goal. The Newcastle clash began a run of six consecutive Premier League games in which the Frenchman's name appeared on the score sheet. Of these matches, United claimed five victories and were held to a single draw, and remarkably they never won by more than the odd goal. The sequence after the Newcastle win, played out between 16 March and 8 April, went as follows: a 1–1 draw at Queens Park Rangers in which Eric equalised with a header deep into stoppage time; a 1–0 home win over Arsenal courtesy of Cantona's perfect chest control and powerful volley; the Frenchman's precise left-foot strike at the end of a strong run was enough to see off Tottenham at the same venue; United overcame Manchester City 3–2 at Maine Road, Eric scoring from the penalty spot; and Coventry City were despatched 1–0 at Old Trafford after a Cantona tap-in.

Gary Neville, the Manchester United and England right-back, described the difference between the vintage side of 1996 and the United team he played in five years later in an interview with the *Guardian* in November 2001. 'We had a period about five years ago when [Eric] Cantona was playing when we won five or six games 1–0. But we were a completely different side then, a lot more solid and nowhere near as adventurous. This is a far more adventurous team, a far better team, far more exciting. You can't have Giggs, Beckham, Scholes, Keane, Verón, Van Nistelrooy, Cole, Solskjaer in your team and expect us to go out and defend.'

It was not just in the Premiership that Eric excelled. The Frenchman had always performed well in the FA Cup, and when United entertained Southampton at the quarter-final stage he scored the first goal and created a second for Lee Sharpe in a 2–0 success. That fixture took place a week to the day after the crucial win at Newcastle, and United's performance was in a similar vein: again they failed to produce their best attacking play but remained resolute in defence before Eric orchestrated the breakthrough at a moment when it was perhaps least expected.

The win over Southampton set up an exciting semi-final against Ruud Gullit's Chelsea at Villa Park. The Dutchman it was who gave the London team a first-half lead, but Cantona, who captained United that day in the absence of Steve Bruce, was in sparkling form and was unlucky when yet another sweetly struck volley rebounded off a post. The Frenchman's involvement was then crucial as his header guided the ball back across goal to create Andy Cole's second-half equaliser. Minutes later David Beckham latched on to Craig Burley' s misdirected backpass to give United a 2–1 lead. Unusually, Eric's most significant intervention in proceedings came at the United end. With Peter Schmeichel stranded after saving a Gullit effort, the United captain appeared on the goal line to head clear John Spencer's fierce volley. Eric's appearance in defence surprised most people, not least the BBC's John Motson, who exclaimed: 'Here's Spencer on the follow-up for Chelsea. Oh! Headed away by Cantona, is that? Goodness gracious, Eric Cantona on the goal line, otherwise it was 2–2. I had to look twice there to make sure that it was the Manchester United captain.'

Manchester United's defeat of Coventry on 8 April had put them into a commanding position at the top of the Premiership. They led Newcastle, who had a game in hand, by six points and boasted a slightly better goal difference. The Old Trafford side knew that if they could secure three wins and a draw from their remaining four fixtures, the title would be theirs irrespective of Newcastle's results. However, on Saturday 13 April, Alex Ferguson's men suffered an unexpected and potentially disastrous 3–1 reverse at Southampton. After conceding three first-half goals, United even changed their strip at the interval since the players complained that they could not see each other because their light grey shirts were not clearly visible in the bright sunlight. There was even a theory that the grey shirts were jinxed – footballers are a notoriously superstitious breed – since United never won on the few occasions they wore them.

The upshot of the Southampton defeat was that United had to win their three remaining matches and score plenty of goals in the process to make absolutely sure they were not overtaken by Newcastle. In that context, Roy Keane's goal in a 1–0 victory over Leeds United at Old Trafford on 17 April was simply priceless. Ahead of the last home match of the season, there was still the possibility that the destination of the title would be decided by goal difference. The 5–0 thrashing of

Nottingham Forest therefore represented a result as close to perfection as possible. Paul Scholes, who was selected ahead of the out-of-form Andy Cole, opened the scoring before David Beckham grabbed a goal either side of half-time. Ryan Giggs then added a fourth. But as the final whistle approached, the home fans were desperate for a Cantona goal to round off a display of typical majesty from the Frenchman. Eric's goal duly arrived when his attempted pass to Lee Sharpe rebounded fortuitously into his path. After an exemplary piece of chest control, he slammed an emphatic volley into the Forest net. The United captain fell to the floor in celebration as the crowd sang his name.

The following day, 29 April, Newcastle beat Leeds United to keep themselves in the title race, but they could only draw at Nottingham Forest later that week, which meant Manchester United held a two-point advantage and comfortably superior goal difference going into the final game of the season, a potentially testing meeting with Middlesbrough at the Riverside. When Eric led his team-mates on to the field on Sunday, 5 May, they knew it was imperative to forget about the game between Newcastle and Tottenham at St James's Park. Win, and the title was theirs. A draw would probably suffice as well, but a defeat would be catastrophic. Cantona and his team-mates responded to the situation in the manner of champions by storming to a convincing 3–0 victory, David May, Andy Cole and Ryan Giggs all on target. Unbridled joy ensued, but the story of Cantona's dramatic and glorious comeback from the depths he had reached the previous season was not yet complete.

Eric Cantona may have been blessed with sumptuous skill and an abundance of natural talent, yet other crucial factors enabled him to translate raw ability into success. Players and coaches who have worked with him always remark upon his assiduous attitude towards training and practice. Moreover, at Manchester United, this was a positive state of mind that rubbed off on many of the other players, especially the generation of youngsters whose impact was now being felt. 'He'd always be out there doing extra training with the lads,' Lee Sharpe recalled. 'There were a few of us at the time, the young lads, we'd look to stay out there and do shooting practice and he'd always be one of the players out there with us.'

Undoubtedly, Eric's ability – as well as that of Steve Bruce, Peter Schmeichel and Roy Keane in particular – to shepherd many of the less experienced players through the trials of the 1995/96 campaign was one of the finest achievements of his career. What is more, Lee Sharpe identified Alex Ferguson's handling of Cantona as the key factor that allowed the Frenchman to flourish at Old Trafford. And the by-product of that was that the manager could hold Eric up as a shining example to his young charges. 'He gave him this free role, letting him express himself, do his flicks, score his goals. I think that's why the lads looked up to him so much. They thought: "If I can be anyone, that's who I want to be. I want to be treated like that, I want to play like that, I want to be loved like that." He was treated differently to everyone else but he played differently to everyone else, so horses for courses.'

Furthermore, Eric Harrison, the youth-team coach who was responsible for much of the nurturing of the group of youngsters that included Paul Scholes, David Beckham, the Neville brothers, Ryan Giggs and Nicky Butt, was able to call upon Cantona's knowledge of foreign coaching techniques. Harrison revealed that he once asked Cantona about differences between young players at United and young French players. 'He replied that, ability wise, they were similar, but he thought that one aspect of the French boys' game was better than ours, and that was that they received the ball better than our young players. I took that onboard straightaway and, as always when I have been given good advice, I acted. In this instance, I introduced more juggling with the ball because five to ten minutes of this exercise developed good ball control. Surely, if it was good enough for Cantona, it was good enough for my boys.'

Harrison also offered an insight into the method behind Cantona's masterful technique: 'I wonder how many fans observed that he rarely passed, crossed or sent in a shot with swerve on the ball. Also, he very rarely passed the ball with spin or swerve on it because – his logic was indisputable – it is easier for a team-mate to control a ball that is not spinning.'

However, Eric also used less conventional methods to fine-tune his performances on the field and ensure he was fully focused on football. Since his early years as a professional in France, he had been fascinated by the subconscious, an area he explored regularly in psychoanalysis sessions. According to Lee Sharpe, the Frenchman employed the expertise of his psychoanalyst to help improve his game. One Saturday night after a match, Sharpe and Cantona, accompanied by their respective friends, encountered one another in the bar of a Manchester hotel. The men all sat down together and chatted over a drink. Sharpe, aware that Eric was interested in an array of areas and issues not traditionally related to football, raised the subject of psychology. It was then that Cantona related his experiences of psychoanalysis. A surprised Sharpe responded: 'I can't believe you do that. I thought you were all off the cuff and had an air of confidence about yourself that said if you didn't play well today you'd do it right next time.'

'No, no,' Eric retorted. 'I always have a look at where I can improve, how the game's gone and what I'm going to do next time.'

From then on, Sharpe realised just how deeply Eric cared about the game and his role within it. 'Eric said, "It's just I have a look into my game and what my game is about and what I can do with it," rather than him having to build himself up full of confidence and talk himself into having a good game.'

The former United winger's recollections of Eric's approach certainly tally with comments the Frenchman made after the end of the 1995/96 season in which he explained his immense self-belief. 'I've said in the past that I could play single-handedly against eleven players and win. I believe in myself. Sometimes it's crazy, I know. There is a place for doubt: doubt makes you question yourself, it makes you want to win. Doubt leads to fear, and fear is what fuels every great challenge. But the trick is to transcend that fear, to believe in your own abilities so that the team can win. I've always had that quality. Even if it's crazy, it's part of who I am. There is something inside me that always believes I can do it.'

The final match of the 1995/96 campaign was the FA Cup final against Liverpool. In the week leading up to the game, Eric received the much-coveted Football Writers' Award for their Player of the Year, a testimony to his reformed character, the immense influence he had had as the architect of United's successful season and the eighteen goals which made him the club's top scorer. However, for many outside Old Trafford it was a controversial decision and one which was pilloried in certain national newspapers by journalists who maintained that it was scandalous to bestow such an honour on a man who, a year earlier, had been cast as football's number one enemy. Joe Lovejoy, writing in *The Times* on 28 April, sensibly took issue with these detractors. 'To dispute that Cantona is the best, and most influential, player in the Premier League is to fly in the face of peer-group opinion and statistical proof,' he wrote.

On the morning of the final the BBC broadcast a rare television interview with Eric in which he told Des Lynam of his admiration for the way United's crop of youngsters had dealt with the demands of the title campaign. 'The young players who have come in have been wonderful, but the most important season for them is next season. After your first season and you win the championship you maybe think that's it, but next season will be the most difficult in their heads, but they will handle it.'

Since Steve Bruce was still struggling with injury, Eric had the honour of leading the United team on to the Wembley turf. As is so often the case with high-profile games around which heightened expectations exist, the teams failed to produce the swashbuckling spectacle predicted. United curbed their attacking instincts and flooded midfield in order to stifle the life out of Liverpool's passing game, and Roy Keane was outstanding, ensuring that Steve McManaman in particular remained anonymous. It was a game of few chances, but as extra time loomed United won a corner, to be delivered by the ever-improving David Beckham. David James, the Liverpool goalkeeper, came to punch the ball away but failed to make decent contact, the ball fell to Cantona and the Frenchman contorted his body to strike a shot into the net from the edge of the area.

Anyone who looks again at the replay of this goal will wonder how on earth Cantona managed to produce such a controlled strike with such accuracy and power when the ball was almost behind him at the point of impact. Martin Tyler, who was commentating on the final, recalled that there was a bizarre mixture of incredulity and inevitability about Cantona's winning goal. 'That whole period, from the October to the May, I was there for many steps along the way and you just felt there was a sort of inevitability about it. I said something like "Would you believe it?" When he scored, you couldn't write that as a fictional story and get any credibility for it. The truth was much stranger than fiction. As a man, he answered what had happened, and as a footballer, he had the tools to do it.'

During a post-match interview live on television Eric was asked whether that afternoon represented the best moment of his Manchester United career. 'It was important to do the Double two years ago and again this season. Now we can go on holiday and have a nice holiday,' he smiled. And when Clive Tyldesley, the interviewer, remarked upon the massive change in the Frenchman's fortunes, Eric, still grinning, responded: 'Yeah, that's life. It's happened now.'

As the United captain climbed the famous Wembley steps to collect the trophy, a Liverpool fan spat at him. It was a tribute to his new-found powers of self-control that he did not retaliate in any way, despite being in striking distance of the miscreant.

Several of the journalists who attended the post-match press conference that day remarked upon Eric's charisma and sincerity as he proclaimed himself, somewhat bizar-rely, to be 'half English, half French and half Irish' before paying homage to the vital role Alex Ferguson had played in his rehabilitation. 'Everybody knows what I feel about Alex Ferguson. He has been a great man, a great manager, for me, for this team and for Manchester United.'

Cantona's lack of retaliation when spat at by the Liverpool fan was another example of his recently dis-covered ability to remain calm in situations where he might previously have exploded. However, Eric would always insist that there had been no great metamorphosis. 'I often get asked about the change in my temperament since the incident at Crystal Palace. The truth is there hasn't been such a big change. People think I've suddenly learnt to feel at ease with myself, but the fact of the matter is that I was never ill at ease in the first place. Everyone has their bad moments. It's impossible for anyone to say definitively that something like that can never happen to them.' The Frenchman's message was, indeed, that he had not necessarily changed completely, he had simply learnt the art of self-control, the quality he had so severely lacked in the past. 'There was a time when I would lose my temper regularly, when I felt that I had to stand up and say something about the things that made me angry. I used to take a stand and rage against injustice all the time. Now I know how things will turn out and that has taken the fun out of losing my temper. There was a time when I could derive a certain pleasure from trying to work out what to say and do next. But not any more.'

On that Cup final day, 11 May 1996, Manchester United became the first team in the twentieth century to win a second Double, at the end of a campaign which had begun with the ignominious defeat at Villa Park. On that night in August the previous year, Alan Hansen had of course asserted that Alex Ferguson's side would win nothing given the inexperience of many of its players. Not only had the normally astute pundit been a long way wide of the mark, his comments had also provided plenty of extra motivation in the Manchester United dressing-room. Lee

Sharpe recalled: 'I don't think it could do anything but inspire you to go on and stuff those words straight back down his throat. It's like if ever someone from an opposing team does an article in the paper the day before [a match], it's usually brought in and pinned on the noticeboard as if to say, "Here you are, that's what they reckon about you." And straight away it saves the manager having to do a team talk because it just riles everyone. No one likes to be knocked.'

The entire United team had defied their critics throughout the season, and none more so than Eric Cantona. For the achievements of 1995/96 alone the Frenchman merits his place in the pantheon of footballing legend.

14 French Leave

Eric wasn't afraid, he has a strong character, he has this power to tell people what he thinks.

FRANCK SAUZÉE

Eric Cantona experienced his first taste of what international football offers when he was called up for the French youth team in May 1982. For that match, Eric and his young team-mates stayed in the same Lyon hotel as the full international side. At meal times, just a few metres separated them from some of the greatest players ever to don the blue shirt of France, men such as Michel Platini, who would later manage Eric at international level.

Eric performed well for his country at youth level, and as his club career began to develop over the next few years he was duly selected for the Under-21 side, mainly on the back of the thirteen goals he scored in 1986/87, his first season as a professional with Auxerre. That young French team boasted a number of players, including Eric himself and Franck Sauzée, who would go on to make an impression at full international level. In 1988, however, their efforts were channelled towards winning the European Under-21 Championship for France.

Eric clearly felt there was something magical about playing in that team, coached by Marc Bourrier. Not only was the side full of excellent players, but as a group they evidently felt no fear. Later in his career, looking back on those days with the Under-21s, Canto, as he was known to the French public, remarked: 'There was a good team spirit and, in time, we realised that we were all pretty gifted. The majority of us played in the France first team and in the First Division. At the same time, bonds of friendship had been formed. We played football with total freedom as if we were children with no cares.'

His own form in the European Under-21 Championship was simply sensational. In the quarter-final second leg against the Soviet Union, he struck twice – the first a towering header, the second a pile-driver from the edge of the area. Then, in the first leg of the semi-final, he put England to the sword as the French gained a famous 4–1 victory. He laid on the first goal before following it up with further magic from his repertoire. After gaining possession not far inside the England half, he beat several opponents, danced into the inside left channel within the penalty area and slammed the ball powerfully into the top corner of the net. Canto went on to create the fourth goal by picking out Stéphane Paille, his strike partner, with an exquisite backheel of the type that was later to be recognised as his trademark. That piece of skill was the talk of the nation for weeks to come. For the record, England's defence boasted both Martin Keown and Tony Adams that night.

In the return leg at Highbury on 27 April, at a time when the French media was going crazy over his announcement that he was quitting Auxerre, Eric produced the sort of match-winning performance that was to traumatise more than a few English defences in later years and in the process bagged another brace of goals, demonstrating on both occasions his finest qualities: vision, deceptive pace and ice-cool finishing.

Franck Sauzée, who could play in defence or midfield, was another important component of the spine of that side, but he insisted that it was Cantona who inspired the players, it was he who really made them tick. 'Oh, when Eric played in the Under-21 team, every time we felt secure, we had a good balance in the team, we needed him because he had a great personality on the pitch and he was very friendly with the players and he wanted to win all the time. It was a fantastic boost for us. He did very, very well.' For Sauzée, recollections of Eric's exploits against England in those Under-21 matches represent his best memories of playing alongside Canto. 'He scored twice at Highbury and he was fantastic. We were very young and it was a good competition for us, but we needed experience, and I think the way Eric played changed something in our mentality. When we went to Highbury it was difficult and we didn't know exactly what English football was about. I think he put away all the complexes of being afraid to play in another country because you don't have any experience there. He helped us a lot.'

France's opponents in the final were Greece, which meant a first leg in Athens where they endured plenty of intimidation from a crowd of some 80,000 fans. Under intense pressure for much of the game, the French held on for a draw. Eric had the chance to settle the match in France's favour but was denied by foul play from the Greek goalkeeper. France soaked up pressure and looked to play on the counter-attack as the Greeks pushed forward, eagerly attempting to take advantage of being the home side. As they went in desperate search of a breakthrough, Greece left themselves exposed at the back and a long ball found Cantona with virtually the whole of the opposition half at his mercy. But he was rugby-tackled by the Greek keeper as he bore down on goal. He was still outside the penalty area which, obviously, meant there was no penalty, and because of the ridiculous rules of the time, the keeper escaped with just a caution.

The young Frenchmen were seen as heroes back home. One newspaper singled out Eric for particular praise: CANTONA, THE MESSIAH its headline purred. However, the hero of the hour soon became the villain and had to forgo the opportunity to complete the job he had started in Greece. Sadly, Eric missed the second leg of the final because it took place shortly after he had received an indefinite ban from international football imposed by the French Federation following the outburst during which he labelled Henri Michel, the French national team coach, a 'shit bag'.

Franck Sauzée scored two rip-snorters in France's victory in that second leg and still insists that he and his team-mates used Eric's absence as a rallying point. 'The players were very disappointed but it was a big, a fantastic, a massive motivation for us. We wanted to win for Eric, and we did. I'm sure he was very glad to see the team win the competition.' At the match, Cantona was not forgotten by one section of the crowd, at least, as they unfurled a banner which read ONE PERSON IS MISSING: CANTONA.

By the time the Under-21 side became European champions, Eric had of course already represented the full national side. On 12 August 1987, he made his debut in a friendly against West Germany in Berlin. 'We lost 2–1 but I scored a goal, which was important since many players had played in the French team, although few have remained, and it's after the first match that determines whether or not you're going to last. And I'm still here!' Eric recalled in the video *Ooh Aah Cantona* during the early part of his career with Manchester United.

The goal itself, as several observers have noted, was similar to Gary Lineker's strike against West Germany in the 1990 World Cup semi-finals. Cantona slipped in behind two German defenders, allowing a long ball to drop across his body. It sat up perfectly for him to fire left-footed, back across the goalkeeper and into the far corner of the net. Despite this dream start to his full international career, Henri Michel awarded him just four more caps in the following two years, a fact which may go some way to explaining his eventual outburst against the France coach.

According to Cantona, his poor relationship with Michel was laced with more than a touch of irony. Eric was full of respect for what Michel had achieved as a player with Nantes in the 1970s; he regarded him as a fine playmaker. But as a manager, Eric argued in his autobiography, Michel was lousy. He was convinced he lacked the strength of personality to cope with the rigours of, and the inevitable criticism involved with, managing a high-profile national team. In short, Cantona reckoned he couldn't handle the pressure. 'In less than two years, Henri Michel had tried all of fifty players. In my opinion, it seemed that he was allowing himself to be influenced too much by the commentaries of the sporting press about the composition of the team.' Furthermore, the player insisted, the majority of his team-mates shared his opinion of Michel. What held them back from speaking out, Cantona claimed, was that the French system had taught them not to ask questions.

Whatever the truth of the matter, Franck Sauzée recognised that the Cantona–Michel personality clash did nothing to further the cause of either man in the long run. 'Eric had, and has, a strong character. He had a very big reaction to that [not being selected for the national team] and of course things became difficult for him after this declaration. It was a hard moment for the manager. Eric wasn't in the French team and he reacted very strongly. I think Eric and Henri Michel suffered as a result of his declarations. Eric wasn't afraid, he has a strong character, he has this power to tell people what he thinks.'

The late 1990s saw the beginning of the most sustained period of success in the history of Les Bleus, culminating in their 1998 World Cup victory on home soil and their Euro 2000 triumph in the Netherlands. However, the early part of that decade was characterised by a series of failures that cast a shadow over the French game as a whole. The country was unable to qualify for the 1990 and 1994 World Cups and produced a disastrous showing at the 1992 European Championship.

On 22 October 1988, shortly after Eric Cantona's verbal assault on Henri Michel, a manager whose CV included taking Les Bleus to the semi-finals of the 1986 World Cup in Mexico, France's inability to overcome Cyprus in Nicosia – the match ended 1–1 – meant they did not qualify for the 1990 World Cup in Italy. That feeble result marked the end of the French Football Federation's enthusiasm for Michel's methods, and he was fired soon afterwards. In times of crisis, those whose responsibility it is to employ football managers often turn to one of the team's former stars to repair the damage and recover the club's or nation's lost pride. So it was that in the wake of Michel's dismissal the French Federation turned to Michel

Platini, the man who had inspired France to two World Cup semi-finals and a European Championship triumph in the 1980s.

At his first press conference, Platini made it clear that his role was to engender a winning spirit and make the French team successful, not to get involved in personal squabbles. He was clearly sending a message to Cantona, a player whom he admired. And as suddenly as he had been banned, Eric was granted a reprieve, evidently an essential ingredient in Platini's recipe for a French revival. Platini and his assistant, Gérard Houllier, were building a team that they hoped would make a serious assault on the 1992 European Championship.

On his return to the side on 16 August 1989, Eric linked up again with Jean-Pierre Papin and the strikers ran riot, grabbing two goals apiece as France defeated Sweden 4–2 in Malmö, thus ending the Scandinavians' long run of home games without a reverse. The deadly duo produced the magic again as France beat West Germany 2–1 just a few months before the Germans were crowned world champions in Italy. After the French had gone behind early in the match, Papin levelled shortly before half-time, and four minutes from the final whistle Cantona stole into the box, rose above the opposition defence and directed a bullet header into the German net for the winner.

Just as the 1990/91 season started well for Eric at club level with him scoring regularly for Olympique Marseille in the early part of the season, his international form was also promising. He and Papin were again on target for the national team on 5 September as they beat Iceland 2–1 in Reykjavik in a European Championship qualifier. However, he was enraged by Platini and Houllier's decision to substitute him for a more defensive player with the score at 2–0. After he had been replaced, Eric made straight for the changing-room instead of joining his team-mates and the technical staff on the bench. According to Houllier, the management team realised that Cantona was a man who needed and demanded to be playing all the time, a fact which no one recognised better during his career than Alex Ferguson at Manchester United. Houllier recalled the incident for the writer Ian Ridley: 'Eric went out of the ground and straight to the changing-room. He got mad and furious, he was in a fit, and Michel and I realised something was wrong so we sent somebody to calm him down in the changing-room. He did, and nobody heard of it. So Michel said to me, with a smile on his face, "I won't take him off again. He plays right to the end!" '

Cantona viewed international football as an essential part of his career since it afforded him the opportunity to pit his wits against the best players in the world. 'The French team is something else altogether,' he asserted on the *Ooh Aah Cantona* video. 'You can compare yourself with all their best players – world-ranking players, European-ranking players – and this is the best way to assess your own value, to know your worth, because you can't always tell when you see your goals on TV, you don't really know. But on this football ground, in front of these players, you can really know your worth. It is only when you play against great international players that you can prove how good a player you really are.'

After that good start in Iceland, France's qualifying campaign for Euro 92 went from strength to strength. In fact, they became the first team ever to win all their qualifying matches (against Czechoslovakia, Spain, Albania and Iceland, twice each) and Eric was an essential influence throughout the campaign. Therefore, when he announced his decision to retire from football in December 1991 at the tender age of 25 after throwing the match ball at the referee while playing for Olympique Nîmes, Messieurs Platini and Houllier were desperate to persuade him to change his mind.

It is to the enormous and lasting credit of both men that they were able to convince Cantona that his future, at club level, lay in England. As has already been mentioned in these pages, Houllier helped engineer a move across the Channel, initially to play for Sheffield Wednesday (although he only stayed there a week) and later, of course, for Leeds United. The two men were surely taking a massive gamble in constructing the national team around and helping find a club abroad for a player with such a poor disciplinary record, but Erik Bielderman commended them for the courage and foresight they displayed. 'They loved the player, rather than judging the man. And they felt that such a player should play football and they knew that he had to go abroad. And Gérard Houllier, with his English connections and his knowledge of English football, felt that it was the right place for him. In Spain or Italy, Cantona would have been more volatile because the people there are more volatile. In England, there is more respect – I don't include the tabloids and the way there is disrespect. Generally speaking, the fans let you live your life without being harassed and most of the clubs have traditions and managers have respect. And there is the way the game is played. You can play football; it's a very quick and physical game, but you play football, you don't only think about destroying and defending. For Eric, it was a chance to play positive football.'

In marked contrast to Eric's achievements at Leeds at the tail end of the 1991/92 season, his experiences with the French team at the 1992 European Championship were extremely negative. As a result of the all-conquering nature of their qualifying campaign, France were one of the favourites to win the tournament in Sweden. France, however, drew their first two games, with Sweden and England, and needed to avoid defeat against Denmark to qualify for the next stage. With just seconds left on the clock and the game apparently heading for another draw, Denmark produced a late winner. The Danes, with the inspirational Peter Schmeichel, Eric's future club team-mate, in goal, were eventually to win the tournament having famously come off the beach to participate because Yugoslavia were unable to take part given the war that was raging in Eastern Europe at that time.

Ironically, the way in which France strode so majesti-cally through the qualifying phase was one of the causes of their abject failure in Sweden. There is no greater ill for a team preparing for a major tournament than peaking too early and allowing complacency to take root as a consequence. 'From the winning team with the spirit, the fighting spirit, they started to feel, three or four months before the competition, that football was so easy that they could lose their concentration, that they could lose friendly games, but that suddenly when the competition came around, they would win,' Bielderman reflected. 'The first game [at Euro 92] didn't work that way, and then the media attacked Platini.' Bielderman also suggested that there was unrest within the camp.

Sadly, although he didn't know it at the time, it was to be Eric's only opportunity to perform at a major international tournament. 'The European Championship of 1992 in Sweden was a great disappointment,' was Eric's verdict on *Ooh Aah Cantona*. 'We won eight consecutive matches in the qualifying group and we hadn't lost a game in three years. Perhaps we arrived a little too much as the favourites, which was probably a bit premature in view of our limited experience. But it's useful nevertheless. Experiences like this are worth living.'

It came as no great surprise to most observers that Michel Platini quit his role as France coach in the aftermath of the Euro 92 débâcle. Gérard Houllier took over the reins, but in September 1992 France still lost their first World Cup qualifier 2–0 to Bulgaria in Sofia. In the following game, however, they made some amends as Cantona created the first goal for Papin and scored the second in a victory over Austria. Finland were next up, and they were also despatched, the usual suspects on target again.

Once a 4–0 victory over Israel in Tel Aviv in which Eric grabbed the first goal had been thrown into the equation as well, France seemed to be cruising towards qualification. In the autumn of 1993, they went into their last two qualifying matches knowing that a single point would secure safe passage to the finals in the United States the following summer. However, an all too familiar problem then took hold: complacency. In October they played host to Israel, one of the weakest teams in the group. Twenty minutes from the end France were winning 2–1 and had virtually secured their place in sport's greatest competition. David Ginola had created the first goal and scored the second, but was then taken off by Houllier. France simply had to resist a modest side for less than half an hour; even if they conceded one goal and the game ended in a draw they would qualify. Inexplicably, Israel scored twice to complete an unlikely 3–2 victory.

The equation was still simple enough: France needed just a point when they played Bulgaria in their last qualifying match in Paris on 17 November. But it appears doubts were beginning to set in and many members of the squad, and perhaps the management as well, were beginning to grow anxious. Against Israel, Houllier had started with a 4–3–3 formation with Ginola and Cantona playing either side of Jean-Pierre Papin, the principal striker. That appeared to work well enough until Ginola was removed from the fray at Houllier's insistence. For the Bulgaria game the manager switched back to a 4–4–2 system, and in the build-up to the match Ginola was told by Houllier that he would not be playing from the start, despite his goal and assist in the previous game. Ginola admitted in his autobiography that he vented his frustration at not making the starting line-up by telling journalists that 'some of the players were being picked on the strength of their personality, which had maybe influenced the manager's decision'.

Perhaps egged on by the media, Eric Cantona took this to be an attack on himself and Jean-Pierre Papin. According to Ginola's account of events, Cantona burst into his hotel room and demanded to know what Ginola had said to the press about him and Papin. Ginola confirmed he had told them that he believed some of the players' personalities were affecting the decisions of the manager, but he denied having mentioned names and insisted the journalists were merely trying to drive a wedge between members of the squad. 'He stormed out just as suddenly and dramatically as he had arrived. I had a lot of respect for Cantona as a player, and the same went for Papin, so I would never have bad-mouthed them,' Ginola stressed.

Despite the less than perfect atmosphere in the camp leading up to this crucial encounter with the Bulgarians, with just seconds remaining on the clock France found themselves heading for the 1–1 draw (Eric had scored the

French goal) that would send them to the World Cup. Ginola, who had come on as a replacement for Papin with ten minutes to go, then won a free kick deep into Bulgarian territory, just a few yards from the corner flag. However, rather than waste the remaining moments of the match by playing the ball into the corner and keeping possession, the winger launched a cross towards Eric Cantona, who was stationed in the penalty area. The ball flew over Cantona's head and was picked up by the Bulgarians. They immediately counter-attacked and, to the horror of almost everyone inside the stadium, scored through Emil Kostadinov's superb strike. There was no time for France to make amends. The referee blew the final whistle, France had lost 2–1 and they were out of the World Cup.

In the inevitable post-mortem and recriminations that followed, David Ginola, the man who had inexplicably ceded possession deep in the Bulgarian half, was made a scapegoat by many sections of the media and even by the French coach himself. For Gérard Houllier, the failure to qualify for the World Cup was a personal disaster. Even so, it is hard to justify the vitriol he directed at Ginola: 'The fact that one player cracked up was like a drop of acid . . . David Ginola is the murderer of the team . . . he sent an Exocet missile through the heart of French football . . . David Ginola committed a crime against the team, I repeat, a crime against the team.' It is hardly surprising, given the strength of Houllier's words, that at the time of writing the two men have still not buried the hatchet.

A more objective review of events shows that blame for France's clutching of defeat from the jaws of victory can be laid at several different doors. Certainly Ginola was far from blameless, but, as Erik Bielderman explained, he was not the only player to have let the team down. 'It's true that Ginola was silly to attempt such a cross because only Cantona was there, but if you look at the other players when Bulgaria got the ball back, everybody was sleeping as if the game was already over. Ginola is the man who made the mistake, but behind him at least five other players are as guilty. But people had to find an explana-tion and Ginola was the obvious explanation.' Moreover, Gérard Houllier must shoulder some culpability, for although he wasn't actually on the field of play, the coach should always accept at least some responsibility for his team's inability to gain a single point from two home games against the likes of Israel and Bulgaria. Bielderman pointed out that the media were not innocent either: 'Another level of blame was on the media because they were so arrogant at the time that they made an atmos-phere where people believed France had qualified before they had actually qualified.'

And what about Eric Cantona? Was he also to blame? Perhaps not as much as others, Erik Bielderman suggested: 'Cantona was not one of the most guilty at that time.' Eric's career figures for World Cup qualifying matches would certainly appear to bear this out: of the eleven games he played, France won seven, drew two and lost just two, Monsieur Cantona notching seven goals in the process.

Although Franck Sauzée still struggles to identify the exact causes of France's failure in the autumn of 1993, he believes that, in the long term, lessons were learnt for the benefit of French football. 'It's difficult to explain. Before the last two games everybody thought it was fine and we would get directly into the World Cup. I think it was a big lesson for French football, a big lesson of humility, and I think after this the French team learnt that every game is not easy and that you have to fight to win.'

Suggestions were rife in the French media at the time that Eric believed France's demise to be the fault of David Ginola. However, that is not an argument Sauzée sup-ports. 'I think if Eric had a real problem with him he would have told him, because Eric was like that. Every-body was very disappointed not to go to the World Cup and maybe afterwards there were suggestions from the press ... people needed to find someone guilty. But I don't remember Eric doing that.' Sauzée himself refuses to blame any one individual. 'I think it's too easy to do that. When you win, you win all together; when you lose, you lose all together.'

Moreover, although Cantona and Ginola appear not to have been bosom buddies, especially after their hotel-room bust-up before the Bulgaria match, the latter is adamant that the pair did not fall out over the controversial free kick. In his autobiography, Ginola recounted a chance meeting with Joël during which he told Cantona's brother to pass on his regards to Eric and suggested the two of them might meet for a drink and a chat after they had both retired from football. Ginola added: 'I think at the moment we are surrounded by people who are not always looking for the best in us, so it is better to meet after our football lives are finished.' And he claims that Joël responded: 'I'm sure Eric feels the same.'

Of course, it is hardly surprising that David Ginola regards Gérard Houllier as the guilty party in the whole débâcle, considering the coach's stinging criticism of the player. However, Ginola's assessment of that team's abilities appears sound: 'We had some very good individuals in the team. In front of goal Jean-Pierre Papin was amazing, and Eric Cantona was a brilliant player. Defensively we were strong too, with players like Laurent Blanc, Marcel Desailly and Bernard Lama in goal, and Didier Deschamps in midfield.' But Ginola contends that for all their individual ability, the players failed to blend properly as a unit and were unable to achieve the levels of consistency required to bring success at the highest level. 'This is where I think Houllier failed us, as it is the manager's job to get the best out of his players and build the right spirit.'

Soon enough, in the late summer of 1994, France began the task of attempting to qualify for the 1996 European Championship in England under a new coach, Aimé Jacquet. As Houllier's replacement sought to rebuild the French team, he appointed Eric Cantona his captain. Although this was a position the Manchester United player cherished, it was one that would bring him into almost constant confrontation with the country's media and French football's hierarchy.

It is important to remember at this juncture that Eric had been regularly crucified by the French press during his club career in France. Moreover, many of his team-mates had been lambasted by the newspapers for their failure to qualify for the 1994 World Cup. The omens were not good when Eric immediately appeared to be at odds with journalists in the lead-up to the team's goalless draw with Slovakia on 7 September. *L'Equipe* was stinging in its criticism of his attitude: 'One of the major problems was his behaviour as captain. He never took on the role as leader, notably with the press. He acted as though he was boss of the whole of French football. He told reporters at the training camp that he wanted them to turn up on two occasions and no more. They were not happy because he was also insulting and said: "If it was up to me I would **** on you."'

In Cantona's defence, he was not the first international captain to fall out with his country's ever-demanding and ever-critical media. The *Manchester Evening News*, through David Meek, who covered Old Trafford for the paper for more than thirty years, provided a slightly different slant on the matter: 'At the same time the French journalists must perhaps question their attitude to the player. Cantona has been a pussycat for the press in England in his two years at Old Trafford. Perhaps the critics in France find it difficult to come to terms with the brilliantly successful career – three successive championship medals – of their exile in England. The fact that an "Anglo" has been made captain of their national team since France's failure to qualify for the last World Cup is also a problem for them.'

Typically, however, the French Football Federation passed on the opportunity to present a public show of unity with their team's captain when the organisation's president, Claude Simonet, announced: 'I regret his attitude and some of his comments which were out of place. I will have to have a meeting and talk with Eric.' The first rule of football man-management: don't humiliate the player by telling the whole world he faces a ticking-off before you speak to the man himself. Whatever the rights and wrongs of Cantona's approach to the French media, matters could only possibly have been made worse by the attitude of the French game's governing body.

Nor was that Simonet's only moment of indiscretion. According to the *Today* newspaper, he disclosed that a team of psychoanalysts had been brought in to study Eric's appearance in the Nike TV advert, which was banned in Britain. 'I asked psychologists to analyse the advert. They tell me his fears that he may never find another sponsor are a sort of confession,' Simonet is quoted as saying. In the same article, presumably cribbed from a French newspaper, Simonet added that Cantona had only been appointed captain because none of his team-mates wanted the job. 'Eric certainly deserves the captaincy as far as talent goes, but I'm not sure about his cultural knowledge.' Cantona's riposte was simple: 'I don't care what Simonet says. Whether a president is good or bad has no influence on the game.'

The following month, France were held to another goalless draw, this time in St Etienne by Romania, quarter-finalists at USA 94. The match was of particular interest in England since Terry Venables' national team were due to play Romania in a Wembley friendly a few days later. The *Daily Telegraph* therefore sent its football writer, Henry Winter, out to France to cover the game. He detected a very different attitude from Eric to the one reported by French journalists at the time of France's previous Euro 96 qualifier. 'Cantona, relaxed and courteous, was adamant his French Revolution with its emphasis on passing over dribbling would continue,' Winter wrote. 'Cantona controlled the flow of the match, the first international in St Etienne since France beat Yugoslavia in 1984. Effortlessly changing the speed and direction of French moves, his contributions resembled one of his better days with United.' Moreover, the *Telegraph* man made the telling assertion that 'of Jacquet's current selection, only Cantona and Milan's splendid Marcel Desailly can be considered world-class'.

However, the French remained unconvinced of Eric's abilities, and after yet another 0–0 draw, with Poland in November, the president of the French league, Noel Le Graet, remarked: 'There are doubts over whether Eric Cantona should remain as captain, or even retain his

place.' And when Aimé Jacquet added that Eric's performance had been 'disappointing and below par', it was
evident that the coach had little intention of offering
public support to the man he had appointed as captain.

Given the bad blood that already existed between the
Manchester United player and the French Football Federation, it is hardly surprising that in the wake of the bad
publicity that surrounded events at Selhurst Park in
January 1995, Eric Cantona was never to be selected again
for his country. In fact, he played his last game for Les
Bleus seven days before that fateful evening, when France
defeated Holland 1–0 in Utrecht; he had scored his last
goal for France against Australia on 26 May 1994 in
another 1–0 victory.

Despite his enormous contribution to Manchester
United's Double-winning season of 1995/96, Jacquet refused to grant Cantona a recall for the Euro 96 tournament in England. David Ginola, whom Jacquet also
refused to select, used his autobiography to convey the
argument that surely Eric should have been given the
chance to prove his worth to France in England,
the country where he had reached his peak. 'Maybe that's
what pushed him into making the decision to retire from
the game altogether. He had had enough, and he was fed
up with football's mentality.' The French coach, though,
saw both Cantona and Ginola as potential menaces to the
harmony he had created within his squad, and asserted:
'We have managed without Cantona for a long while. I feel
a moral obligation to keep faith with the players who have
taken us to the finals.'

For his part, the Manchester United player felt he was
being persecuted for his outburst at Selhurst Park, a
misdemeanour for which he had already been punished
by his club, the Football Association and the legal system.
'I think a lot of officials thought I was dead after the ban.
But since I was not completely dead and since I was even
resurrected, they have done everything they could to
make sure I died a second time. We'll see who dies in the
end,' Eric said by way of riposte in an interview with a
French magazine. 'I thought my 45 caps and 20 goals for

France could have been taken into consideration,' he added. Cantona certainly detected a very different attitude in his dealings with French football's governing body and the national team's coach to the support he had experienced at Old Trafford in the wake of Selhurst Park. 'I never believed I could be treated so well at a time when I was in the depths of despair. I felt I owed everything to these people who treated me in such an elegant manner.'

Perhaps it was tough on Eric, but Jacquet's decision not to include him was a crucial step in the construction of the team that went on to win the 1998 World Cup and the 2000 European Championship. It could be argued that France, who appeared solid and dependable at Euro 96 but lacked real flair, losing their semi-final on penalties to the Czech Republic, could have won the tournament with Cantona's creativity on board. However, history will recall that Jacquet had a long-term and ultimately successful strategy and that, in spite of the striker's impressive goals-to-appearances ratio, the decision to omit Cantona was eventually vindicated.

It always seems puzzling that the class of 1988, which promised so much by winning the European Under-21 Championship, failed to live up to expectations at full international level. While Franck Sauzée, whose five-year full international career saw him win 39 caps and score nine goals, admits that it is difficult to explain the group's failings, he also observes that perhaps it was those very expectations that stifled their ability to perform. 'I don't really have the answer. It's a fact that we had a fantastic side with the Under-21s and everybody played for the team. It was fantastic, and we didn't have any pressure on our shoulders. I think that's why we did well. The pressure was on the French national team, not on the Under-21s, and that's why I think we did well. We were all very good friends. Maybe the pressure was too great for us [at full international level], but it [the Under-21 team] was a great experience for us.'

15 Great Expectations

You are limited in Europe and in international football with how many chances you get and how many good things you can do. I'm sure he produced a few wonderful things, but when you're used to him doing that all game and he's just showing one or two flashes people say he's not as good as he thinks he is or as everybody else thinks he is.

LEE SHARPE

After winning a second Double in three attempts, Alex Ferguson made it clear that lifting the European Cup was now his burning ambition for Manchester United. It was an aspiration Eric Cantona certainly shared, especially as in the summer of 1996 it appeared certain that he would never again have the opportunity to prove himself at a major international tournament.

Cantona had given a clear indication of his priorities when interviewed by Des Lynam before the FA Cup final. 'I think the next very important target for Manchester United will be the Champions League next season,' he remarked. 'We all want to win it. It is important for English football, for us, for everybody. If we don't win it the people will forget us. If you just win in your country you have no credibility.'

However, Ferguson's plans to strengthen his squad for the added challenge of an assault on Europe suffered a major setback when Alan Shearer, who had once and for all proved himself a world-class striker at Euro 96, opted to sign for his hometown club, Newcastle United, instead of teaming up with Eric at Old Trafford. A Cantona–Shearer axis, with all due respect to other United strikers, would have been the dream ticket for the 1996/97 season at least. Ironically, however, one of the reasons why

Ferguson had bought Cantona in the first place was because Alan Shearer had snubbed his advances in favour of a move to Blackburn Rovers from Southampton.

While Shearer went to Newcastle for £15 million, Alex Ferguson spent less than £9 million on his five new recruits. The manager purchased Jordi Cruyff from Barcelona after being impressed by the Dutchman in Euro 96, and expected to deploy him as a striker or as cover for Ryan Giggs on the left wing. Another star of the European Championship, Karel Poborsky of the Czech Republic, was brought in to provide pace on the opposite flank with, it was hoped, the style rather than the attitude of Andrei Kanchelskis. Ronny Johnsen, the versatile Norwegian, could play in the heart of midfield or defence, while his young compatriot Ole Gunnar Solskjaer was viewed as one for the future, although in reality he would make the greatest impact of all the new boys. And the experienced Raimond van der Gouw would offer back-up for Peter Schmeichel in goal. What is more, Cantona was made club captain after the summertime departure of Steve Bruce to Birmingham City, while Lee Sharpe joined Leeds United for £4 million.

Once the new campaign got underway, Shearer's name was forgotten as United went about their business with customary style and determination. In the Charity Shield, Eric combined well with the blossoming David Beckham to open the scoring in a comfortable 4–0 victory over Newcastle United. The season proper then began on 17 August with a trip to Wimbledon, where Cantona again broke the deadlock, taking down Nicky Butt's pass with his left foot before hammering it effortlessly into the top corner of Neil Sullivan's net. The Frenchman raised his hands to the heavens in celebration as he received his team-mates' congratulations.

Despite its fine blend of sublime skill and ferocious power, Eric's goal was to be overshadowed that day by the exploits of David Beckham, who propelled himself into the public consciousness by scoring famously from his own half of the field. Even so, it was a mark of Cantona's influence that Beckham was delighted, above all, to receive great praise from his captain after the game. When the Frenchman had seen Beckham's audacious strike from the bench (he had been substituted), he grinned and exchanged knowing glances with Alex Ferguson. It was the beginning of a new order for the Old Trafford club.

That Eric Cantona's influence at Old Trafford was a significant factor in the development of David Beckham is not open to debate. 'Cantona was a big influence at Old Trafford,' Beckham remarked, 'especially the way he used to stay behind after training to work on skills. I have done that all my life. I used to find a bag of balls and take free kicks and corners until the training staff ordered me in.'

After draws against Everton, Blackburn Rovers and Derby County, Eric was next on target on 7 September in a 4–0 hammering of Leeds United. Although he performed well, the Frenchman surprised everyone at Elland Road by missing a first-half penalty, the first time he had failed to convert a spot-kick in a competitive match for Manchester United.

Four days later, the team launched its European campaign with a trip to Juventus, the European Cup holders. United were one of two seeded teams in a group that also featured Rapid Vienna, the Austrian champions, and Fenerbahce of Turkey. The Old Lady, as the Turin club is known, presented the toughest of challenges for Ferguson's young players, many of whom were inexperienced in Europe's elite club competition.

The manager's game plan for the clash at the Delle Alpi Stadium consisted of Eric playing up front on his own, while Jordi Cruyff and Karel Poborsky had instructions to provide him with support from their wide positions in a five-man midfield whenever possible. However, it was a tactic that was fundamentally flawed: Eric had never been happy leading the line since his strength was to pick up possession from deep and feed a more advanced striker or players breaking down the flanks; his forte was certainly not holding the ball up in the manner of, say, Mark Hughes. To make matters worse, in the absence of the injured Roy Keane United's midfielders had their hands so full that they were unable to provide Eric with adequate support. It was a problem Ferguson later fully recognised, insisting that Cantona had received unfair criticism in the wake of the game. 'Much of Eric's effectiveness is geared to people moving around him. In Turin it just didn't happen, so of course he was quiet.'

Even though United rallied after half-time, the Italians were superior throughout the encounter and the 1-0 scoreline did little to emphasise their overall domination. Yet for Alex Ferguson and his team the game offered an abundance of important lessons, and if they worked on certain weaknesses in tactics and concentration there was no reason why they should not progress, at least beyond the group stage of the tournament.

The next Premiership visitors to Old Trafford, Nottingham Forest, duly suffered the backlash of United's disappointing display in Italy. And a certain Frenchman continued to recover his goalscoring form with a 25-yard thunderbolt and a penalty kick. A draw at Aston Villa then followed on 21 September, before United faced Rapid Vienna in a must-win Champions League clash at Old Trafford. The emerging talents of Ole Gunnar Solskjaer and David Beckham were once more on display as the pair grabbed the goals in a 2-0 win. On this occasion, Ferguson was happy with the way he had deployed his captain: 'I knew he would be man-marked so I asked him to play further upfield – which he did perfectly. Both he and Solskjaer did extremely well.' Furthermore, it was a performance that led Ernst Dokupil, the Austrian team's coach, to suggest that United were genuine contenders for the European Cup.

So all the signs were positive. Back in the Premier League Cantona and his team-mates completed important home victories over Tottenham Hotspur and Liverpool, Solskjaer and Beckham again to the fore, then, on 16 October, United continued their European odyssey with a journey to Turkey to face Fenerbahce. The side's previous Turkish experiences had provided little delight, and the omens were not good when Peter Schmeichel received death threats from local fans before the match. However, the atmosphere inside the stadium was less intimidating than expected, even if the public-address announcer did his best to whip the crowd into a frenzy.

United showed that they were fast learners in European football, soaking up pressure and hitting the Turks with devastating counter-attacks that saw David Beckham and Eric Cantona score in a 2–0 success. Cantona played well, operating behind a front pairing of Cruyff and Solskjaer, with Messrs Beckham, Butt and Johnsen patrolling mid-field. The Frenchman's goal was particularly satisfying since his performances in Europe had yet to convince many observers of his pedigree at that level, despite his unquestionable thirst for glory on the continental stage. Eric punched the air repeatedly after converting Cruyff's cross at the end of a move he had himself begun. It was an unusually emphatic celebration of a type rarely seen in the final year of his career, clearly indicating just how important European success was to Eric.

Of course, the demands of playing against the Continent's elite teams were, in the main, far greater than and extremely different to those encountered by Eric and his team-mates in the Premiership. Lee Sharpe offered his view of Cantona's European record and the scrutiny he came under: 'It is harder to play in Europe. I don't think he produced as many sparks of magic in Europe as he did in the League. But I don't think anybody does. When people play for their country or in Europe they do a couple of brilliant things whereas when they're playing in League football they might do half a dozen to a dozen brilliant things. You are limited in Europe and in international football with how many chances you get and how many good things you can do. I'm sure he produced a few wonderful things, but when you're used to him doing that all game and he's just showing one or two flashes people say he's not as good as he thinks he is or as everybody else thinks he is.'

United's season was beginning to take shape: a strong position in the Premiership was complemented by improving European form. However, heavy defeats at New-castle and Southampton, punctuated only by a League

Cup victory over Swindon Town, were followed by narrow reverses at home to Fenerbahce in the Champions League and Chelsea. Even the return from injury and suspension of Roy Keane, the heartbeat of the United midfield, did nothing to stop the rot. Eric Cantona found himself in the middle of a barren spell that saw him fail to score in the Premiership for eleven games, a statistic that, given the benefit of hindsight, may now perhaps be interpreted as an initial indication that his powers were on the wane.

Under the circumstances, the Premiership clash with Arsenal on 16 November carried immense significance, as did the Nigel Winterburn own goal which afforded the Reds a 1–0 victory over the League leaders. But another setback arrived the following week in the shape of a second 1–0 defeat at the capable hands of Juventus. At least, though, there were signs that United were beginning to get the measure of their Italian rivals as they were denied a positive result by a combination of good goalkeeping, the woodwork and ill fortune. Cantona, in particular, extracted a string of fine saves from Angelo Peruzzi. Even so, Alex Ferguson was beginning to experience twinges of anxiety regarding Eric's form. 'The confident Eric of old would have buried it,' was his verdict on one goalscoring opportunity, while his overall assessment went as follows: 'Eric Cantona, for all the hard time the press are giving him at the moment, could have scored five by himself. Their goalkeeper makes one fantastic save from Eric, who also hits the top of the bar. It is then that I have to admit he has lost a wee bit of confidence. I would normally expect him to do better, though he wasn't the only one.'

Whatever the signs that United were developing in Europe, they would now have to win in Vienna and hope Juventus overcame Fenerbahce if they were to claim a place in the quarter-finals. The side warmed up for the Rapid Vienna showdown in the first week of December with a draw at Middlesbrough and a League Cup exit at the hands of Leicester City, before overcoming the latter 3–1 in the Premiership on 30 November.

And so to Austria. For once, Alex Ferguson could select a team that resembled his first-choice eleven and his players seemed relaxed ahead of the crucial encounter at the Hanappi Stadion. Eric enjoyed the company of his room-mate Peter Schmeichel, even if the two were unable to beat the dynamic partnership of David May and Gary Pallister at table football and pool. When it came to the real football, though, the Frenchman and the Dane showed their true worth. Schmeichel produced the finest save of his career, not dissimilar to Gordon Banks's from Pele, to deny the Austrian team an early breakthrough. Thereafter, United were in the ascendancy as Eric created the opener for Ryan Giggs before sealing the victory as he swept David Beckham's low cross into the back of the Vienna net.

After draws with West Ham United and Sheffield Wednesday, Eric finally ended his Premiership goalscoring drought when Sunderland visited Old Trafford four days before Christmas. His first was a penalty, coolly slotted past his former Olympique Nîmes team-mate Lionel Perez; the second was destined to live in the memory for ever. Collecting the ball just inside Sunderland territory, he outfoxed two opponents and strode in the direction of the goal before playing a one-two with Brian McClair. When the ball returned to him on the edge of the area, Eric took a quick glance and chipped it over Perez, who had advanced some distance from his line. The ball sailed into the top corner of the net. Cantona stood where he was and milked the applause that reverberated around Old Trafford. Maybe the United captain had not lost his magic touch after all. The goal certainly appeared to have strengthened the manager's faith in him. 'What remains most vividly in my mind,' Ferguson wrote, 'is Eric's response. It was the look of him, as if he was saying, "Don't ever doubt me. I know I haven't been playing as well as I can, but I'm back, and here's to the memories." '

Ole Gunnar Solskjaer also continued his fine form with two well-taken goals against Sunderland as his partnership with Eric showed increasing promise. The pair certainly appeared happy playing together, and there were even suggestions from some quarters that Eric preferred lining up with the Norwegian to having Andy Cole as a partner. The latter, despite great application, had struggled to deliver the quantity of goals expected the previous season. And there had been rumours that the Frenchman, who from time to time had appeared to glower at Cole when he failed to convert a chance the former had created, simply did not rate the former Newcastle front man. Some newspapers even went so far as to claim that there was a major rift between the two, an assertion the England striker wholeheartedly denied in his autobiography. 'It was all a myth about Eric and me. The myth being that we hated each other's guts, that we despised each other with an absolute passion.' According to Cole, the pair didn't even know each other particularly well, but that was not to say that they were enemies. 'I didn't have a problem with Eric. He had his own life to lead, his own career to protect, and yet some misguided and ill-informed people constantly attempted to create the conflict between us.'

Even so, there were certainly signs in Eric's last season of professional football that he was more comfortable playing alongside the Norwegian. In purely footballing terms, Solskjaer had proved thus far to be a better partner for the Frenchman since, like Cantona himself, the Scandinavian excelled in situations where he only had the goalkeeper to beat – which, of course, was the sort of opportunity Eric was so adept at engineering. Cole, on the other hand, at that stage of his career at least, was more likely to convert chances through instinct when there was no time to think, no choices to be made. In other words, he was still struggling to adapt his style of play, with which he had had such tremendous success alongside Peter Beardsley at Newcastle United, to meet the demands of the type of football employed at Old Trafford. However, that was a situation that would change dramatically in the months and years ahead.

Further evidence that the champions were finally finding their best form came at the City Ground on Boxing

Day as United thrashed Nottingham Forest 4–0. Significantly, Andy Cole returned from a long absence, the result of injury and illness, to register his first goal of the campaign and embark on his best spell of form since his arrival from Newcastle two years earlier. Cantona's penalty in a 1–0 home success over Leeds United on 28 December then ensured the Manchester club would enjoy a happy new year in the Premiership.

16 I Know It's Over

*When I do quit football, it'll be at the top. I certainly
wouldn't contemplate playing for teams that are any less
successful than Manchester United, or playing for the
reserves. Once I feel I'm not at the top any more, I'll quit.*

                                                ERIC CANTONA

On Sunday, 18 May 1997, a crestfallen Alex Ferguson
addressed a press conference during which Manchester
United announced Eric Cantona's decision to retire from
football. 'He's been a fantastic player for us in the four and
a half years he's been with us and we've won six trophies
in that period, so obviously it's a sad day,' said the United
manager, who later remarked: 'He had a wonderful
balance and presence, a sort of a good arrogance that
transmits itself through the team.'

Four and a half months earlier United had started 1997
in a strong position both domestically and on the Continent. In the Premiership they were two points adrift of
pace-setters Liverpool, while the prospect of a Champions
League quarter-final with Portuguese champions Porto in
March set many a pulse racing.

Goalless draws at Old Trafford have traditionally been a
rarity, yet that was how the year began as United were
held by Aston Villa in the League. There then followed a
double-header with Tottenham Hotspur. On 5 January,
United defeated the London side 2–0 in the FA Cup before
travelling to White Hart Lane a week later. Although the
second match, which United won 2–1, was a far tighter
affair, both encounters featured further evidence of the
development of David Beckham, now a full England
international, as the midfielder struck spectacular goals
on each occasion.

Although Eric was still playing well enough, the emergence of Beckham in particular was a sign that the United youngsters were now coming of age. Cantona had for so long been the master at Old Trafford; now the pupils were catching up and even matching their guru's exploits. Later in the year, Beckham was also voted Young Player of the Year by his fellow professionals. Indeed, there were indications of Beckham's long-term if only partial inheritance of the Cantona mantle, as well as his number seven shirt. Although never destined to be complete, this phenomenon functioned on two levels: the young midfielder was taking over the role of the man who scored the spectacular goals and, especially after he developed a relationship with Victoria Adams (now Beckham) from the pop group the Spice Girls, it was the young Englishman who began to attract the media attention that had hitherto been focused primarily on the mature Frenchman.

The success in north London marked the beginning of a consistent spell of form that would have a significant bearing on United's title aspirations. The side achieved six wins and a draw before succumbing to Sunderland at Roker Park on 8 March. Surprisingly, however, Eric Cantona registered just one goal during that period, albeit the crucial winner against Southampton. He did miss two games through suspension, though, and despite his lack of goals he was still performing well and helping to create chances for others to convert.

But as Eric sat out the vital clash at Arsenal, by now one of United's main title rivals, on 19 February, there was a growing sense that United could manage without the man who had hitherto been their talisman. Roy Keane donned the captain's armband and Andy Cole partnered Ole Gunnar Solskjaer in attack. All three performed brilliantly, and the two strikers claimed expertly finished goals in a 2–1 victory. Moreover, Peter Schmeichel was at his imperious best as he continued his long-standing ability to foil Ian Wright, the Arsenal striker.

As he enjoyed the match from the bench alongside the Manchester United substitutes, Eric may well have realised that his team-mates had matured in such a way that a previously unimaginable scenario now prevailed: they were capable of winning the big matches despite his absence. Doubtless he would also have been delighted by the way the side followed his own mantra on teamwork that night. 'It comes down to instinctive communication and understanding,' Eric had written a few months earlier. 'There must be a kind of unity of purpose in a team. The mind of every player must be focused on the same strategy. The more in tune the members of a team are, the greater its strength is and the better their game is to watch. There should always be a balance between attack and defence. That's the key to success.' The question now taking root in Eric's mind was whether or not that United team would benefit from his services in the long term. It would be erroneous to suggest that Eric no longer possessed the ability to produce his wonderful football of the previous campaign. Yet, as the season wore on, one or two doubts regarding his focus emerged. Alex Ferguson observed: 'Certainly, Eric is an important player for us, but we aren't quite as dependent on him as we once were.'

The surprise defeat at Sunderland in early March, United's first Premiership reverse in sixteen outings, was, in all likelihood, the result of a major European hangover. Three days earlier the team had marched to one of their most memorable successes in European competition as a highly rated Porto side was crushed 4–0 at Old Trafford. It was without doubt, on both a collective and an individual level, the greatest performance of the season. Ryan Giggs and Ronny Johnsen were outstanding in midfield. And there were certainly no complaints about Eric's contribution as the Frenchman scored the second goal and helped create the third and fourth for Giggs and Andy Cole respectively. Again, there was an extra show of emotion when Eric celebrated his goal as he sprinted towards the crowd and kissed his shirt in the way footballers do to show their solidarity and identification with a club and its fans. Moreover, his hugging of Cole and his high-fives with Ole Gunnar Solskjaer in celebration of Cole's goal betrayed a level of delight that suggested European success provided Eric's prime source of motivation in the autumn of his United career.

Two days after the Porto clash, Cantona and Ferguson visited a Stretford school where they planted a tree to mark a landscape project for the nursery the United manager had opened eighteen months earlier. Ferguson later expressed his delight at the way his captain had handled the situation. 'The kids are brilliant. So is Eric, who has even brought photographs of himself to give out.'

A 0–0 draw in Portugal two weeks later ensured United's progress to the semi-final stage of the competition. Eric gave a rare, if brief, television interview after the match in which he stressed: 'We always have a difficult month in October, November or December – we've had it now. And now the season is nearly finished, we're in a race for the Premiership, in the semi-finals of the European Cup. In this kind of situation we are always better.' In reality, his assessment of the situation turned out to be only half true. United would indeed prevail again on the domestic front, yet fail to clear the hurdles that stood between them and glory in the European arena.

In the Premiership, Eric rediscovered his goalscoring form with strikes in the win at Everton, the home defeat by Derby County and the away victory over Blackburn Rovers. In the latter, he created a goal for Andy Cole before claiming what turned out to be his last goal in a United shirt as the Old Trafford club won 3–2. Liverpool were by now United's closest title rivals, the Manchester team enjoying an advantage of just two points as well as a game in hand at the top of the table. The clash between the two at Anfield on 19 April therefore adopted the air of a decider, and United's 3–1 win contributed much to their push towards the championship. Despite drawing their next three matches, none of United's title rivals could take advantage of this minor blip and the Premiership trophy remained in Manchester.

Eric's form, though not spectacular, was decent enough during the run-in, but his infallibility was no longer unquestionable as once it had been, nor did he provide the type of timely interventions that had made the ultimate difference between success and failure in the previous campaign. On 11 May he played his last game for United, creating the second goal, for Jordi Cruyff, in a 2–0 home win over West Ham United.

It was the outcome of United's two-leg Champions League semi-final against Ottmar Hitzfeld's Borussia Dortmund that appears to have cemented in Eric's mind the decision that it was time to bring his football career to a close. The denouement of those two encounters is crucial when one analyses Eric's impact in Europe. The Germans were strong, resilient opponents and deserved to win the competition, as they eventually did by defeating Juventus 3–1 in the final. Yet United would rue a glut of missed chances and misfortune, as well as Dortmund's spectacular last-ditch defending. All in all, it was a case of ifs, buts and what-might-have-beens.

For starters, observers might have held a very different view of Cantona's contributions in Europe had Nicky Butt or David Beckham been able to convert the chances created for them by Eric in the first leg at the Westfalen Stadion on 9 April. Both received inch-perfect, slide-rule passes from the Frenchman with, seemingly, only the goalkeeper to beat, yet were unable to score. Butt's effort struck a post, Beckham's was cleared off the line by a rapidly retreating defender. The result was a 1–0 scoreline in Dortmund's favour, courtesy of a deflected goal that Raimond van der Gouw reached but was powerless to repel. Schmeichel might have saved it, yet it would be harsh to criticise the Dutchman who was making only his fourth appearance of the season after the Dane sustained an injury only 45 minutes before kick-off.

In the return leg, a fortnight later, Dortmund grabbed an early goal, but United still had enough goalscoring opportunities to secure a place in the final. Twice they had apparently legitimate goals strangely ruled out by the referee. Thereafter, however, it was United's own profligacy that was their downfall. The luckless Andy Cole, a perennial scapegoat for those outside Old Trafford, bore the brunt of the ensuing criticism, but other players also missed gilt-edged chances, among them Gary Pallister, Ryan Giggs and, more surprisingly, Eric Cantona.

Just imagine for a minute how differently Eric's European record would have been viewed had Butt and Beckham scored in Dortmund, and had he converted his own chances back home. Even Alex Ferguson has admitted to being puzzled by the sluggish nature of his overall performance in the two games. And while the Manchester United manager does not concur with the critics who assert that Cantona never played well in the major European matches, he revealed in his autobiography: 'I do admit that there was something, perhaps some kind of mental block, that stopped him from being the best player in the world. I'm sure he had the ability to achieve that status but there was an element in his nature that seemed to prevent him from realising the full potential of his incredible gifts.'

David Meek has observed almost all the great European occasions at Old Trafford and he too remains surprised by Eric's apparent inability to produce his best football when the eyes of the Continent were trained upon him. 'It's the big mystery for me. I honestly don't know. He never seemed comfortable, and I don't know why. He always seemed irritable – that was evident when they played Galatasaray. He was easily rattled, easily provoked. English football suited him and he was happy with it and comfortable; it suited his talents. Maybe playing foreign teams didn't suit him, and maybe that would explain why he was more successful in England than he was in France.'

There is certainly one theory that Eric's outstanding success in the Premiership could be attributed not just to his own brilliance but also to the ineptitude of English defences when it came to coping with a striker who plays the withdrawn role Eric enjoyed so much. Meek believes there is mileage in this assertion. 'I think there's some substance to that idea because, let's face it, English football as such has only improved since we've brought foreign players into the game. If you were to judge English football by English players, you need look no further than the England team, who – it sounds disloyal to say it now – struggled to qualify for the [2002] World Cup.'

In the wake of United's European exit, Alex Ferguson spotted that Eric was unhappy in a way that suggested something deeper than mere disappointment that the team would not be playing in the final. 'There's an air of depression about the place,' he wrote. 'Eric Cantona in particular is in a broody mood. I suspect success in Europe has become very important to him, a personal Holy Grail, and I think he has reached a crossroads in his career. It looks as if the chances he missed, not to mention his relatively quiet performance, have prompted him to question his future.

'I believe Eric is seriously wondering whether he has now run his course at Old Trafford. Maybe he's influenced by this last season. By his own high standards, he's been disappointing. I don't think he's ready to throw himself off a bridge just yet, but he knows he hasn't had the same influence of late. He is still a charismatic figure with great vision, but at 31 [in fact, he was still 30 at this point], perhaps he's lost his cutting edge.' His goalscoring record for 1997 certainly supported that theory. Eric scored just four Premiership goals after Christmas 1996, whereas he had struck on ten occasions in the equivalent period the previous year. More importantly, perhaps, for a man who usually thrived on the big occasion, throughout the season he had failed to find the target in the majority of the crunch games – against Liverpool, Newcastle, Arsenal, Borussia Dortmund and Juventus.

Perhaps the clearest indication, discerned by Ferguson, that Eric Cantona was losing his affection for the game was the way he filled out in his final season. There was no doubt that he had put on weight. You just had to look at his jaw-line to realise that, and pictures of him leaving the field bare-chested after the second Dortmund defeat also betrayed the fact that he was no longer quite so svelte around the midriff.

On Thursday, 8 May, Eric finally delivered the news Alex Ferguson definitely did not want to hear. 'I received a bombshell on my arrival back in Manchester. Eric

Cantona comes to see me to say that he wants to retire from football this week. I thought he'd been very preoccupied; now I know why. Of course I'm enormously taken aback by Eric's decision. But I try not to get too heavy on him, and by the end he's laughing a bit,' he revealed in his diary of the season.

Ferguson confessed to respecting Cantona's decision to quit while he was still pretty much at his peak rather than simply fade away. However, there are crucial differences between Ferguson's first account of how and why Eric quit, recorded in his diary, and the version he recounted in his autobiography, published two years later in 1999. In the latter Ferguson asserted: 'He [Eric Cantona] said he felt he had become a pawn of Manchester United's merchandising department and that he was not going to accept such treatment any longer. His second complaint was that United were not ambitious enough in the purchase of players. I had a lot of sympathy with him on both counts.'

Ferguson had for many years battled with the United board over their intransigence regarding transfer fees and players' salaries. The manager firmly believed that special financial arrangements should be made for, perhaps, two or three top players who could lift the rest of the team to a higher plane. Yet the club's directors refused to break the long-standing wage structure and Ferguson was therefore unable to recruit big names from Italy like the Brazilian striker Ronaldo, Gabriel Batistuta and Marcel Desailly, the French defender.

No footballer in his right mind would not want to play alongside a Ronaldo, a Batistuta or a Desailly at his peak, but would Eric really have liked another player to be the main attraction ahead of him? History also reveals a flaw in this contention since it seems to suggest that United were not capable of winning the Champions League unless they snapped up players who were established stars on the world stage and paid them wages that recognised that fact. In the event, the club bought Jaap Stam, the Dutch defender, and strikers Dwight Yorke and Teddy Sheringham from Aston Villa and Tottenham

Hotspur respectively, and won the European Cup just two years after Eric's departure. Perhaps it is also worth highlighting the fact that Sheringham is in fact older than Cantona.

Only the Manchester United manager and Eric himself know what reasons the Frenchman gave for his departure in their private meetings. Certainly, Eric would not have cared for the commercial exploitation, yet he made it very clear after leaving the club that he wanted his share of income from profits made off the back of his name. Image rights are an increasingly significant issue in football, and Cantona, while he apparently deplored commercialisation, was not a man to give up what he felt was his by right.

While the two reasons cited by Ferguson were perhaps contributing factors, it is highly unlikely that they were the only things to determine Eric's decision. There is little doubt that in the latter months of the 1996/97 season he had lost some of the sharpness that set him aside from other players. As a man who had always said he would stop playing when he could no longer produce his best form, his retirement was a logical step. Eric was fatigued by the demands of the past two seasons and his best years were behind him. He certainly did not want to fade away, he wanted to be remembered as a player who was always on top of his game. And, crucially, one thing he would never have been able to abide was sitting on the bench or being substituted on a regular basis. Cantona was not given to cameo appearances. For him, it was all or nothing.

If one considers that Andy Cole was at last finding his true form since his move from Newcastle United and Ole Gunnar Solskjaer was showing great promise, it is easy to imagine a scenario in which Eric would have been cast in a supporting role behind younger men, in a similar manner to the way in which Dennis Bergkamp is now used at Arsenal. Cantona would not have coped well with such a situation, and David Meek believes Alex Ferguson would not have cared much for it either. 'I think the manager would have found it hard to put Eric on the bench, to see such a great player playing a support role as opposed to a major role. I think that's one of the reasons behind his decision to let him go, so to speak. I think he felt that he wasn't able to give as much as he had because he was getting older and the team had reached a level, and I don't think he fancied playing a support role. That theory is supported by the fact that he didn't go and play for anybody else, other than beach football, which nobody is really going to compare.'

Eric had always reacted badly to a manager's decision not to select him, and the intensity of these reactions had got him into extremely hot water in France, with both the national team and Olympique Marseille. He would certainly not allow the same situation to develop at United, a club that had stood by him in his darkest hour. Moreover, he had always enjoyed a wonderful relationship with the manager and would not have wanted that to deteriorate. So, in fact, he probably did Alex Ferguson a favour by not giving him the dilemma of whether or not to select Eric as he grew older and his powers diminished.

The key for Eric was that he always had to be playing. In January 1993, just two months after signing for United, he was asked in an interview how he would react if Alex Ferguson were ever to leave him on the bench. 'I'd be upset. Who wouldn't be? I want this team to win, but I want them to do it with me. A victory without me would be a hollow victory,' was his telling response.

Furthermore, it is highly unlikely that Eric would have been able to cope with the acrimonious end to his love affair with Manchester United that would undoubtedly have materialised had he no longer been regarded as the team's key player. Lee Sharpe was able to shed some light on what Eric required of his relationship with United and what United gave him in return. 'There's no two ways about it, he needed to be loved. And to be loved on such a grand scale was exactly what his personality and his game needed. To come in and just to be given no responsibility, no defensive duties, no "you've got to do this and you've got to do that, Eric; go out and play your game and win the game for us, thanks very much" – he thrived on it and he loved it.'

There is another probability: Eric was bitterly disappointed by his and the team's failings in Europe. Come the end of the 1996/97 season, in all likelihood, he must have been resigned to the fact that European glory was never to be his. He had always cherished the opportunity to test himself on the biggest stage, yet he was now excluded from this by Aimé Jacquet's decision not to select him ever again for the French national team – a fact which, according to Jean-Jacques Bertrand, left Eric with 'no hope'. Cantona was dismayed not to have the chance of playing for his country of origin in Euro 96, in the land where he had become a superstar. His comments in his autobiography, published prior to the tournament, had revealed how much he relished this prospect: 'I hope that England will prove a happy hunting ground for me again in 1996 when France will, I pray, reach the final of the European Championship. What a dream it would be to play at Old Trafford en route to the final at Wembley. I have a vision of France playing in England and bringing to the English supporters the sort of style, panache and magic which has been associated with many of United's games at Old Trafford.'

At 6.11 p.m. on 11 May 1997, a supporter's home video captured Eric's exit from United's title celebrations. As the United captain, who had appeared a little subdued throughout the festivities, disappeared down the Old Trafford tunnel, he gave one final, wistful wave to the crowd. His glittering career at Manchester United had come to an end, although he would wear the red shirt one last time in a testimonial match the following week. 'My eyes keep straying back to Eric Cantona. He seems deep in contemplation, especially when he lifts the Premiership trophy at the end,' was Alex Ferguson's recollection of the day.

Four days later Eric met with Martin Edwards, the United chairman, and told him formally of his decision to retire. United arranged a press conference for the Sunday at which they would make the official announcement, while Eric escaped the media glare by taking his family to

France for a holiday. A press release had been prepared for the occasion which included a brief statement from Eric himself: 'I have played professional football for thirteen years, which is a long time. I now wish to do other things. I always planned to retire when I was at the top, and at Manchester United I have reached the pinnacle of my career. In the last four and a half years I have enjoyed my best football and had a wonderful time. I have had a marvellous relationship with the manager, coach, staff and players, and not least the fans. I wish Manchester United even more success in the future.'

The great affair was at an end.

17 Making Movies

Film star, propping up the bar, driving in a car, it looks
  so easy,
Film star, propping up the bar, driving in a car tonight,
Film star, giving it class, living it fast, it looks so easy,
Film star, giving it class, living it fast tonight.

                                        'FILM STAR', SUEDE

By coincidence, elements of Eric's professional life mirror
that of his favourite poet, Arthur Rimbaud, the nine-
teenth-century French symbolist. Rimbaud, pronounced
'Rambo' but certainly not to be confused with the Vietnam
veteran played by Sylvester Stallone in the film of the
same name, displayed enormous if precocious talent as a
writer of poetry from the age of fifteen. However, he was
also noted for his immense volatility, and there was a
streak of violence in his make-up. He cut short his career
as a poet in order to enlist with the French army and
sample a life of action, which led to his death in May 1891,
in Marseille. Only in later years was his influence on a
generation of French poets recognised.

Eric Cantona certainly had the desire to do things other
than play football, and these were things he could now
experience fully. The movie industry had captured his
imagination in the past, as had the possibility of living
in Barcelona, which would be his home for the three
years immediately following his retirement. As ever,
liberty and flexibility would be crucial elements in Eric's
life after football. Even before his retirement he had
talked of the way he wished to live: 'When I stop playing
football I don't want to have to work ever again. I'll
put money in the bank, let it generate interest and live
on that for the rest of my life. No one will tell me what

to do. I won't have a boss and I'll be able to do whatever I like.'

Alex Ferguson has traced Eric's desire to reside in the capital of Catalonia back to the fact that he fell in love with the city when he played in a charity match there early in 1997. This is perhaps only partially true, for the Frenchman had already developed an affection for Barcelona, especially during the visit that followed the shirt-throwing incident at Sédan in 1989 when he was playing for Olympique Marseille.

As Eric embarked upon his new life, his former Manchester United team-mates were still trying to deal with the shock of his departure. Gary Neville recalled that the last time he had seen Eric was as the players got off the coach after returning to Manchester from an end-of-season testimonial match in Coventry. According to the United defender, Cantona simply wished everyone well and said he would see them 'later'. However, he failed to reveal how much later it would actually be. In the Neville brothers' diary, published in 1999, Philip expressed his admiration for the outgoing captain after hearing the news of Eric's retirement on Sunday 18 May: 'As captain, Eric never gave motivational speeches in the way Tony Adams does with England. He was a different kind of leader. The opposition were just frightened to death of him. They put two or three men on him and that gave the rest of us more room to play.'

Meanwhile, Alex Ferguson moved rapidly in the transfer market to fill the void left by Eric's sudden exit, paying £3.5 million to secure the services of Teddy Sheringham from Tottenham Hotspur. Ironically, Sheringham, a late developer, was older than Cantona, albeit by just a month. Even so, Sheringham would play a crucial role in United's future success. The England striker was certainly no mirror image of the Frenchman, yet his ability to drop into deep positions marked him out as the most similar player available at the time. Besides, David Meek believes Cantona's influence during his time at the club had left the rest of the squad in pretty fine fettle. 'Eric had done his job so well and brought on the young players so well that, in reality, he wasn't missed as much as he might have been. That was one of the factors that made him feel he was ready to go; that he'd done his job, that he was now being overshadowed by his pupils, if you like, because he was getting older.'

Acting had long held an appeal for Eric. Indeed, he had had a small taste of life in front of the camera in the various advertisements he had done, particularly for Nike. It was clear for as long as a year before his retirement that his passion for the cinema would one day see him involved in films. He even recorded in print his desire to write his own screenplay for a short film – which he intended to produce himself, of course. Eric was a long-standing admirer of Mickey Rourke and enjoyed the streak of honest rebellion the actor revealed in his films. 'I like actors and actresses who give off a certain passion-ate sense of who they are and who remain true to themselves whatever the part they portray. That passion is what I like best about the cinema.' In fact, this is not really dissimilar to his view of football and footballers.

He had always had an enormous passion for creativity in whatever form, and that was a feature of his personality he was able to convey in the way he played football. He inherited his interest in painting from his father and also enjoys poetry and a wide variety of music. 'I choose my music carefully to match the mood I'm in. I listen to a lot of British and American bands. But every so often, I feel the need to listen to French lyrics, to hear words sung in my native language.'

Eric made his movie debut while he was still at Old Trafford, during his eight-month suspension in 1995. *Le Bonheur est Dans Le Pré* ('Happiness is in the Field'), a satirical comedy about a businessman who turns his back on commerce in favour of life as a duck farmer, was well received in France. Eric won excellent reviews for his brief appearance as Lionel, a rugby-playing libertine. It was enough to earn him his first major role in the 1997 short film *Question d'Honneur* ('A Question of Honour'), another comedy in which he plays an intimidating boxing promoter. Interestingly, Joël, Eric's brother, also features in the two movies.

While the rest of France celebrated Les Bleus' World Cup triumph of 1998, Eric was busy filming his part in *Elizabeth*, Shekhar Kapur's epic film about the early life of the Virgin Queen. Cantona's first English-speaking role saw him play Monsieur de Foix, the French ambassador to the Elizabethan court. It is an ironic piece of casting since the ambassador's job is to forge diplomatic links between England and France, as well as to gloss over the indiscretions of the Duc d'Anjou, one of Elizabeth's suitors. It is certainly a great contrast with the straight-talking Eric seen in other real-life situations. He demonstrates all his usual straight-backed haughtiness while sporting a particularly bushy goatee beard. However, he attracted mixed reviews for the role – although that is hardly surprising given the pedigree of the rest of the cast, which included Cate Blanchett, Christopher Ecclestone, Joseph Fiennes and Richard Attenborough. The *Guardian* described his portrayal of 'a rather menacing French ambassador' as 'odd', and *Empire* magazine insisted Eric's inclusion in the film was merely an example of stunt casting.

Tim Bevan, the film's producer, rejected such a suggestion: 'It is going back to our original concept of not wanting to see actors popping up who had been seen in other "frock flicks". It was a deliberate strategy, and one that helps give the film its freshness. The look of the film is extraordinary, and coupled with a very tight story and powerful performances, it is a cracking good yarn – which is basically the first rule of any movie.' Furthermore, when Shekhar Kapur did his initial casting he travelled to Paris to meet several French actors. Over lunch with Cantona, he was convinced that the former footballer's imposing presence would translate to the screen.

Eric's second film that year could scarcely have been more different to *Elizabeth*. In *Mookie*, another well-received French comedy, he plays Antoine Capella, a boxer who is on the run in Mexico. Capella befriends

Brother Benoit, a French monk, and a talking chimpan-
zee, Mookie. Together, the unlikely trio flee Mexico City
to avoid the chimp being captured by evil scientists and
Antoine falling into the hands of the Mexican mafia, who
have a vendetta against him for not throwing a fight.

In 1999, as Manchester United enjoyed winning the
Premiership, the FA Cup and the Champions League, Eric
starred again as a boxer. This time he played Jo Sardi, a
fighter who is as violent out of the ring as he is in it, in
Les Enfants du Marais ('Children of the Marshland').
Although this light, sentimental drama set in the Rhône
Valley received only lukewarm reviews, it was a resound-
ing success at the box office as over one million people in
France flocked to see it. Eric's character has a grudge
against the town drunk and ends up ransacking a bar,
attacking policemen and being thrown in jail. Meanwhile,
most of the rest of the community is still haunted by
World War One and suffering from unrequited love.

Cantona's next film appearance was in the comedy *La
Grande Vie!* ('The Great Life!'), released at the end of
November 2001. Eric, Joël and Albert, their father, portray
three petanque players who are looking for a fourth
person to join their game; he duly arrives in the shape of
Marcello, a Parisian who has travelled to Marseille in
search of the meaning of life. His meeting with the
petanque players is just one of several humorous incidents that are recounted in flashback form as Marcello lies
in a coma on a hospital bed. Initial indications at the time
of writing suggested that the film would do well.

However, towards the end of 2001, Eric appeared
inclined to bring his acting career to a close. His final role
would be that of a bisexual pirate for a French television
adaptation of a well-known strip cartoon. 'My character is
a gay, or more precisely bisexual, pirate. I don't have any
problem with playing this role, on the contrary: most
homosexual people often take on a macho appearance,'
he told the press before also indicating that it would be the
last time he featured on film. He had already hinted in a
previous interview, published by the Manchester United
official magazine in July 2001, that his acting days were

perhaps numbered. While he admitted that he enjoyed acting, he revealed that he did not regard himself as a particularly good actor. Nor had he derived the same pleasure from appearing in films as he had from playing football.

In the immediate aftermath of his retirement from football, Eric displayed a definite reluctance to return to Old Trafford, turning down the club's invitation to a championship celebration banquet in September 1997. However, he would eventually be persuaded that the time was right for him to appear again in front of the fans whose adulation of the Frenchman is still mightily intense. On 18 August 1998, fifteen months to the day since the announcement of his retirement, Eric played in a special match to raise money for the Munich Memorial Fund. He captained an international all-stars eleven which included Mark Hughes, Bryan Robson and Laurent Blanc against a Manchester United eleven.

As Cantona emerged from the tunnel, accompanied only by his son Raphael, the Marseillaise was blasted out as a fanfare over the Old Trafford Tannoy. He received a standing ovation to the usual chants of 'Ooh Aah Cantona'. In the second half of the match, Eric played for United. David Beckham swapped his usual shirt for the number sixteen to allow Cantona, who also donned the captain's armband, to wear the number seven once again – collar upturned, of course. Between them, the two sides even managed to engineer a goal for the returning hero.

At the end of the game, there were handshakes and hugs all round as the United players renewed acquaintance with their old friend and former team-mate. Then, at last, Eric said a proper goodbye to Old Trafford. Taking the microphone in his hand, he cleared his throat and told the United fans: 'It is a special night for me. It was a wonderful feeling. I thank you for coming and I hope to see you soon.' He paused briefly before adding: 'Yes, I quit football because I lost my passion for the game. I am sorry, I gave everything, but I had five wonderful seasons here, the best ones of my career, and I love you all very much. Thank you very much.' His voice faltered slightly towards the end; the great man appeared even to suppress a tear. He then embarked upon a lap of honour as the fans applauded and sang his name once again to the tune of the Marseillaise.

Eric's relationship with United in his playing days was simply an affair of the heart. Had it ended acrimoniously, years of embitterment might have ensued. Instead, the two have remained the best of friends, catching up with each other from time to time. Cantona has played at Old Trafford twice since that first return, in testimonial matches for the Manchester United manager – by that time *Sir* Alex Ferguson – and, more recently, Ryan Giggs. The Frenchman remains very much in demand for such occasions, and he also appeared in a match in Barcelona to celebrate Johann Cruyff's period of management at the Catalan club.

Martin Tyler commentated on his most recent return when United took on Celtic in August 2001 to mark Ryan Giggs's tenth year at the club. 'He brought the house down. That was a secret [that Cantona would be playing]. I was actually not supposed to be let into the secret, even as a commentator, but Gary Pallister had bumped into him in Manchester and he said "What's Eric doing here?" in my earshot. We kept it as a secret, we just said that there was a surprise coming up, and of course he stole the show again. That is star quality. It is a pleasure to talk about him, really.'

Although Eric has not really kept in touch with any of his former Manchester United colleagues – because of, in part at least, an apparent dislike of speaking on the telephone – he has been happy to support them, as he did by playing in Ryan Giggs's testimonial. He still refers to the club as 'we' and was delighted to see United crowned champions of Europe in Barcelona in May 1999. In the run-up to the match, he had even gone public to offer his backing for Andy Cole, despite allegations that he did not hold his former strike partner in high regard as a footballer. Cantona insisted that United would win the European Cup thanks to the exciting attacking partnership of Cole and Dwight Yorke. 'When I read those words,' Cole revealed in his autobiography, 'a shiver went down my spine. There it was in black and white, the very proof I needed of what Eric Cantona really thought about his old sparring partner.'

Despite his adventures in the movie world, it is hardly surprising that Eric did not sever his ties with football for too long. By the summer of 1998 he was appearing regularly in beach soccer tournaments for a French team that has also often included Joël Cantona and Pascal Olmeta, another flamboyant character who played in goal during Eric's time at Olympique Marseille. Needless to say, Eric was soon made captain – and, later, manager – of the French team that plays in the European Pro Beach Soccer League, patronised by Prince Albert of Monaco, every summer.

The circuit has twice brought him to London to play, in July 2000 and 2001. On both occasions several hundred Manchester United fans made the pilgrimage, many of them from far away, to see their idol play again. He has generally kept himself in good shape and clearly enjoys the high skill level required in beach soccer, as well as the opportunity it provides for the most natural of showmen to display his exquisite control and rapier-like volleying of a football. In the July 2001 tournament he won that leg of the competition's Most Valuable Player award. His prize consisted of several large bottles of lager, which he duly handed over to a group of Manchester United fans who had sung his name incessantly during the three days of the tournament. However, one or two spectators, both in England and abroad, have chosen to abuse Eric while he has been playing beach football. On at least one occasion the Frenchman has responded with a one-fingered salute. Not that anyone would really have expected anything different. Ironically, he picked up a FIFA fair play award for his performances in the European Pro Beach Soccer League in 2000.

Clearly, Cantona is now a massive advocate of the beach game, which is receiving increasing levels of recognition across the globe. Moreover, tournament organisers are always keen to have him on the bill for his understandable ability to pull in the punters, whatever the location. And he seems to be happy playing the role of ambassador for the version of the beautiful game played on sand. Furthermore, the Cantona brothers appear determined to be at the forefront of the game's development worldwide, and especially in France, where Joël in particular is one of the driving forces behind the creation of a French national beach soccer league. 'We wanted to organise courses to identify the talents of tomorrow, making everything well structured and taking our time so as not to make errors,' the younger Cantona brother said in an interview with the French beach soccer team's official website.

In October 2001, Eric returned to Barcelona, his former home, to publicise the fourth European Beach Soccer Tournament, due to take place in the Catalan capital the following February. There, in a newspaper interview, he revealed why he enjoyed his new game: 'I like beach soccer because it is new and it has enormous potential. It's not for retired players, there are stars who shine with their own light.' And he indicated that beach football served the purpose of keeping him active while appealing to his instincts as an innovator. 'Beach soccer helps me get all the adrenalin out that I have inside. I train and I play with the same passion as before.'

Later that month Eric and Joël travelled to Mauritius to promote the sport and encourage the local authorities to host a stage of the Pro Beach Soccer World Championship. On this occasion, though, it was reported that Eric refused to speak to journalists, which was a shame because he usually has some interesting opinions to proffer at the pre-tournament press conference. For instance, when there was intense speculation that Patrick Vieira, the French midfielder, would leave Arsenal in the summer of 2001, Cantona opined that his compatriot should certainly quit Highbury if he felt the club offered him only limited chances of success. What is more, he suggested the Manchester United board should seriously consider appointing Johann Cruyff as Sir Alex Ferguson's successor after his expected retirement as the club's manager in May 2002.

Cruyff has always been a massive admirer of the Frenchman's talents. According to a story published in *Sport*, the Catalan daily sports newspaper, in May 2001, the Dutchman missed out on the chance to sign Cantona when he was manager of Barcelona. During Eric's visit to Barcelona in January 1989, when all was certainly not well at Olympique Marseille, it is claimed he turned up unannounced at the Nou Camp and offered his services to the club. The then Barcelona vice-president, now president, Joán Gaspart rejected his offer without even consulting Cruyff. Five years later, the Barcelona coach referred to Eric as his 'frustrated dream' and admitted that he was one of the few players he would have signed with his eyes closed despite his disciplinary problems because he believed so greatly in Eric's talent.

With a charismatic figurehead like Cantona, beach soccer could well develop as a serious sport in the future. In the meantime, Eric's unquestionable appeal will put bums on seats and attract other professionals to get involved. For instance, Franck Sauzée has expressed an interest in playing alongside Eric again. 'I think when I stop my career, I know he has a big passion for beach soccer, and I would like to play a few games with him,' he told me.

Martin Tyler recalled bumping into Eric at Nice airport in August 2000, just before the Frenchman flew off to play in a beach soccer tournament. The TV commentator was glad to report that the former Manchester United player had lost nothing of his enigmatic charm. 'I had a little chat with him. We were going in to watch Real Madrid and Galatasaray [in the European Super Cup Final, in Monaco], so there were lots of contemporary football things around, but there was Eric, retired and still radiating that star quality – not deliberately, he just has it. I suppose the star quality comes from the talent at his feet, but you don't always get the same thing. There are lots of very good footballers who don't naturally dominate rooms or airports as personalities.'

Even though Cantona has never exactly been regarded as media-friendly, Martin Tyler never personally experienced any difficulties with him. 'I found him very well mannered, very respectful, very private in his way but not so private that he turned his back on you. He came [to Old Trafford] with a reputation and left as a legend. That is the extent of his achievement, really. I can only say I was lucky to see a bit of that.'

Doubtless, Eric's star quality was one of the things that prompted Gérard Gelas, a French playwright and director, to pen his *Ode à Canto* ('Ode to Canto') on the very day in 1995 when his compatriot was sentenced to 120 hours' community service as punishment for his misdemeanour at Selhurst Park. The play takes place on a grass-covered stage which is surrounded by the audience as if they were watching a football match. It consists of a dialogue between Canto and Lorenzo, a loyal if fictitious ballboy, in which the pair discuss Cantona's sentence and a variety of other issues that are important to Eric both in the fictional world and in reality.

Ode à Canto received rave reviews throughout France. Eric even took his family to see the play in July 1995 and gave it his seal of approval. As testimony to its popularity and quality, Gelas's touring company has regularly performed the work throughout France ever since. In one interview, Cantona was asked why he thought Gelas had chosen him as a subject about which to write a play. 'Because I am in the public eye,' he responded. 'He has been able to get a lot of messages across, notably about the National Front. Things that I would not perhaps have said, but it is good that he has made me say them.' Gelas had indeed sussed Eric's attitude towards racism and the National Front, and Cantona would later play in a match at Real Madrid's Santiago Bernabéu Stadium as part of the international football community's Day against Racism. Perhaps Gelas was aware that Eric had once revealed his abhorrence of racism, saying: 'Racism is an abomination. I don't understand why people are afraid of different races coming together. When races come together, cultures are enriched.'

*   *   *

Diego Maradona is the footballer Eric rates as the greatest of all time, arguing that not even Pele can match the feats of the diminutive Argentinian. 'For me, Maradona represents football. He is football. He is the greatest footballer of all time. He managed to win the World Cup without the sort of team and the calibre of team-mate that Pele had at his disposal. In 1986, it was Maradona who carried Argentina to victory, and in 1990 he carried them to the final.'

During Eric's suspension from English football in 1995, he got to know Maradona and became involved in the latter's Players' Union. 'Players need representation. Diego Maradona and I got together to ensure that they got it. The international governing bodies never consult the players before making their decisions,' was Eric's explanation of the union' s *raison d'être*. Strangely, yet amusingly, at the press conference given by Maradona and Cantona to launch the new organisation, both men had placards in front of them bearing their names. One has to pity any journalist at the event who did not recognise two of the most famous players in world football. They need not have worried anyway since the union never really developed beyond its infancy.

However, the bond between Cantona and Maradona has remained a strong one, and the Frenchman travelled to Buenos Aires in November 2001 to participate in an emotional farewell testimonial match for the former Argentina captain. Maradona lined up in a full-strength Argentina side which included Juan Sebastián Verón, the new playmaker at Old Trafford, who within a few weeks of making his United debut had to put up with comparisons with the Frenchman. Eric, meanwhile, represented a strong rest of the world team, and even made his way on to the score sheet.

There is little doubt that Eric has long considered the possibility of returning to football as a manager, and press reports have in the past linked him with vacancies at Fulham, Olympique Marseille and, even, Manchester United. And though he once expressed an interest in managing the Old Trafford club, his stance on the overall issue of whether he would like to become a manager seems to have altered little since his initial comments on the matter, written in 1996. 'I haven't yet decided if I would contemplate becoming a football manager. If I did, it would be on the strict condition that I could bring something new to the game. I would never contemplate becoming a manager simply to do what other managers have done before me. All my life I've wanted to do new things, to break new ground. If ever I had the sense that I could do this as a manager, I'd certainly consider it.'

Even so, opinion is divided as to whether, in fact, Eric would make a good football manager. Sir Alex Ferguson believes he would, and has even invited him back to Old Trafford to coach young players on an informal basis, although it is an offer Eric has not taken up thus far. And United's youth-team coach Eric Harrison wrote in his autobiography of the possibility of Cantona becoming a manager: 'As a profound thinker, he would produce a team full of invention and exciting possibilities. I believe that his side would be an attacking one but well organised. His tactics would be very interesting.' Erik Bielderman, however, insists that the various demands involved in top-level football management would not suit Eric. 'I can't see him becoming a manager because you have to be every day, every single hour concentrated on football and you have to deal with 20 or 25 people around you and the media, and I can't see Eric being able to handle that. He's too volatile. Something he could do one day is to work with young players, but I doubt he will be a new Alex Ferguson. I regret that. I would be very happy to see him [as a manager] because he has great ideas on football and he has a very positive image of what football should be.'

Whatever the future may hold for Eric Cantona, whether he makes a spectacular return to football, wins an Oscar or simply carries on enjoying beach soccer, he has always been confident that he will adapt well to each new phase of his life. During his football career, he insisted that he was not afraid of growing old, yet he does, in some ways, fear death. 'It's not death itself, not the darkness of death that worries me, but the thought of no longer existing in the bright light of living.' Still, he remains open-minded about the possibility of reincarnation and would like to come back to earth as an eagle. 'I love the way eagles move, the way they soar, the way they gaze.' That would certainly be apt.

18 There is a Light and It Never Goes Out

I'm in love with Manchester United. It is like finding a wife who has given me the perfect marriage.

ERIC CANTONA

Eric Cantona's legacy at Old Trafford is both profound and durable. The Frenchman is still revered at the Theatre of Dreams, and on match days his name is regularly sung by fans, both at Old Trafford and in the various public houses close to the ground. Moreover, he influenced an entire generation of young players, especially David Beckham, the Neville brothers, Paul Scholes and Nicky Butt, who, two years after their mentor's departure, played a crucial role in Manchester United's unforgettable Treble-winning season. And how appropriate it was that United should finally grasp their Holy Grail, the European Cup, in Barcelona, the city where Eric lived for three years after the end of his Old Trafford career.

The influence of Cantona could still be detected within Old Trafford several years after his departure. Jaap Stam, the former Manchester United defender, revealed in his much-maligned autobiography that he would often hear Eric's name mentioned around the club; he was presented as a classic role model everyone else should follow. 'His dedication to the game is legendary at United, and Cantona's good habits, such as extra training, rubbed off quickly on his team-mates,' Stam wrote.

Eric certainly had a crucial impact on the fabric of Old Trafford as he helped the club move out of its era of torment when for 26 years, try as they might, scores of players and several managers were unable to deliver the cherished League title. David Meek maintains that one of

Eric Cantona's greatest achievements was to help educate the club's young players and its fans to accept a more patient, possession-based, more continental style of football. 'He educated Manchester United fans as much as the young players in a style of football that was a little bit foreign to what Old Trafford had been used to. By that I mean, traditionally, United fans expected, and I think this influenced the players, a kind of forward-motion football with the ball going backwards very rarely, even sideways very rarely. In fact, Ray Wilkins was mocked in his day and called the "crab" because he believed in possession football and tended to pass the ball sideways.

'What Eric Cantona eventually taught the young players and the fans was that movement on the pitch and off the ball is so important that sometimes if A passes to B and B passes to A, even without either player moving, that can, in fact, be creative because other players might have moved and therefore there are new options open. I think Cantona was a master at this. Sometimes he was like a circus ringmaster with all his acolytes around. He would play the ball and get it back, and you would think: "Well, they're no nearer the penalty area." But suddenly there would be an opening which all this play had created, and Cantona was a master at spotting that opening having played the sort of football that created it.'

George Best is always an essential reference point whenever one attempts to assess the impact of any great player at Manchester United, both in terms of footballing ability and the adulation inspired among the fans. Best was the original footballing icon, a man blessed with the most exquisite talent and a lifestyle that defined the word 'sensational', yet a person who has suffered tragically from his addiction to alcohol.

Promising youngsters at United are perennially labelled 'the new George Best', but because Eric did not come through the club's youth ranks, that was never a burden he had to bear. However, for any player, even to be mentioned in the same breath as Best should be esteemed an honour. And, ultimately, in the modern era, Eric Cantona became the only United icon to be genuinely comparable with the great Irishman. Yet he did so by being the original Eric Cantona, not the new George Best. That is the challenge for all the top players at Manchester United, not to be constantly compared but to stand alone, above all others, as Cantona and Best do, and as Duncan Edwards would surely have done had his young life not been lost so tragically in the Munich air crash.

However, many observers, especially ones who grew up watching players like Bobby Charlton, George Best and Denis Law, dispute the assertion that Eric Cantona is Manchester United's greatest player of all time. For instance, David Meek cites his apparently disappointing performances in European matches as one reason why Eric cannot be regarded in the same light as a few other Old Trafford legends. 'There was a gap in his armoury and that would count against him. Also, he didn't do it for as long as the players who, to my mind, may be ahead of him, like George Best. Although people say George Best finished early, George played first-team football for ten years at Manchester United, from 17 to 27. Then there's Bobby Charlton, and even somebody like Nobby Stiles, who won a European Cup winner' s medal plus a World Cup winner' s medal. He's got to be ahead of Cantona, and that's not to knock Cantona but to put things into perspective.' In defence of Cantona's European record, however, it is worth noting that he played only one full season in the Champions League, in 1996/97 when, arguably, his powers were beginning to wane.

The Cantona era at Old Trafford was the first time the club had been dominated by the personality and playing ability of someone who was not born and brought up in the British Isles. United had employed some good foreign players in the past, most notably the Dutch midfielder Arnold Muhren, yet none of them had the epoch-defining influence of Eric. In pure playing terms, of course, it could well be argued that Peter Schmeichel, undoubtedly the best goalkeeper in the world when at his peak at United, had as crucial an impact as Cantona by making save after vital save in the most important matches. Yet for all his bawling at the back four, the Dane's more straightforward personality never afforded him the intangible quality that gave Eric such immense presence.

Indeed, it was the attractive combination of Eric's charisma and his supreme footballing talent that won him such a special place in the hearts of Manchester United fans. Andy Mitten was able to explain the phenomenon: 'First things first, he was an outstanding footballer, and that's the bottom line. If he hadn't been, then all the other traits in his personality which made him so popular would have counted for little. He had an aura that is hard to define. I've only been star struck twice in my life, and I've been lucky enough to meet scores of famous people from Michel Platini to George Best – and plenty of non-footballers. Cantona was one of those people. I was sat alone in an annexe at the Cliff training ground waiting for a player. Cantona came into the room and said, "Hello, how are you?" before walking out. Sad though it sounds, I was buzzing. I didn't even interview him. It was a small gesture, but at no time did he give off the feeling of superiority that so many famous people do.'

Former United players like Mark Hughes and Bryan Robson have always been warmly received on their return to Old Trafford, but Eric's name is the only one regularly sung at matches by fans. Mitten believes that that can, in part, be attributed to the fact that Cantona's time at Old Trafford was more recent, but he also points out that Eric actually had more songs composed about him and that he was even more popular than Hughes and Robson. 'He just walked away and made all the right noises about United and United fans. The enigma remained intact. Much as Robson and Hughes were and are respected, they both went on to play for other clubs and their professionalism saw them try and defeat United in future battles for their new clubs. Cantona didn't go there.'

Manchester United supporters love players who have come back from the brink of catastrophe. Perhaps it is because such players mirror the club's own re-emergence after the Munich air tragedy. Eric Cantona's exploits in the 1995/96 season, when he was the essential figure in United's glorious campaign, constituted an amazing rebirth of a player whose career might easily have ended in January 1995 at Selhurst Park. Also, football fans love no one more than the player who is most reviled by the supporters of their rivals. A parallel can be drawn between the way in which Cantona was a target for abuse during his time at Old Trafford and the more recent experiences of David Beckham. The England midfielder, had he possessed less strength of character, could easily have been hounded out of English football following his sending-off in the 1998 World Cup for aiming the slightest of kicks at Diego Simeone. But when the going got genuinely tough, Beckham played some of the best football he has produced in a United shirt, just as Cantona had done on his return from disgrace a few years earlier. By and large, the England captain is a more palatable figure for the general public and, as a consequence, is likely to be less of a folk hero with United supporters than Cantona. It's simple really: Beckham is the boy next door, Cantona the beautiful stranger.

If Eric achieved undoubted legendary status at Old Trafford, it is far more difficult to make a concrete assessment of his impact on the French national team and French football as a whole. Erik Bielderman insists that Cantona remained a source of frustration for the French and that national coaches like Gérard Houllier and Michel Platini were seduced by his talent yet sometimes disappointed by what he delivered. 'They hoped that one day he would give what they supposed he had. That's why Chris Waddle and John Barnes played fifty or sixty games for England, never reaching their peak. Each time you felt that the new manager or the new system or the new season would see Waddle and Barnes achieve, but they didn't. And it's the same story with Cantona. We were desperate to see him achieve the ultimate, and after what happened with Man United we felt, "Why is he doing that in England and not with France?" '

Eric did, of course, score 20 goals in 45 appearances for France, a record that hardly suggests failure on the international stage. Even so, Bielderman is adamant that he failed to lift the team as a whole on a regular basis, a fact which does not rank him alongside the game's greatest figures. 'He did play well, but when we had crucial games he was not the man who saved the team as Maradona saved Argentina, as Zidane can save France. He was good when the team was good, but when the team struggled he would underachieve compared with expectations and what he was achieving with Manchester United.'

While it is true that Cantona did not reach the same heights for France as Platini before him and Zidane in later years, he was unfortunate not to have the opportunity to shine for his national team while he was at the very peak of his powers. Eric's club performances as a creator and goalscorer in the 1995/96 season, during which Manchester United won the FA Cup and Premiership Double, were quite simply without equal, but they were not enough to earn him a recall to the French team managed by Aimé Jacquet for the 1996 European Championship held in England, the very country where Cantona had found his best and most consistent level of form.

Above all, Eric Cantona was a pioneer: he was the first Frenchman to build a successful career in England, paving the way for many others. And this key influence is one that David Ginola, for instance, has openly acknowledged. 'If it wasn't for Eric I don't think so many French people would be involved in the game in England. English clubs had some bad opinions about French players, but Eric changed all that with his success and made them keen to have French players in their team in the hope they would be like him.'

Certainly, Cantona appreciated what England had to offer him. He had always craved excitement and passion in football and he found those qualities in abundance in the Premiership. And he always insisted that English football benefited from a level of integrity which was non-existent in other countries, including, presumably, France. Moreover, Eric's move to England clearly rescued his career, as Franck Sauzée recognised. 'I think he maybe needed to change the atmosphere around him. I think perhaps he was tired of the press, of the people. Sometimes it's not easy to be a good player in your home country. Do you remember when David Beckham, in the

World Cup in France, had the incident with the Argentinian lad? I remember it was really difficult for him [back in England]. OK, afterwards he did well and now he is fantastic. Maybe Eric was tired of this sort of context.'

Eric's former team-mates have identified the different qualities that combined to make his career in England so successful. Sauzée stresses that his technical ability brought something new to the English game. 'Eric was a very good player, he was skilful and he brought his technique with him. He was able to change the game with a free kick or a goal. He was a player who came to England with French ability and he brought something new with his technique. People were very interested and enjoyed seeing him play.'

On the other hand, Lee Sharpe believes his strength of character was equally important since it allowed him to produce flashes of skill in matches that most players would only dare attempt in training. 'Mentally, he was very tough. He played his own game no matter how much pressure was on him and no matter how the game was going. Some games he would be trying flicks and you could see they weren't coming off, but he would still try them, and in the last couple of minutes one would work and it would end up in a goal or something. So he definitely had a mental toughness about him.'

Furthermore, many of his colleagues, both during his short time at Elland Road and throughout his spell in Manchester, appreciated a level of humility in Eric that those who did not know him could rarely detect. Shortly after Leeds United's victory over Liverpool in the 1992 Charity Shield, David Batty and Gary Speed called round to Eric's house. For a few minutes they joined Raphael, his son, in kicking a ball against the garage door. But when they picked up the ball to look at it, both Batty and Speed were stunned to discover that it was the match ball from the Charity Shield, which had been given to Eric because he had scored a hat-trick. 'But that was Eric Cantona,' Batty summed up, 'an immense talent who had more than enough self-confidence and self-contentment not to be concerned with the trappings of his success.'

Still, Erik Bielderman establishes the fact that there are very definitely two sides to Cantona's character and makes the following assessment of his personality: 'He's a very kind person. You can't know him without having a feeling about him – either you hate him or you like him. Sometimes you can love him and hate him at the same time, you have mixed feelings. He is nice, he's clever, that's the positive. On the other side, you can say he's volatile, he's difficult to handle and sometimes he has such a strong feeling of the good and the bad that he doesn't understand that between the good and the bad there are ten different steps and you have to accept that the world is not white and black, it's grey.'

Opinion is divided on the subject of whether, indeed, Eric Cantona was one of the truly great players in world football. On the one hand, it could be argued that he was not: Eric never played in Italy, which is football's New York on the basis that if you can make it there you can make it anywhere; nor did he play in the World Cup finals or win the European Cup. However, he did win a remarkable four championship medals in consecutive years, at Olympique Marseille, Leeds United and Manchester United (twice). The Old Trafford club, of course, lifted the Premiership trophy four times in five years and only missed out on the title in 1994/95 because of Eric's absence.

Bald statistics do not always provide compelling evidence of a player's greatness or otherwise, but they do offer some interesting food for thought. During his two spells at Manchester United, Mark Hughes scored 115 goals in 345 appearances at a rate of a goal every three games; Eric Cantona scored 80 goals in 181 appearances at a rate of a goal every 2.275 games. For France, Eric scored 20 goals in 45 appearances at a rate of a goal every 2.25 games. At the time of writing, that represents a better goals-to-game ratio than, for instance, Thierry Henry (a goal every 3.1 games) or Christophe Dugarry (a goal every seven games), both of whom have won the World Cup and the European Championship with France. Like Cantona, neither Henry nor Dugarry could be regarded as a straightforward goalscorer; all three prefer to operate in the space behind the main striker. In fact, only the most prolific French strikers of all time have a goals-to-game ratio that is superior to Cantona's. In the 1950s, the legendary Just Fontaine bagged 30 in just 21 outings at an astounding rate of more than a goal a game. In more recent times, Jean-Pierre Papin, so often Eric's strike partner, notched 30 in 54 games at a rate of a goal every 1.8 games.

Whether Eric Cantona was a world-beater or not, whether or not he totally fulfilled his rich and undeniable potential, are issues that are clearly open to debate. What is certain is that he was instrumental in creating Old Trafford's golden age of the mid to late 1990s and his influence helped give other players the confidence to move on to greater success even after Eric had turned up the collar of his Manchester United shirt for the last time. It is also true that the esteem in which he is held at the club has barely diminished with the passing of the years. So there is ample testimony to the man's genius, yet perhaps the most telling remark on the subject was made by Ole Gunnar Solskjaer, a man who has scored the winning goal in a European Cup final. 'In thirty or forty years' time,' he remarked, 'I'll probably boast about having played with Eric.'

Epilogue

Eric Cantona's time at other clubs was littered with disagreements, fights with team-mates and clashes with the manager, yet none of these problems seem to have existed at Manchester United. Lee Sharpe's explanation for this is a straightforward one: 'He realised how good the team was and he realised how good he was in the team and how important he was to the team, how much he was respected by the manager and the players. I think it was just a great stage for him to play on.'

Cantona always did what came naturally to him; his reactions were from the heart. On the plus side, that meant his play was so fearless that he would attempt complicated pieces of training-ground skill during a match. On the other hand, there was the negative side: his gut instinct at Selhurst Park in January 1995 was to assault Matthew Simmons, and he did so; his heart told him to publicly criticise Henri Michel, the French coach, and he landed himself in serious trouble. While it is clearly not possible to condone Eric's violent outbursts, a common theme can be detected in each of them: he was reacting to a perceived injustice and, with his black-and-white view of the world, meted out his own punishment. Cantona's own view of himself was as follows: 'Perhaps I should be an example to people, but I do not think that way. I do not react that way. I'm simply me.'

Lee Sharpe's final remarks about his former team-mate shed a little more light on the real man behind the football persona: 'Everyone thought he was aloof and so beyond everyone, but I think he was the only player in the team at the time who was living in a three-bedroom, semi-detached house. Everyone else had to get the big house and the nice car, and he would turn up in his club car and still live in this three-bedroom, semi-detached house. He was quite happy to stay at ground level with his little family home. I think that just sums up the bloke. There was a modesty about him. Sometimes after training he would bring his little one in and be out playing for an hour with the kid. We'd see a side of him that people don't see.'

It is also worth remembering that for all the bad publicity Eric generated, he remained a highly respected figure among the country's professionals. Richard Shaw, who experienced no repercussions in his later meetings with Cantona after the Selhurst Park incident, described what he was like to play against: 'He got the ball and no matter how tight you were, how close to mark him, it seemed like he had that extra bit of time. People say that all great players have that bit of extra time. As tight as I felt I got to him, or if I watched him on TV and other players got to him, I always felt like he had that little bit of trickery, that little bit of skill, and I think as a defender you stand off possibly a bit too much and maybe admire him a bit too much.'

Gary Speed retains fond memories of the Frenchman even though Cantona spent most of his English career at another club. 'I think the lasting impression of Eric would be sitting down watching *Match of the Day* and Eric scoring another fantastic goal for Man United.'

So which Manchester United player has adopted the Cantona mantle since he took early retirement? The answer is simple: no one. What has in fact happened since his departure is that his former team-mates have taken over elements of the Cantona contribution, yet no individual has managed the whole effect. David Beckham inherited the number seven shirt and the media attention; Roy Keane wore the captain's armband and got into trouble with referees; Teddy Sheringham, Dwight Yorke, Ruud van Nistelrooy, David Beckham and Paul Scholes have all played in Eric's withdrawn striker role. Each has, at times, excelled, yet thus far none could claim to have performed with the same level of effectiveness as the Frenchman. Yorke has even been known to wear his collar upturned *à la* Cantona, yet never with the same panache. Ryan Giggs has, at times, been capable of those moments of genius that nobody else could quite produce. Denis Irwin, Paul Scholes, Dwight Yorke, Ruud van Nistelrooy, David Beckham and Teddy Sheringham have all taken penalties with differing degrees of success. Again, none of them has managed to make the role their own.

So much in football is about chance. There are so many imponderables in the game that things often don't work out in quite the way you expect them to. Eric Cantona's dream move to his hometown club, Olympique Marseille, appeared the perfect scenario, but it ended in mediocrity and ignominy. However, at Old Trafford, Eric was, in the words of David Meek, 'the right player in the right place at the right time'. It is for that reason that Erik Bielderman insists Cantona is a more important figure in English football history than in the history of the game in his own country. 'I would give more space to Eric Cantona if I were writing about English football than I would with French football because Eric Cantona never played in a World Cup, never won a European Cup. All his achievements as a world-class player were at Man United and never with French clubs or the French national team.'

Indeed, despite his brushes with authority, Eric Cantona's time at Manchester United was without doubt the most successful of his career. The club, its players, the manager and the fans all deserve credit for providing Eric with the ideal environment in which he could blossom. But Cantona himself deserves his fair share of the plaudits. United gave him the platform, but his actions and his long-lasting influence helped deliver riches and glory beyond the wildest fantasies ever to circulate around the Theatre of Dreams in the modern era. For that alone he should be remembered.

Fact file

FIRST DIVISION CAREER IN FRANCE
1983/84: Auxerre, 2 appearances, 0 goals
1984/85: Auxerre, 4 appearances, 2 goals
1985/86: Auxerre, 7 appearances, 0 goals
1986/87: Auxerre, 36 appearances, 13 goals
1987/88: Auxerre, 32 appearances, 8 goals
1988/89: Olympique Marseille, 22 appearances, 5 goals;
Bordeaux, 11 appearances, 6 goals
1989/90: Montpellier, 33 appearances, 10 goals
1990/91: Olympique Marseille, 18 appearances, 8 goals
1991/92: Olympique Nîmes, 17 appearances, 2 goals

Total: 182 appearances, 54 goals

CLUB CAREER IN ENGLAND (ALL COMPETITIONS)
1991/92: Leeds United, 15 appearances, 3 goals
1992/93: Leeds United, 20 appearances, 11 goals;
Manchester United, 22 appearances, 9 goals
1993/94: Manchester United, 48 appearances, 25 goals
1994/95: Manchester United, 24 appearances, 13 goals
1995/96: Manchester United, 38 appearances, 19 goals
1996/97: Manchester United, 49 appearances, 14 goals

Total: 216 appearances, 94 goals

Total with Manchester United: 181 appearances, 80 goals

INTERNATIONAL CAREER
45 appearances, 20 goals

HONOURS
1990: French Cup with Montpellier
1991: French Championship with Olympique Marseille
1992: English League Championship and Charity Shield with Leeds United
1993: Premiership title and Charity Shield with Manchester United
1994: Premiership title, FA Cup and Charity Shield with Manchester United; PFA Player of the Year
1996: Premiership title, FA Cup and Charity Shield with Manchester United; Football Writers' Association Footballer of the Year
1997: Premiership title with Manchester United

TIMELINE
24 May 1966: Eric Cantona born in Marseille
May 1981: Cantona joins Auxerre as an apprentice, making debut in French national youth team the following year
12 August 1987: Eric makes first of 45 appearances for French national team, against West Germany
June 1988: signs for Olympique Marseille for French record fee of £2.3 million
September 1988: banned from international football for labelling French manager Henri Michel a 'shit bag'
January 1989: Cantona is loaned out to Bordeaux after throwing his Marseille shirt to the ground during a friendly against Torpedo Moscow
July 1989: signs for Montpellier
Summer 1990: returns to Marseille
Summer 1991: transferred to Olympique Nîmes for £1 million
December 1991: Eric retires from football following suspension for throwing the ball at a referee and insulting members of French Football Federation's disciplinary committee
31 January 1992: Howard Wilkinson brings Eric to Leeds United on loan deal
27 November 1992: Cantona moves to Manchester United for around £1 million

26 May 1994: Cantona scores last of his 20 goals for France, against Australia

25 January 1995: Eric attacks member of public at Selhurst Park, an outburst that sees him banned from football for eight months and serving a period of community service

1 October 1995: Eric scores against Liverpool on his return to Manchester United after suspension

18 May 1997: Manchester United announce that Eric Cantona has retired from football

Bibliography

BOOKS

Absalom, Steve, Bellers, Lance and Spinks, Simon: *The Unseen Archives – a Photographic History of Manchester United* (Mustard/Parragon, 1999)

Barnes, Justyn (ed.): *The Little Book of Man Utd* (Manchester United Books/Carlton Books Ltd, 2001)

Batty, David: *The Autobiography* (Headline, 2001)

Beckham, David: *My World* (Hodder and Stoughton, 2000)

Broadbent, Rick: *Looking For Eric* (Mainstream Publishing, 2000)

Cantona, Eric: *The Illustrated Cantona* (Headline Book Publishing, 1996)

—— and Basse, Pierre-Louis: *Un Rêve Modeste et Fou* (Robert Laffont, 1993)

—— and Fynn, Alex: *Cantona on Cantona* (Manchester United Books/Andre Deutsch Ltd, 1996)

Chapman, Lee: *More than a Match* (Stanley Paul, 1992)

Cole, Andy and Fitton, Peter: *Andy Cole, the Autobiography* (Manchester United Books/Andre Deutsch Ltd, 1999)

Ferguson, Alex and McIlvanney, Hugh: *Managing My Life* (Hodder and Stoughton, 1999)

—— and Meek, David: *A Will to Win* (Manchester United Books/Andre Deutsch Ltd, 1997)

Finn, Gerry P. T. and Giulianotti, Richard (eds): *Football Culture: Local Contests, Global Visions* (Frank Cass, 2000)

Ginola, David: *David Ginola: Le Magnifique, the Autobiography* (CollinsWillow, 2000)

Harrison, Eric: *The View from the Dugout* (The Parrs Wood Press, 2001)

Hughes, Mark and Meek, David: *Hughesie: The Red Dragon* (Mainstream Publishing, 1994)

McIlvanney, Hugh: *McIlvanney on Football* (Mainstream Publishing, 1999)

Neville, Gary, Neville, Phil, Barnes, Justyn and Pilger, Sam: *For Club and Country* (Manchester United Books/ VCI plc, 1999)

Radureau, Vincent: *Cantona: L'Aventure Anglaise* (Canal + Editions, 1995)

Reid, Joyce M. H. (ed.): *The Concise Oxford Dictionary of French Literature* (Oxford University Press, 1989)

Ridley, Ian: *Cantona, The Red and the Black* (Victor Gollancz, 1995)

Ruddock, Neil and Smith, Dave: *Hell Razor* (CollinsWillow, 2000)

Rühn, Christov (ed.): *Le Foot* (Abacus, 2000)

Schmeichel, Peter and Balsby, Egon: *Schmeichel, the Autobiography* (Virgin Publishing Ltd, 1999)

Somerscales, Jillian, Murrell, Debra and Pritchard, Louise: *The Official Manchester United Illustrated Encyclopaedia* (Manchester United Books/Andre Deutsch Ltd, 1998)

Stam, Jaap and Butler, Jeremy: *Jaap Stam, Head to Head* (CollinsWillow, 2001)

White, Jim: *Always in the Running* (Mainstream Publishing, 1998)

Wilkinson, Howard and Walker, David: *Managing to Succeed* (Mainstream Publishing/Edinburgh, 1992)

NEWSPAPERS AND MAGAZINES

Daily Mail
Daily Mirror
Daily Telegraph
Empire
Express
FourFourTwo
Guardian
L'Equipe
Manchester United
Marca
News of the World
Observer
Sport

Star
Sun
The Times
Today
Total Film

VIDEOS

Alex Ferguson's Ultimate United (Manchester United/Paul Doherty International/VCI)

Au Revoir Cantona (Manchester United/Paul Doherty International/VCI)

Cantona Speaks (Manchester United/Paul Doherty International/VCI)

Elizabeth (PolyGram Filmed Entertainment)

Manchester United: Champions of Europe (Manchester United/Paul Doherty International/VCI)

Manchester United Official Review 96/97: Champions Again! (Manchester United/Paul Doherty International/VCI)

Manchester United: The Double 95/96 (Manchester United/Paul Doherty International/VCI)

Ooh Aah Cantona (Pickwick)

The Munich Memorial Match: Farewell to Legends (Manchester United/Paul Doherty International/VCI)

Index